Whisper

Your Name into My Ear

a memoir of survival

Marguerite Lévy-Feibelman

Marguerite Lévy-Feibelman

September 11, 2014

Cincinnati

Published by River Road Press

The Library of Congress has catalogued this book as follows:

Lévy-Feibelman, Marguerite
Whisper Your Name into My Ear: a memoir of survival
Control Number: 2011935496

ISBN: 978-0-9834930-8-2

Special quantity discounts are available on this book for educational institutions or social organizations please see above contact.

Printed in the United States of America

Designed by Joyce Faulkner

To Papa

Il n'est pas de commune mesure entre
le combat libre et l'écrasement dans la nuit.

~ Antoine de Saint-Exupéry

Acknowledgements

I wish to thank Professor Elie Wiesel for his encouragement at a critical moment of my project, and Dr. Michael Berenbaum for recognizing in my book a unique story worthy of telling. Among the many people of goodwill who helped me along this history-steeped journey, I especially wish to thank Marie Lainez, archivist at the Memorial de la Shoah, Paris. Her assistance with exact texts and dates of French laws under Vichy and other official information was invaluable.

To the employee at city hall in Roanne (Loire) who photocopied a stack of war news from the Journal de Roanne on a Saturday morning after closing time, I bear lasting gratitude.

To Joyce Faulkner of River Road Press who enhanced the looks of the book with graphic arts, I extend my deepest appreciation. Her smile and her patience were inexhaustible. Joyce, you are a real trooper. I never knew how much work it is to create a book. To Pat McGrath Avery, I humbly say: Thank you.

Heart-felt thanks go to my son Allen for the generous sharing of his editing and computer skills. My husband Leonard was an indispensable supporter. Without his love and caring I could not have written this book

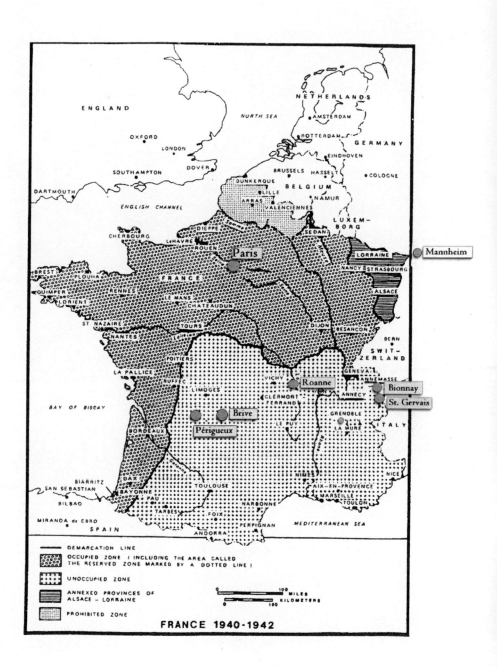

FRANCE 1940-1942

DEMARCATION LINE

OCCUPIED ZONE (INCLUDING THE AREA CALLED
THE RESERVED ZONE MARKED BY A DOTTED LINE)

UNOCCUPIED ZONE

ANNEXED PROVINCES OF
ALSACE – LORRAINE

PROHIBITED ZONE

Contents

Foreword

By Michael Berenbaum

In his classic work *Survival in Auschwitz* Primo Levi wrote:

If the drowned have no story, and single and broad are the path to perdition, the paths to salvation are many, difficult and improbable.

Marguerite Lévy Feibelman's, *Whisper Your Name Into My Ear* is more modest than a story of salvation, but it is a difficult and improbable story of survival. Written with charm and grace, it tells of her family's journey through the years of darkness. Her father Albert Lévy was a prominent and enormously successful German businessman who understood early on that the rise of Adolf Hitler meant danger if not doom to the Jews of Germany. Unlike many of his peers, well rooted, accomplished and moderately powerful titans of industry, who presumed that they would be insulated from what might follow, Lévy understood the danger of Hitler and acted accordingly. He liquidated his holdings and resettled in France precisely because he had internalized the dangers that faced his people. Accustomed from his business experience to taking swift and decisive action to protect against danger, he moved his family to France, which he assumed was far enough away from the Nazi menace to provide a safety net. There he rebuilt his business career by establishing the second largest paint company in France.

Born Margot Lévy, the child was forced to change her name from German to French and became Marguerite; so too, she changed her culture and her language. The pattern would repeat itself again and again. The Lévy family lived comfortably in an elegant apartment in a plush section of Paris where they enjoyed the cultural activities of a splendid city. Cosmopolitans, the cultural adjustment was not difficult. Successful, their transition was eased by the comforts that money can buy. Albert Lévy prepared for the difficulties that were on the horizon. As Marguerite makes clear, he stored gasoline and the raw materials

xi

for ongoing manufacturing activities knowing that war would bring scarcity, and he who prepares for scarcity wisely can not only endure, but prosper.

The Lévy family was cautious, not clairvoyant.

They believed the French conceit that the Maginot Line would hold, that the French Army was prepared and well equipped and they were persuaded that Hitler's Germany would expand in the East and not in the West. Once the Germans invaded, the Lévys again took flight, moving to the Loire department, an area that seemed to be within the zone of quasi-independent Vichy France. There as Frenchmen with the great tradition of Liberty, Equality and Fraternity, they felt they would be protected. And then the reality of French acquiescence to Nazi Germany set in and once again the Lévy family took flight.

As I read Feibelman's memoir, I was struck by two insights from another work.

In his introduction to *Daring to Resist*, the catalogue of an exhibition at New York's Museum of Jewish Heritage, David Marwell wrote: "just because Jews were powerless does not mean that they were passive." The Lévy family was anything but passive. False identity cards were prepared, possessions were hidden, all evidence of their Jewishness was concealed and when Albert Lévy was not able to provide a way out for his family, young Marguerite stepped into the breech and took over the leadership of this effort.

David Engel has written of Jewish time. Though we tend to think of the Holocaust within the context of time as set forth by the perpetrators moving from persecution to systematic annihilation, from mobile killers to gassing, Jews experienced time differently. Ruth Bondy has argued that a gigantic gap exists that is more than chronological between the German schedule and the Jewish one. The Lévys intuited that they had to respond to the German schedule actively. On December 11, 1942 Pierre Laval, the Vichy Prime Minister published his infamous edict 108. "All Jews in the former Free Zone must get their IDs stamped 'J' by January 11, 1943." Marguerite recalled: 'J' stamped on my identity card means one thing: we, the French Jews are being assembled for deportation. Her response was immediate. "Cannot be!" Angry, she fumed. Wrath eliminates all ambivalence... "We shall not get our IDs stamped 'J.' We shall not be shipped east."

Thus, they took bold action just before all Jews had to register with the Vichy authorities. It was then that they changed their names and places of birth, Lévy became Lengel. With their falsified documents they sought a place of refuge in a small town in the French Alps, remote enough to attract little German attention but still in a situation that provided more than its share of danger. The Lévy/Lengels escaped in part because they internalized the danger and acted accordingly. They had the energy and the spiritual resources to act. They were not, as so many around them, paralyzed by the danger. To procrastinate was to invite impending doom.

Whisper Your Name Into My Ear is the story of a girl coming of age, moving away from her parents, setting off on her own and even going through the ordinary rebellions of teenage years under the most extraordinary, the most precarious of circumstances. All that is missing is a sexual awakening but as Marguerite was well aware, intimacy was exceedingly dangerous when one is living on false papers, when one's true self must be hidden even from one's own self. Still one marvels at Marguerite's bold decision to climb Mont Blanc, the highest peak in Europe, a brave decision even in the best of times and one made all the more bold by the times.

I read with appreciation her description of her mother's anguish when her hosts offer her Ham — the daughter of pious Jews she had never eaten Pork — but any gesture of discomfort could have blown their cover. One also admires her mother for hiding a Jewish calendar in her shoe. A Jewish woman should know when Rosh Hashanah occurs. She struggled to retain the last scaffold of her former life.

Marguerite came of age during the war and could strike out on her own. She is recruited into the French Resistance and suddenly discovers that others around her are living double lives, concealing far more than they are revealing. All the while she offers us a glimpse of life within France during this turbulent era. One senses the joy of her participation and the reader celebrates with her the liberation of France and the end of so great a jeopardy.

Were this a fable and not an autobiography one would have anticipated the return, the restoration. Job, who had lost his ten children and his wealth, recovers his wealth and has ten new children. The Bible remains mute about the scars from his earlier loss. But the Lévy's return is far from complete. Her father returns to his factory Géo Gignoux and resumes earning his livelihood, but a hernia operation costs him his life before the family fortune could be restored. The strains between the Lévy brothers exacerbated by the dangers of war are never healed and Marguerite must live in tension with her uncle who becomes CEO. Life is messy, endings are not necessarily endings and new beginnings are difficult. One does not return to the same place because circumstances have changed and one has changed.

One senses that Marguerite's efforts at gaining compensation for the family's losses prolonged the unsettled past and only magnified the sense that something precious had been taken from this young woman, something that even a lifetime in the United States married to a man she loved could not restore. There is no happy ending to this memoir, but many happy moments and an exuberance of spirit and an exhilaration of the soul that come through page after page, chapter after chapter.

Historical Context

LAW No. 1077 of 11 DECEMBER 1942
(For brevity called EDICT 108 by the Jewish community)
relative to the affixation of the mention "Jew" on identity cards delivered to French and
foreign Israelites. (J.O. 12 December 1942)

According to constitutional orders 12 and 12b:

Article One — Any person of the Jewish race according to the terms of the law of 2
June 1941 is requested to present him/herself, within a delay of one month from the date
of the promulgation of the present law, at the police station of his/her residence or in
want thereof to the gendarmerie to get a stamp "Jew" affixed on his or her identity card
or on a document taking its place and to his or her individual food card.

Article Two — Offences against article one of the present law will be punished by a
penalty of one month to one year in prison and a fine of 100 to 10,000 francs or of one of
these two penalties only, without prejudice to the right of the administrative authorities to
decide on the internment of the delinquent.

Any false declaration with the objective to dissimulate belonging to the Jewish race
will be punished with the same penalties.

LOI No 1077 du 11 DÉCEMBRE 1942

relative à l'opposition de la mention "Juif" sur les titres d'identité delivrés aux Israélites
français et étrangers. (J.O. 12 décembre 1942.)

Vu les actes constitutionals 12 et 12 bis ;

Article premier. – Toute personne de race juive aux termes de la loi du 2 juin 1941
est tenue de se présenter, dans un delai d'un mois à dater de la promulgation de la
presente loi, au commissariat de police de sa résidence ou à défaut à la brigade de
gendarmerie pour faire opposer la mention "Juif" sur la carte d'identité dont elle est
titulaire ou sur le titre en tenant lieu et sur la carte individuelle d'alimentation.

Art. 2 – Les infractions aux dispositions de l'article 1er de la présente loi seront
punies d'une peine d'un mois à un an d'emprisonnement et d'une amende de 100 a
10,000 fr. ou de l'une de ces deux peines seulement, sans préjudice du droit pour
l'autorité administrative de prononcer l'internement du délinquant.

Toute fausse déclaration ayant eu pour objet de dissimuler l'appartenance à la race
juive sera punie des mêmes peines.

Chapter 1

To War

In Paris on the avenue des Champs Elysées near the Etoile in 1936 on a summer evening about 6:30 PM, Papa and I watch the *Anciens Combattants,* the veterans of World War I, lay a wreath on the tomb of the Unknown Soldier under the flagstone beneath the Arc de Triomphe. I am eleven years old. The fires of patriotism burn bright in me. I push to the curb where I may see.

Suddenly, chaos erupts!

The socialists have just won a majority in the elections and Albert Lebrun, the president of the Republic, has asked Léon Blum to head the new government. The far right under the influential sway of Charles Maurras, the inflammatory anti-Semitic editor-in-chief of l'Action Française, a daily, is angry at the choice of Léon Blum, a Jew.

Shouts break out: *A bas Léon Blum! A bas les Juifs! La France aux Français!* Down with Léon Blum! Down with the Jews! France to the French!

The left is backing their leader with brawls of: *Vive Léon Blum! A bas l'Action Française! Mort à Maurras!* Death to Maurras.

I shudder.

I venerate the medals worn on the chests of the Anciens Combattants who lost their legs, their arms, and their lungs at Verdun, in the trenches, on the Marne River. Many parade in wheel chairs. The sight of the white gloves, the sounds of the marching bands, the multicolored wreaths wrapped with wide golden ribbons, the bouquets of red poppies, pink gladioli, white carnations; the blue corn flowers, and the decorated veterans — overwhelm me with the sacrifices made for France. I fear that the fanatical far rightists and the fanatical far leftists are destroying her.

At the same time I am curious.

I follow the actions of the Riot police. They use their truncheons to separate the fist-fighting demonstrators. I follow the kicking bodies being dragged to the waiting vans parked on the rue de Marignan, rue Marbeuf, and rue La Boétie, the side streets. There, the militants are being dumped one body on top of the other pell-mell into the white paddy wagons, hissing: A bas! Vive! Oust!

Margot Gerda Lévy — I was born in Mannheim, 1924, into a good Jewish family, though not a citizen of that country; my Alsatian-French father having repatriated two years ago to Paris.

My genealogy can be traced quite a way back. Papa comes from Soultz (Haut-Rhin) next to Guebwiller. Colmar about 20 km to the north is the nearest large town. My paternal great-grandfather, Félix Lévy, was born in 1795 "10 Pluviose Year VI of the French Revolution" in nearby Jungholtz. (Before that, civil records were kept in churches and synagogues). Félix had a son Joseph Lévy who married Josephine Kahn of Nancy and begot my father, Albert, and his three brothers and a sister.

Albert left school at fifteen to support his mother and younger siblings because his father (my grandfather Joseph Lévy), died in 1900; and an older brother, Louis, was in Breslau studying for the rabbinate. After three years of apprenticing at Cousin Jacques' Kosher deli in Mulhouse, Albert bought his first commercial property across the Rhine River in Mannheim. He was only eighteen.

In Mannheim, the entrepreneurial Albert sold or manufactured radios, I'm not sure which, but eventually he was drafted into the German army; survived World War One as a cook on the Russian front, and, in the midst of post World War I scarcity, started importing margarine from Holland. Albert was made of the cloth that wears well in a city. Soon he had a direct phone line to the Dresdner Bank.

The margarine scarcity abated; Albert moved on to paints. He bought a patent, and began stirring in a rented garage at night; by day he sought out painters and wholesalers. The business was

2

named ALÉDY, an acronym of Papa and his brother's first names and surname: Albert and Edouard and Lévy — ALÉDY G.m.b.H. "Grandma Lévy made Papa take Edouard as a partner," Maman told me later. ALÉDY developed within ten years into one of Germany's largest paint companies.

My parents met over tea.

Marthe, brown-haired, modern and vivacious, from the cigar manufacturing Oppenheimers, was visiting big sister Jenny at her apartment next to dad's building on H 2-16 avenue, Mannheim. Jenny invited Madame Lévy to tea. Suitably impressed, Grandma Josephine had Marthe over to meet her second son, Albert — at tea. "Well, he had curly red hair, was tall, energetic, and successful..." Maman told me with a little nuanced mischievous smile that tells the best truth. Marthe very soon brought Albert home to meet her parents. Grandpa liked Albert so much that he asked him on the first visit, "When is the wedding?" The courtship hadn't progressed that far. "I must first find out if Miss Oppenheimer likes me," the bridegroom to be answered. *"Ob ich Fräulein Marthe gefalle."*

No problem. Marthe had fallen in love with Albert at first sight.

In May 1920, at age thirty-five, Albert married twenty-five-year-old Marthe Oppenheimer from Gemmingen, near Heilbronn, in the state of Baden. Marthe was the youngest of Abraham and Babette Oppenheimer's eight children. Father Abraham Oppenheimer, the founder of a tobacco business of the same name, was an alderman and the head of the local Social Security.

When Marthe Oppenheimer became Albert Lévy's wife and had to switch from an executive role to raising a family, it was hard on her. She had been accustomed to running Oppenheimer Cigars since the age of seventeen "Up to the morning of my wedding" she blended and smoke-tasted tobacco leaves like a wine taster, handled the bookkeeping, and hired and fired. Oppenheimer Cigars was a national brand.

Nutrition classes, piano, bridge, and tennis besides a wide social circle helped her get over the domestic drudgery. Ilse came along in eleven months, and I three and a half years later. Mother applied her nutritional knowledge and fed me freshly squeezed carrot juice "from six weeks on." She grated the carrots and squeezed the juice out through a cheese-cloth. She fed her family crudités and salads. Maman had a stillborn baby between Ilse and me. "How did it die, Maman?" "When I was pregnant I lifted Ilse into the high chair and the cord broke," she says with a pinched smile.

A large, spacious, balconied apartment near the Rosengarten is where I was born with the help of a midwife. In our private garden I cut up worms with Leonard Feibelman, the upstairs boy who becomes my husband some twenty-plus years later.

Our eight-room apartment had Viennese voile curtains, moire drapes, and turquoise velvet and silk upholstered salon chairs and sofa. There was a live palm tree in the salon (I too water one, once monthly, in my dining room); the sun shone through the half-drawn voile curtains. The rosewood piano in the salon is where my sister had to practice and where Mother played Mozart sonatas and sang. I liked to climb into the rugged leather armchairs in the day room; of the formal Chippendale dining room and Papa's library I was in awe. Tabriz rugs covered the floors. Lisbeth and Fräulein help Maman. Papa never enters the kitchen. Mother cooks, bakes. She makes sauerkraut in a deep grey with blue-stripes stoneware pot covered with a flat slate stone. She cans, buys the vegetables and other provisions. We children play and live in a parallel world under the care of Fräulein. Later, Ilse and I were bribed with sugar cookies that had broken or caramelized almonds that had stuck together (the imperfect pieces) whenever we were sent on errands to Herschel, the corner grocer. On Sunday evenings my parents played bridge with the upstairs Feibelmans. On that occasion the pretty hand-hammered small silver cream pitchers with matching small hand-hammered silver plates (for sugar cubes) were used.

Under the class veneer Papa and Mother believed in a hardy brood. "These children have to fit into the world!" (Papa). A fall, a scraped knee? "Go into the kitchen, break an egg, peel off the inner skin of the shell and apply the soft membrane to the wound. It will disintegrate as you heal." (Maman, when I was seven). Swim, roller and ice-skate, scooter, play hula-hoop, and ball — get hardened. Every evening after our bath, Maman would give us a cold water spray with the hand-held shower in the tub.

Happy children invent practical jokes. On Saturday night, we knot dad's nightgown sleeve or slide a wet sponge under Mother's bed sheet or an alarm clock goes off at 3 AM under their bed. Maman screams at the sight of a June bug. Really? A chocolate bug sits on her bed sheet as she folds back the cover! Although we decide many times to stay awake and listen to their reactions — always we fall asleep.

Sunday mornings we crawl into their bed. Papa pretends his arm is stiff or his back all wet or he yawns: "Couldn't sleep last night!" He plays with us. The rules are simple: have fun — within the perimeter permitted by the family. We are naturally respectful and neat. Not to be on time for meals — hands washed, hair brushed, clean — never enters our minds. We follow the example of our elders. We entertain ourselves. We read books and play with our Wertheimer and Oppenheimer cousins at Post Office, stamp set, checkers. In the street, we spin tops, and hopscotch. On Tuesdays I sit on a footstool next to Fräulein Bardman, the visiting seamstress, and sew doll clothes from the age of four on. Later, I embroider napkin holders and shell peanuts for buttered sandwiches. I am grateful to my parents to have born me into a creative household and given me my space.

Every day in Mannheim Maman meets or talks on the telephone with her sisters Selma and Jenny. I see Maman at the top of the Oppenheimer and the Lévy clans similar to a well-tended rose in a cared for garden. Later, I realize how dependent Maman really was on this nourishing sub-culture, and when that is destroyed, she just shrivels like a pinched flower.

On the other hand, Papa's brilliance and his humor inject into our household a sense of individuality. "The ancestors," Papa once said with a mirth-filled smile as he pointed to the oil canvases of his father, mother, and Mother's parents set in heavy rococo gilded frames on the walls of his library. "Albert!" A slight mockery of her parents provoked an immediate gentle rebuke from Mother who adored her parents. My surname is a source of strength.

5

On Saturday mornings, Papa stands on the bima, the altar in the synagogue. He wears a new business suit and top hat. He reads from the Torah and gives charity. Charity is not a private affair back then: the smiling rabbi announces to the congregation the amount in a loud voice: "He schnudert... he gives..." The congregation gasps. Warmly, the rabbi shakes Albert Lévy's hand. An aura surrounds Papa as he descends the steps of the altar; head high under his black silken top hat. I think: When this Lévy grows up... — she too wants to earn the respect of the community.

Hitler breaks the family circle when I am nine. The adults around me speak in hushed voices.

In Papa's library Maman whispers to me: "*They* burned down the Reichstag and accuse a crazed Dutchman of the crime." Mother's face turns white. By then, I had seen brown-shirted men goose-step and make the Heil Hitler salute in the streets of Mannheim.

On the day Papa calls Ilse and me into his library, I know something important is about to happen. Seated in his black and brown striped velvet armchair behind his desk, he says: "Children, fear not. Your father will protect you," and he opens the center drawer of his heavily polished dark brown Chippendale desk and sets a small revolver on the desktop. I feel Hitler has nothing bigger than my father's mother of pearl-handled revolver.

Papa's protection isn't just the emotional sort. Father goes to Soultz — his birthplace in Alsace. On his return (I remember the evening with blazing gravity) at the dining room table, dressed in the semi-formal attire that he always wears — a suit, vest, and a tie — he announced: "We are moving to Paris." He had turned the pages of the register in Soultz and found right away the birth records of Edouard, Alphonse, and himself. "The mayor said he will issue our papers of reintegration as French citizens at once." My parents cut deep smiles. Because the Versailles treaty had returned Alsace and the Lorraine to France in 1919, Papa obtained French citizenship for his, Edouard's, and Alphonse's families. We had become French by rightful re-integration of all Alsatian-Lorrainers.

I am excited. My older cousins from Strasbourg: Hélène, Robert, and Louis Meyer laugh a lot when they visit. They are so much fun. They speak their mind. They are irreverent. Once, Robert said to dad: "Uncle Albert, the world is not your factory!" No one in our family circle would have dared! Gay Hélène taught me "Frère Jacques" and "Il court, il court le furet." Once dad sat on a tray of chocolate cookies she had baked. He controlled his temper and with a dry cough, went to change his suit. Hélène had put down — over a board — one large tray to cool on dad's upholstered leather armchair. The idea for my wholesale import business I later glean from Hélène's gift shop.

With my cousins from Strasbourg, Papa speaks Alsatian. My sense of heritage is further strengthened when Papa explains that members of the Lévy tribe had walked to the Rhine Valley hundreds and hundreds of years ago in small bands after the fall of the Second Temple in Jerusalem.

Without letting on to the children, Father sells ALÉDY and goes with Mother to find an apartment in Paris.

Ilse and I are shushed off for two weeks to our maternal Grandma Babette Oppenheimer in Gemmingen with three or four little gift boxes of yummies: dates, prunes, apricots and almonds.

We would ceremoniously kneel and open the lower drawer in grandma's room after dinner, pick one date, one prune, one apricot and several almonds in the hollow of our palms. They would last ten contentedly chewing, self-disciplined, grinning minutes.

Mannheim, we left before *they* did something to Papa. Papa had sent two workers home on SA Intimidation day. (Ernst Roehm, the head of Hitler's Sturmabteilung, the SA, a special faction of thugs, had ordered his adherents to report at work in all Jewish-owned businesses in their brown-shirted SA uniforms on that day in order to intimidate the Jewish owners). Later, Roehm was murdered on the Führer's orders and to empower the SS). At ALÉDY two workers showed up dressed in their brown-shirted uniforms. "Today I sent two men home," Papa announced at dinner with a dry cough. "I told them that in my factory, the workers wear the

ALÉDY uniform. They both hopped on their motorcycles and returned wearing their ALÉDY-issued blue overalls."

"Albert, this is risky!" Mother had exclaimed with a grimace of alarm.

The next day in Papa's library, Maman whispered to me: "I hope we can get out before they do something to Papa."

Papa also fired Lisbeth in disregard of Hitler's orders that Jews cannot dismiss Christian employees. Father had returned early from work and, opening the front door, he found Lisbeth reverse reading the carbon copy of a letter he had written by holding it up to the mirror with all the lights on. Papa exploded, "I will have no spies in my employ!"

My sister and I crossed the border into France in Forbach by train in a first-class compartment with Papa. Maman had stayed in Paris to ready the apartment while Father fetched us from Grandma Oppenheimer. It was March 1st, 1934. I observed that when Papa presented the brown hard cover French passports to Hitler's henchman, the brown-shirted SA saluted respectfully. Much later I reflect: Germany had no army, no navy; the Luftwaffe did not exist. France still had the edge. In my new blue and white taffeta dress with a white bow in my hair, a new life is starting.

From the moment I set foot on the quay of the Gare de l'Est railway station, I think Paris is magic.

Our apartment at 76 avenue de la Bourdonnais is located near the Champs de Mars. It is furnished with our Mannheim furnishings, and beautifully wallpapered. Our crystal chandelier hangs over the dining room table; the Tabriz rugs cover the parquet floors. The large Romantic painting of a young couple in a boat on a lake hangs above the silk sofa in the salon; the other more impressionistic one hangs on the wall behind the dining room buffet.

The French windows extend from floor to ceiling. I am disappointed though: six rooms instead of eight. No long hallway to roller-skate in, but impressive glass doors separate the three

8

formal rooms. The apartment is divided into formal and private quarters divided by an opaque glass door, each built around an inner rectangular hall, so the whole looks like a number eight.

On that first night in Paris, Papa takes us to the café on the Place de L'École Militaire. Five broad avenues fan out: avenue de la Bourdonnais; avenue Bosquet; avenue de la Motte-Picquet, avenue Duquesne, and avenue de Tourville. "Look, look!" Under a street lamppost, a pair of young lovers hold each other and kiss. The École Militaire is flooded in light. A statue of Maréchal Joffre on his horse faces the entrance to the Champs de Mars.

Papa clears his throat; folds furrow his high forehead. In a stern tone of voice he says: "We are in France now. We will do like the French. Not one word of German will be spoken between yourselves from now on at home or in the street." My sister and I look at each other; we burst into fits of laughter. *"Comment vous appelez-vous?" "Je m'appelle...* What is your name? My name is..." are the few words of French we had been taught in private lessons. It is here at the glass-enclosed Café de l'École Militaire in Paris that the pattern of taking punches on the chin with a grin — is cast. Who wants to sound like a Boche in France 1934? Later, Papa's executive order saves our family's lives.

Promptly I change my name to Marguerite from Margot Gerda. My sister Ilse changes hers to Ghislaine. I unclasp my gold neck chain with a gold medallion engraved Margot on one side and on the other the Star of David. The necklace stays in my jewelry box for years. I take it out from time to time to remember.

Perceptions and thinking change. Rhythms and cadence change. Papa gets up at 6:00. I hear the front door close at 6:45AM sharp. Papa leaves 76 avenue de la Bourdonnais and takes the commuter train at the Orsey rail station to Savigny-sur-Orge. He has bought a disused brewery with enormous cellars, called Géo Gignoux. Maman tells me: "Papa has to start all over, work very hard, take great risks. He must hire workers, staff, salesmen, a chemist, and buy all new machinery." He must convert the old brewery into a modern paint factory.

Soon the Schmidts — Papa's old foreman Helmut from ALÉDY, wife Hilde and five-year-old Rolph from Mannheim — arrive for dinner at 76. Papa has hired Helmut Schmidt to supervise the new factory, Géo Gignoux, in France. Within five years, the Nazi Schmidts steal back to Germany. In 1940, Helmut would return in his SS uniform to arrest Papa and "show him who the boss is now." Luckily we had left!

At home Papa says that the work ethic in France is different. The concierge has to inspect the satchels of the workers at the gate and let pass one only liter of wine daily. The French workers had been accustomed to bringing two liters of *gros rouge* to work each morning.

When Papa returns home at 7 PM, he directly goes to his Chippendale armoire in the salon and pours himself a Cognac.

After dinner, my parents go for a walk in the Champs de Mars. Papa would much rather rest. In Mannheim, my parents had subscriptions to the theater and the Opera. In Paris, more tired and thriftier — they go and see the lighter fare of Mistinguett and Josephine Baker. "Papa needs to relax."

Ghis and I at first attend the free Rothschild school. My first report card, oh pain! I am fourteenth in the class. Mother consoles me. "Listen to my own mishaps," she says lightly. "Today at Félix Potin's (Paris' famed grocery chain) I asked for a 'window of cheese' instead of a 'slice' because in the dictionary the German word 'Scheibe' means in French both: *une tranche* (slice) and *verre* (glass, window). And Aunt Martha told me yesterday that she went to the hairdresser, pointed to her neck, and asked the operator for a shave of her butts. She misconstrued the translation for the German word *hintern*. (In French, "hintern" is used for both "behind" and "buttocks.") Smiles replace tears.

Within three months, I am head of my class, allowed to wear a medal on a red ribbon on my school uniform.

It's the director of the Rothschild school who cures my perennial winter ear and throat infections. He asks me to tell my mother to put a beret on my head and a scarf around my neck.

10

Soon, Maman invites the director and his wife to our apartment for an elaborate dinner. A newcomer, she needs to show where we come from. I am sure side doors and drawers of the buffet were opened for proper glimpses at the silver, the crystal, the Rosenthal and Meissen dinner and tea sets.

By then, I had done my own innocent impression on René. The nephew of the director regularly threw his ball over the wall into the girls' playground at recess near the exact spot where I was standing, then scaled the bricks and watched my reaction. Catch! I threw the ball back.

Soon a group of us meet on the Champs de Mars after school. We play dodge ball and prisoner's base; in the fountain I launch my rubber-band-propelled boat that Papa had brought me from a client who is a toy manufacturer. "I told him I have two daughters."

Sometimes Maman brings to us and to our playmates on the Champs de Mars fresh warm croissants in a white paper bag from our favorite bakery on the rue Saint-Dominique. Buttery and flaky. Later I realize that with Papa at his factory all day and her sisters in Germany, Maman pined for company in Paris.

In Mannheim, Mother would say: "Papa gave a very nice Bar Mitzvah to your cousin Ludwig." Or: "Papa funded Hélène's dowry. She is getting married to Julien Ruffel, a Christian of Strasbourg. We are attending the wedding." In Mannheim, strangers would ask me: "Are you Albert Lévy's daughter? Please give my best regards to your parents." Proudly, I delivered the messages. In Paris, no one knows us.

In July, the Rothchild school year ends. I have my eye on a lycée. I'm nine. Maman says: "Papa thinks the free Rothchild School is adequate for another year. He doesn't yet know what his earning ability is." I really want the best education. I insist. Maman confides: "I will pay for your tuition and books with savings from my household money." The seventh form is a paying grade.

At Lycée Victor Duruy on Boulevard des Invalides I excel in math and in French composition. The teacher calls me "Marguerite Gautier" after a famous French novelist. Proud and happy I learn everything about France. Her history, the names of her rivers: le Rhin, le Rhône, la Garonne... and her mountains — Les Alps, les Pyrénées... At school, France is referred to as "the hexagon." I'm especially interested in the Revolution of 1789, the people fighting for Liberté and Egalité. The teacher reads my composition aloud to the class. I had written something to the effect that the king and the nobility lived in luxury and trampled the serfs' wheat crops in pursuit of wild game and that they kept the serfs down while they led a life of pleasure and dissipation. At the same time, I felt very sad at the fate of Marie Antoinette's two children.

Victor Duruy teaches us that Germany is lacking in chivalry and had barbarians as ancestors. Visigoths, Goths, Ostrogoths. Vandals. That Germany remained fragmented until Bismarck unified the Principalities and the Duchies into one country; while France has been one realm since Charlemagne in 800 A.D. I bathe in bubbles of French superiority.

French culture molds me. I read Jules Verne; *Les Lettres de Madame de Sévigné;* Alexander Dumas' *Les Trois Mousquetaires, Monte-Cristo* and *La Reine Margot; La Petite Fadette,* by Georges Sand — and many more. Ghis and I go to a matinée at la Comédie Française. We see Corneille's *Le Cid.* Papa and Maman take Ghis and me to an evening performance of Madame Sans-Gêne. The next day I impersonate the char woman — crude, vulgar. I put my fists on my hips, make fun of cops. "Have you ever..." Maman smiles.

Once, I invite Claudine, a lycée classmate, "Come and play at my house." The next day she delivers a formally worded: "My parents have not the honor to know your parents." Yet, my father is an industrialist and we live on the fashionable avenue de la Bourdonnais, while Claudine's is a simple bailiff at the court house, and her apartment is above stores on avenue Bosquet. Snubbed!

Agnès Lecourtois doesn't snub me. Her father, Daniel, is a famed Parisian character actor, and her mother: a Bolshoi ballet dancer in exile. Daniel Lecourtois adopted Agnès at the age of two.

Both Agnès and I are unconventional. Agnès becomes my best friend.

At the lycée, every teacher quotes at least once in her class *"L'Homme est un roseau pensant,* Man is a thinking willow." Pascal's heritage is inculcated into us whenever we deviate, whenever we respond to a question with a stupid answer. *Avez-vous bien réfléchi?* Did you think that through? The teacher would say in a singing intonation, her authoritative inflection of the voice leaving no doubt. Think! In Paris I become a thinking willow. Thank you Blaise Pascal!

In 1935, Papa is fifty years old. When Maman goes to the Champs de Mars to watch us play prisoner's base after school she would sit on a bench; benches are free. To occupy a chair you need to buy a ticket.

When Ghis and I join the Scouts, we buy yards of khaki fabric and a bag of down blended with goose feathers. On the foot-pedaled Singer sewing machine, I sew my own sleeping bag; I stitch my own scout skirt. Maman has to buy the jacket (too difficult to cut and sew), the blouse, and the neckerchief. My huge sleeping bag weighs a ton and resembles a duffel bag. It's warm and I schlep it!

While I sew I look over the common courtyard into the dining room of the very wealthy on avenue Frédéric le Play whose apartments border directly the Champs de Mars (one street over from avenue de La Bourdonnais). I look through the window of the (at eye-level) third-floor apartment and watch the goings on of the butler in white gloves, and the maid in a grey-and-white uniform arranging fresh bouquets of gorgeous gladioli, carnations, and roses into wide-mouthed crystal vases. Once I interrupt a tête-à-tête candlelight dinner of the exquisite daughter with her dashing young man. Unabashedly, I stare at the fine gestures of her arms and hands and at his pleasure. The maid is summoned to draw the curtain on me. *Tant pis!* I act out the romantic scene for Maman.

But I feel seriously excluded when my peers discuss the various forms of old polite address between parents and children *Vous-tu, vous-vous, tu-vous, tu-tu,* and Jacqueline warbles: "My parents

13

address us with the formal 'vous' and we are allowed to use the intimate 'tu' talking to them,'" and Gail solemnly hoots with a hint of superiority: "My parents address us as 'tu' and we speak to them in the formal 'vous.'" I have experienced Hitler's threats and am aware of the dangers that lurk out there on the other side of the frontier. To myself I think: Rome burned while Nero fiddled.

In the Tuileries Gardens, one Sunday afternoon, a beautiful little blond boy about four dressed in an expensive light blue sailor suit comes over to watch me wind up my rubber band-propelled 12" boat. He looks so nervous and excited that I let him set the boat into the fountain. His grandparents seated on two chairs nearby address him as "Monsieur." "Monsieur, you may touch the boat." He appears rather sickly, translucent. The excessive formality and his frailty sting my vitality. I feel too strong. This is just one of many instances of hollowed decadence in the old stock crawling all about me that fills me with a deep malaise hard to understand. The nervy, withered branches.

At the lycée in the hallway waiting to enter a classroom, I ink algebra equations on my hands. I solve mathematical problems as a form of entertainment. Once I have to copy one hundred lines of "I shall not exchange stamps in the classroom." ONE HUNDRED LINES are the normal redress for transgressions. I loathe the "hundred liner social embarrassment and the repetitive work" so much that I stop exchanging stamps in class. But I continue making my own stamp books and go often with Papa on Sunday mornings to the stamp market on the Champs Elysées between la Place de la Concorde and le Rond Point where vendors set up their displays and I would buy a packet of 100 or 500 stamps from around the world, many from the French colonies. Large stamps printed in exotic blues, greens. Orange, yellow, red, and purple with artistically rendered ethnic figures.

My peers select me as *chef de classe o*f my 4th form. This entitles me to stand at the head of the class as we enter a new classroom. From classroom to classroom I carry the heavy ledgers which are half the size of an artist's portfolio holder into which the teachers set down the grades. I open and close the book on the teacher's desk at the beginning and at the end of each class. Few of my fellow students want the honor of the weight.

Closeness corrupts. My history and geography teacher whispers to me as I pick up the ledger on her desk: "If you have time, Mlle Lévy, you may wish to review what we have studied so far in history for next Wednesday…" For the rest of that school year, she gives me advance notice about a forthcoming surprise quiz. I kept "our" secret until today.

Before school starts, the students buy their textbooks at la Librairie Gilbert-Jeune on the Boul' Mich by the quais. We cut and fold paper covers. I eagerly memorized a whole year's worth of curriculum in advance. Classroom time is mostly spent raising my right arm. "Call on me! On me! I know the answer!" Math is my favorite subject.

Paris is freedom. At home I take to straddling chairs backwards. Toilet seats as well — I sit backwards to pee. *A bas* bourgeois conventions! I test my ground rules. Bedtime at 8 PM? Never mind. I read by flashlight under the covers those titillating sexy magazines bought at the kiosk until Maman confiscates them. I quickly discover that all those eight o'clock bedtimes encourage 4 AM wake ups. Under my coverlet, bright early and fresh and with a flashlight — I memorize poetry, English irregular verbs, geology. Good for perfect grades on that day's tests.

Scouting is widespread in France. Soon after our arrival in Paris, a young lady blond and blue-eyed in a slim skirt and pretty shoes introduces herself at Synagogue Chasseloup-Laubat. She asks Ghis and me if we would like to join her troop. We really wish to, but Papa says "No." Mother is closer to us, and she wants us to be happy. Papa is very involved with his factory. Weeks pass, and we join the Swallows. Ghis earns the totem name "*Albatross fidèle*, faithful Albatross" and I: "Salamander coquette." The girls are cliquish, and conceited.

We join the Maccabées at the opposite end of the socio-economic-idealistic arc. Months of motivational songs and slogans eventually dim our fervor to become chalutzims in Israel, pioneers digging the earth and making the desert bloom. I like living at 76 avenue de la Bourdonnais, I like my Lycée Victor Duruy. I hate hypocrisy. Unbeknown to myself, Ghis and I are exploring our inner inclinations, constructing our identities. After the Swallows and the Maccabées we move over to the Robins, a non-denominational upper-middle-class troop. The girls speak about their lycée and their teachers with detached humor. Their freedom of mind and openness appeal to me. Our cheftaine is a mature career woman, I don't know which profession: she always arrives at outings carrying a briefcase.

At avenue de la Bourdonnais, Papa every now and then hints at Edouard's high spending. "I saw another entry for 5,000 francs in the cashbook today...;" but one particular evening he adds: "I told Edouard today his sons Norbert and Jean are idiots. They have to attend private school in order not to flunk out of class. Edouard replied: 'And your daughters change Scout troops like handkerchiefs.' 'At least they are independent! I told him.'" and Papa's eyes twinkled. I never really gave my parents credit for their support. They brought us up free to experiment.

Freedom to experiment ends in near disaster at Le Printemps department store. On the first time there, I go up and down the moving escalators, up and down, while Mother and Ghis shop. When I had ridden enough, where is Mother? I am nine. I am lost in Paris, I cry. An elegantly coiffed Parisian with a chic little blue felt hat, the epitome of French sophisticated savoir-faire and lightness, takes me home to 76 avenue de la Bourdonnais by bus which was more expensive than subway at the time. She rings the bell, and delivers me with a cheerful smile to Francine. "Voilà!"

A gloved handshake.

Mother arrives home in a state of hysteria. "*Mein Sonnenschein! Mein Sonnenschein*! My Sunshine! my Sunshine! If I had lost you, Dad would have given me a very hard time!" So Papa cares about me, too, I smile to myself. (Father is rather the strict, powerful type). So, I'm loved by both parents!

French words sound delicious on the tongue. They gently vibrate the vocal cords; they touch the taste buds. I savor their flavor. On a subsequent trip to Le Printemps — Maman, Ghis, and

I go to the department store on the Boulevard Haussman to buy a bra, *un soutien-gorge* in French. The vowels "ou-ien-o" tickle my tongue. Head high, I repeat aloud along the crowded boulevard a dozen times the musical monosyllables *"Sou-tien-gorge, sou-tien-gorge..."* with Maman and Ghis trailing a distance behind bent in two with laughter. People look up; eyebrows arched, and go on on their way.

At what age did I really start exploring *mon* quartier? The Eiffel Tower, the Champs de Mars from Le Trocadéro to L'École Militaire; le Musée Rodin; the shopping street — rue Clerc. The rue de Grenelle is filled with staid ministries and foreign consulates. I remember pushing once with Agnès along the broad avenue de la Bourdonnais to the Seine and noting that all the multi-storied grey stone apartment buildings look solidly solemn. No stores. Eventually I must have extended my flaneries along les quays of the Seine. I never have enough time to really browse through the many open-air stalls of the *bouquinistes,* the famed antique booksellers. On Sundays I protest, "Le Bois de Boulogne? Not again! It's boring!" "But I have been to le Parc Monceau!" Maman calls me "my Little Gypsy." I like best my rucksack and going camping.

At Easter, Pentecost, and in the summer — with whatever troop we happen to belong to at the moment — we hammer spikes into the ground, attach our tents' cords. Our days start with reveille around six. Cheftaine blows a horn. Sleepy, we crawl out of our warm feather bags. Mother mails me the daily Figaro newspaper to scout camp.

One of my favorite chores at camp is to walk a mile or two in the morning to the village baker and fetch the round boules of fresh country bread. Once, two Girl Scouts and I eat a large chunk of crust off a warm, croustillant five-pound round *pain de campagne*. Back at camp, we had to listen to a sermon about self-discipline. Oh well!

The worst time in Paris was in the early dark of winter on the way home from school at the corner of the avenue de Tourville and the Boulevard de Latour Maubourg. A man would emerge holding

17

his wiggling penis in his hand, walking straight at me. I would break into a run, cross the Boulevard de Latour Maubourg, and, at a safe distance, turn around. If he had left, I would continue walking along the avenue de Tourville at my normal pace, heart pounding. At home I'm tight-lipped.

In le Bois de Meudon, once, our troop had scattered about on a treasure hunt. Suddenly Cheftaine blew an insistent whistle. We run up. She leads us out of the woods to the road. My patrol leader whispers to me: "Cheftaine saw a man with his pants down exposing himself."

Paris!

Every two weeks, Mother stuffs a Kraft clasp envelope with Gruyère and butter for each of her sisters Selma and Jenny in Mannheim, and once a month for her sister Bertha Hanauer in Heilbronn. I stand by the kitchen table and watch her lovingly wrap the slice of yellow creamy butter into wax paper, then wrap the cheese into a piece of white cloth. Butter is bought by the pound and cut with a metal string from a *motte,* a beehive shaped mound. With sensual pleasure, Maman gives a pat to the fleshed-out golden envelope and says, "This will give them something to eat and bake with."

In the summer of 1934, Maman and I again visit Mannheim and Grandma Oppenheimer in Gemmingen. Grandma's veranda looks over the vineyards heavy with purple and green grapes. She shares the peace of her vineyards with me. I, her grand-daughter, am dressed in pink bloomers. I'm nine years old, and French. I have learned of Liberté, Egalité. I sing the Marseillaise, and the Gauls have become my ancestors. On the veranda I turn the picture of Kaiser Wilhelm against the wall. "He made war on France!" Grandma Oppenheimer wipes a tear with her starched, embroidered white handkerchief. In silence, she suffers this outrage to her dignity by her favorite grandchild whose little bug of patriotism feels triumphant.

Every morning in Paris, I read Le Figaro while dunking a slice of buttered toast into my café au lait before setting off for school. Politics are my passion. I hope to discuss the news with Papa in the evening at 6:45 PM.

In the salon, I wait for Father's key to turn the front door lock. After a long commute from his factory, he will first hang his coat in the hall closet, then enter the salon, take out a key from his vest pocket, and open the side door to his armoire. There he pours into a snifter a Courvoisier. For a moment he pauses, stares at the light reflected inside his hand (or is it a *Brocha,* blessing over the liquor?) and next in one gulp downs the fiery Cognac. Only after the ritual of passage from business to the closed family circle is completed, will he recognize me. Seated in one of the silk and velvet upholstered armchairs, impassioned for justice and burning with political fever, I pounce. "Papa, Mussolini used mustard gas on barefoot, ill-armed native troops in Ethiopia. What will the League of Nations do?" They must set wrong things right. At once! I feel. And I shove under Papa's nose the picture in Le Figaro of the poor little Ethiopian donkeys lying on the road, jaws smashed to pieces, eyes blown out from their sockets, their stomachs opened.

Papa would like a moment of peace. He resents my assault. Nevertheless he takes me seriously. I am his preposterous child who dares speak to him before being spoken to. He clears his throat: "Mussolini is no better than Hitler," he says. "Eventually we will have to go to war, but then it will be too late."

I am still wrapped in an aura of innocence, quiveringly ready for happiness. I expect grownups to right things. "The democracies are paralyzed," says Papa.

Papa is a fighter. He has been there in the Great War that was supposed to end all wars less than twenty years ago. He doesn't like war, but he lets me know that you have to fight when an enemy threatens, and the sooner the better.

In Mannheim — Mother's brother-in-law Uncle Max Wertheimer, his son Fred (my seventeen-year-old cousin), and Uncle Elias Strauss are sent to Dachau Concentration camp for six

19

weeks, then sent home — all to frighten them into leaving. In Paris, we tiptoe on our silky Tabriz rugs as if in a morgue.

Papa wastes no time. He immediately sends a sum of money to Stanley Oppenheimer, a cousin of Maman's in Philadelphia. "Please issue affidavits for Marthe's sisters Selma, Gida, Jenny and their families so that they can immigrate to the United States." Papa has to prod, and prod, and prod. "Please hurry! We haven't heard yet! Have you exchanged the French francs I sent you as a guarantee that they will not become a burden to you nor to the American government? The French francs are devaluating. Please hurry!" Eventually, eleven people are issued visas to immigrate to America. The Strausses do not make it. I learn that money can save lives. I feel evil licking my skin like vipers' tongues.

1938. Uncle Louis and Aunt Gretel arrive from Czechoslovakia at the Gare de l'Est, weary but smiling with two suitcases and five Louis d'or (equivalent to five American Gold Eagle dollars) glued to the pipe under the lavabo in the W.C. But W.Cs. are locked before the trains pull into the rail station in Paris, so Uncle Louis had to fetch the conductor. *"Le conducteur* thought I was very clever," I hear Uncle Louis say to Papa. Papa winces at "clever."

That night at home alone with us, Father says: "Louis is a professor with an empty head. He forgot to provide for himself and his wife. The five gold pieces are all he could take out of Czechoslovakia." Louis left a valuable collection of paintings on the walls of his apartment in Bruno. Papa now has to support Uncle Louis and Aunt Gretel. I learn that you must prepare for bad times.

The slogan "Peace with Honor, peace for our generation," has failed. In 1938, Germany overruns Czechoslovakia.

Czechoslovakia, her defenses dismantled by Hitler, is a little friend. I am angry. How could France and England sacrifice un petit ami in need? I no longer trust Daladier, nor Chamberlain, nor people who govern us. But here my anger is tempered by pleasure.

In the salon with Uncle Louis and Aunt Gretel, I play games of lapsus linguae. My uncle has spent a vacation in the Carpathian Mountains with Dr. Sigmund Freud. In *On Dreams*, Freud quotes

Uncle Louis' doctoral thesis, "Sexual Symbols in the Bible". Uncle Louis analyzes my dreams: The train ride through green meadows means you wish to take off, he says. He reads character into my handwriting; he reads the lines of my palm. I have a long head line, and my heart line stretches all the way across. Both lines run parallel and separate. "That's very good," he says. "Marguerite is coming into her own." My chest swells. The self-confidence with which I handle the Dean of Admissions at the University of Grenoble a few years later is due in part to the influence and the admiration of a learned uncle who came into my life when I was thirteen.

For the next year I enjoy the presence of my worldly and once richer relations. They show me a new perspective. Uncle Louis paints for me a stark geo-political-military picture. "Now the Skoda Works produce weapons for Hitler." In my mind I see Hitler like a boa constrictor devouring one country after another, and edging closer to France for his next meal.

1939. The little town of Savigny-sur-Orge where Father bought his factory doesn't look the same. A white poster glued on the stucco wall of the mairie calls for General Mobilization. Antoine, Noel, Lucien, and several other workers of Papa's paint factory stand reading their orders effective the next day, Saturday September 2, zero hour. Glum, in blue overalls, navy berets pulled over one ear, empty canvas satchels slung over their shoulders, their faces show bewilderment. Poland is far away and Stalin last month signed a friendship treaty with Germany. The recruits of 1914 had put flowers in the barrels of their bayonets as they marched off to the front...

Out of respect I move behind the recruits. To myself I repeat the old adage: "The French soldier may look sloppy, but the army is fit."

War has come. We give up the apartment in Paris. Papa and Maman decide we should stay on in Savigny-sur-Orge at the cottage. I take algebra classes at the École Communale, public school. English, Geometry, History, Geography, and French literature I study on my own. I take up typing and shorthand as well. These skills later offer havens.

In Savigny I walk or ride my bicycle over the railroad tracks up the plateau to school, and to the neighboring villages of Viry — Morsang — and more. At Géo Gignoux, I sit on a high stool next to Mlle Jeanne at a table in her "lab." We fill little metal boxes with white Géo Barium powder for hospitals. At home, I knit a white lamb's wool sweater for myself and dye it navy blue. More practical.

One day Monsieur Kaiser arrives at our cottage. He carries a wooden box. It is easy for me to remember Monsieur Kaiser for his strong build and the middle age noticeable on his visage. His heavy German accent disconcerts me. I think: "Another boring visitor of my parents' generation. How can I make my exit?" He stands in the living room of our cottage inside the Géo Gignoux compound. Solemnly he declares: "Monsieur Lévy, here are our valuables. We may be interned as stateless Jews. Please take care for us," and he hands his wooden box to Papa. I wonder what my father will say. I stare from one to the other. A gentle look appears on my father's energetic face; a sigh wells up to his lips. Monsieur Kaiser turns to me, the offspring. He says: "I have known your father since 1920. He's a man of principles. I would entrust him with my life."

I have always felt proud of Papa. Monsieur Kaiser praises him even more. With German precision he says: "I met your father once in Mannheim, he was pushing a huge leather valise on a cart in the street. When I asked him what he was doing, he said: 'I am taking the morning's receipts to the Dresdner bank. They need my money to meet their obligations.'"

Monsieur Kaiser sets his rough wooden box on our Chippendale dining table. From that day on, and all throughout World War II, the fate of the Kaiser treasure is entwined with the fate of the Lévys.

When I am fifteen, we school children take gas masks to school, and spend time in air raid shelters. My father installs ours inside one of the deep damp caves of Géo Gignoux. I knit while waiting for the "All clear." At home, thick purple curtains cover windows. At night, our foursome plays bridge by candlelight because the fall leaves plug up the Géo Gignoux dam and the generator fails. The electricity flickers. Ghis and I appropriate a wheelbarrow at Géo Gignoux for our private clothing drive: "Your donation, s'il-vous-plait, for the Alsatians and Lorrainers evacuated from their homes..."

Our cart — filled up with knitting yarn, blouses, skirts, scarfs, petticoats, socks, and even a wool coat — jumps over the cobbled sidewalks to and from the collection site inside city hall. Ghis and I, laughing, steady the one wheeler.

In Savigny, our garden borders the river. On the Orge River, Ghis and I can go rowing. As a dare I pluck a dead rat out of the water by the tail and swing the rodent into the air. Fly! Very close to my sister's face. So sorry!

Emilio, an Italian worker at Papa's factory, presents Ghis and me with a pair of pigeons; we are delighted. A fenced-in pigeon house stands next to the cottage. One day, by mistake, the door is left open. Mine flies away. For hours, Ghis and I walk up and down the streets of Savigny with the second pigeon attached by the feet to my shoulder. We think her cooing should attract her mate. No such luck. Disconsolate, I return home. Within two days Emilio offers me a new male pigeon.

That same generous Emilio, who could not read or write and noted down the weight on the lids of the buckets of paints as 50 + 3 or 50 + 6, exactly as the scale indicated, instead of 53 or 56 kilos, regularly beat his two daughters who both worked at Géo Gignoux and regularly committed incest with them. Papa installed two beds in an attic at the factory where they could escape their father. When I hear about it, I think: To me, Emilio gives two pigeons — to his two daughters incest and violent beatings. I wanted to do something about the inequality, and for a moment I ponder: Should I return my pigeon to him and say, "Stop treating your daughters so badly," but I didn't feel up to it.

Ghis the first born, stronger by three and one half years, scratched me in my tender years. Her scratches, I'm sure, helped

23

develop in me a strong empathy for human suffering and injustice. When on the Route de Morsang about 5 PM, on the way home at a time Géo Gignoux let out, I sometimes met one or the other of Papa's workers on their bicycles (they always saluted me kindly with a hand to their beret) I thought: Marguerite, you should deserve their respect for your own deeds, and not because you are the boss's daughter. I couldn't stand the unearned esteem. Hypocrisy!

During the inevitable summer of 1939 at the cottage, Papa eats lunch with us. He likes his wife and daughters. He entertains us with happenings at the factory as when Mlle Jeanne is given a silver watch and a plaque to celebrate her 25 years of service at the brewery and later at Géo Gignoux paints. "She shyly asked me if Gilbert could stand next to her at the ceremony because they had been living together for twenty-plus years." (Gilbert likewise worked at Géo Gignoux). "We didn't want to get married; they cut our social security benefits." All summer I had been sitting next to Mademoiselle Jeanne in her upstairs work place. We packed Géo Barium powder into small metal boxes. Thin like a match, she always wore the same blue-checkered apron. I didn't see her smile once. We never spoke a word. We just quietly filled and weighed the small paper bags with the white powder, dropped them in the rectangular 6 ounce metal containers, and closed the lid. Mlle Jeanne had a white pet mouse that played around her stool. To me, Mlle Jeanne looked as mousy as her pet. She didn't seem the least bit in love or impassioned. I enjoyed her gentle silence. Whenever I pushed the creaking door to her "lab-under-the-eaves," I felt happy. "Bonjour, Mademoiselle Jeanne."

An explosion shakes Géo Gignoux. It happens in the boiler room where lacquers and resins are mixed and boiled. François, one of the young workers, is severely burnt. Ghis and I had spent the day in Paris at the dentist with Maman; we had missed the fire engines, the ambulances, and the sirens. When we return home, Papa coughs; he looks gray. Within a day or two, he says: "Ghis and Marguerite, I want you to please take turns and visit François in the hospital. Cheer him up." Poor François, his head and arms all bandaged up, reduced to lips and tearing eyes expressing pain. I sit there on a chair by his bed asking "Ça va?" in a low voice. Eventually François loses his battle. I feel cold.

The next day at lunch Papa says: "This morning a lady in black came to see me at the office. She asked if she could come to the funeral tomorrow, and where she should stand. She is François' mistress and his wife and mother do not know of their liaison. I told her to walk behind the immediate family." For a moment my grief breaks while I think about the place of a mistress at a funeral of a man loved by three women. But François' death shakes us up. Oh sadness!

War letters arrive from my cousins Robert and Louis who serve in the Ligne Maginot: "We have World War I rifles, the wrong ammunition. When we drive up a hill, we must dismount our trucks, the 1929 models haven't enough engine power."

Papa coughs, he believes in the Maginot Line. At the cottage, he says: "I have to stock up on raw materials so that I can give work to my people." Father fills the vaults of Géo Gignoux with row upon row of steel drums heavy with gums, pigments, and resins imported from Indo-China. He expects overseas shipping to be disrupted and military procurements to take precedence over civilians. The parking lot at Géo Gignoux resembles a truck terminal. Papa secures the fief against a long siege."He is using up the family's private money for stockpiling," whispers Maman to me. "It is imprudent." I watch the barrels roll down the ramps.

At night, we hear the trains clank. "They are carrying fresh troops and material to the front." Géo Gignoux has large orders for camouflage paints. "For tanks and trucks." Papa's optimism is sure of victory.

That fall, Ghis and I dig a deep hole under the shed near our cottage. Like people in the countryside, we store potatoes, leeks, carrots, and cabbages. We carefully cover our winter provisions with straw and wooden boards.

Quel hiver! What a winter! Our potatoes turn into bluish mush; our vegetables freeze. Phew! In the spring, Ghis and I scoop out the first of our family's miscalculations — it takes days. Dumb!

The second miscalculation is that Papa — like William Bullit, the ambassador of the United States to France — thinks we will win the war. The Maginot line is impregnable!

The well defended Maginot Line, engineered with defensive passion along the Rhine River since the early 1920's and which has cost France billions of French francs and nearly bled her to death economically, actually leads the nation and the Lévys into disaster.

When Hitler's mobile Panzers roll around the fixed blockhouses of the so-called invincible Maginot Line, and the roads to the capital are blocked by refugees fleeing north-south on the main arteries out of Paris, Papa no longer can drive — south-north — from Savigny to his bank deposit box at la Société Générale in Paris. Helpless in the kitchen at the cottage after he's turned back, "I couldn't get through," my father, said. Circumstances had overtaken Papa.

A crumbling stone wall surrounds the old castle grounds next to the Géo Gignoux compound in Savigny-sur-Orge. Trudging home on May 27, 1940, from the pharmacy in the village center after hearing on the radio: "King Léopold III of Belgium ordered the capitulation of the Belgian army to the Germans without informing his British or French allies," I brush the wall's length with my arm in utter dejection. Oh God! It's not so! Can't be! The son of World War I hero-warrior King Albert I, a traitor! The pharmacist and I had shared the pain of his betrayal. "It's bad! Very bad!" she had said. Although quite older, she's my friend; at her drugstore she and I listen to the radio together. She advised me: "If I were your family, I would leave."

I factually reported her words at home and Papa was pensive. And here is what impressed me — and it is not only true of Papa, but true of all true believers in the world — how steadfastly they believe in the object of their faith. My father believed in victory. He also liked to work very hard. He was so immersed in his factory that he didn't realize how dire was the military situation. The pharmacist had told me that the trains — whose iron axles we hear

26

squeaking and creaking throughout the night — rolled to the front empty and returned south filled with the wounded.

One consequence of King Léopold's treason was that German troops rushed into the gap between the Channel and the Franco-British lines — held by the Belgian forces — like water through a levee breach. My heart aches.

The nine days of "Dunkirk" give their name to a miracle in defeat. It took Hitler less than six weeks to send the British Expeditionary Corps back to Dover in tatters, and to destroy the French army thought of as the most powerful in the world. Thus, I become aware of my country's vulnerability long before I'm cognizant of my own.

Ghis and I, most unusually, are admitted to a family council around the dining table. My cousin Jean, four years younger than I, is not. Maman and Aunt Martha both talk at the same time: "When do we leave? What shall we take?" Papa and Uncle Edouard discuss who will sit next to Monsieur Marquerre, the Géo Gignoux truck driver, and learn how to drive the two-ton. Papa jokes: "We are in good company, the government also is fleeing Paris for the Touraine."

Le *tout* Paris is moving out.

For the next two days we fill cartons with cans of salmon, prunes, dried fruit, rice, and noodles. We pack the silverware and the china. Towels, and bed linens — all are taken off the shelves. Closets are stripped of clothes. Aunt Martha, ever competitive with her sister-in-law, visits us at the cottage. "You are not taking your crystal, are you? There isn't room in the truck!" she exclaims. Maman reluctantly returns her deep-etched lead crystal vases, bowls, decanter, and candy dishes to the buffet. Later on she finds out that her rival smuggled her own heirlooms into the camion.

I slide my two favorite thin volumes of the Romantic and the Symbolist poets into the outer pocket of my backpack. They are my dearest companions. Papa and Maman together go to the vegetable garden and water the lettuce, the peas, the beans. Together — they bid good-bye to the fruits of their loves' labor.

27

Ghis sets her textbooks back onto the shelves in her room: on the radio we heard that the baccalauréate examinations scheduled for the next day, June 8, are cancelled "for reasons of national emergency."

Only later do I realize how extraordinary the prewar period in Paris was. When the social order was crumbling, and the inner and outer signs of military defeat to come were in place. The inescapable sinking. The imploding of a worm-eaten old order — a house hollowed by termites — and how I witnessed the dissensions and the betrayals with a heart torn by love and despair.

On the last night, I stand in front of our kitchen cupboard at the cottage where my mother keeps her preserves. I pull the latch. I stare at the Mason jars filled with *confiture aux quatre fruits,* jam made with strawberries, raspberries, red and black currants that I like so much — all this work! And pouf! I open two-three lids. I break two-three seals. The Boches won't eat my mother's jams!

The following morning, the Ford and the truck make a right turn at Place de la Mairie. The bistro proprietor in a denim apron over his potbelly is sweeping the sidewalk with his bristle broom. He's so close to the curb that he has to straighten up and let us pass. I hear him mumble: "*Merde alors,* the Géo Gignoux crowd is getting out! Shit!"

It's market day. On the square, the vendors are setting up their stalls. The charcuterie, the patisserie, the boulangerie — all are lit up. Sheepishly I look at the grocer's store. Sorry, Monsieur Pierre, no more money from these hoarders. My sister and I won't be coming daily anymore to buy your cans of salmon and sardines, pounds of rice and flour. I would have liked to say good-bye to my friend the pharmacist. Oh, well! It is June 8, 1940. I roll down the window in the back seat of the Ford...

Chapter 2

Exodus

(Summer 1940)

Access to la Nationale 20, the highway in the direction of Tours, is clogged at Longjumeau. Cars, hay wagons, pushcarts, taxis, horse drawn carriages, camouflaged canvas-covered government trucks — a sea on wheels — block the southwest main road out of Paris.

This is no ordinary traffic jam.

It's a massive exodus of people fleeing from the advancing German armies. Mesmerized, I stare out the rolled down window of the Ford.

Hitler's hordes are closing in. In 1918 the Boches were stopped short of Paris on the river Marne. This is the new battle of France. 1940. I etch on my mind the images of:

the slow moving ox-carts from Belgium piled high with household goods and family. They lumber under the blistering summer heat, wooden axles creaking.

A young woman in a black ruffled skirt and white blouse, strings of blond hair glued to her sweaty forehead. Alone, on foot, she is pushing a baby carriage ahead of her. Her sole possessions (besides her baby) are a water canteen and a tin cup that dangles from the handle bar. On her feet she wears ankle-strapped sandals.

A French soldier, buttons torn off his long coat, hurries alongside the Ford. From his pocket sticks out a bottle of Calvados. He hasn't shaved in days. Helmet turned backward in a sign of disaffection, every few steps he turns his head. Nervous, gun discarded, an empty satchel bouncing on his hip, he runs straight south, AWOL.

A Citroen, windows rolled down, crawls next to the Ford. Inside, four French officers. Braids and ribbons. They pass a bottle

29

of Calvados from hand to hand. They laugh, they joke, their faces red with drink. Here bolts the world's most powerful army.

I'm in shock.

This morning I still had believed in the Bastille Day parades. In the handsome St. Cyr officer cadets, their famed plumed headdresses — the white Casoar — fluttering in the wind. I had believed in the power of the exotic Spahis draped in their red cloaks. The Senegalese giants marching in cadence to their drums under the protective roar of the French Air Force flying in close-winged formation from Place de la Concorde up the Champs-Elysées to L'Arc de Triomphe had filled me with confidence and pride in my country's imperial invincibility.

This is different.

Through the open window of the Ford, I see an old man dressed in a black suit and white shirt tied to a mattress lying atop a hay wagon. Two strong oxen pull the loaded wagon. The skin on his face is waxen. A swarm of black flies buzz about his eyes.

A CORPSE!

Feverish voices rise inside me. So in wartime dead grandfathers aren't buried in graves! Their bodies rot under the searing sun, strapped to a mattress, and flies suck the moisture out at the corners of their closed eyeballs. So life isn't sacred! So...

Something cracks in my inner self, something I had been standing on.

A few teenagers on bicycles wheel between the traffic as if in a game.

Suddenly Stukas — black swastikas painted on the wings — pierce through the blue blazing skies. They swoop at car-top height releasing their whistling bullets. All traffic freezes. Directly ahead of the Ford crawls the Géo Gignoux truck. It holds dozens of jerry cans filled with gas.

Oh God, if you get us out of this one, I'll serve you forever. Positively forever!

The skies are pure blue.

In the car, no one speaks. Even Aunt Martha holds her tongue. She knows that a burst of fear will get her no sympathy from Papa.

When I was little I suppressed shivers under the cold spray after my daily bath, I cleaned and dressed my skinned knee after a bloody fall. I clench my teeth, duck, and cover my head with my arms.

Infantrymen in the French uniform brush against the cars. Their faces glisten with sweat and fear. Haggard, disheveled, their long open winter coats are covered with summer dust. In flight from German Panzers, they walk, battle-shocked, as if in a daze.

I'm fifteen years old, a citizen of the second largest Empire; I witness the rout of France's Third Republic. I do not yet know that this military defeat would change my world forever. Today, I see the exhausted faces of the troops.

An ambulance, sirens wailing, attempts to get through. A slow wave of wheels slithers to one side like one huge snake. As soon as the Red Cross van passes, the cars again spread back over the full width of the buckling asphalt. People help save the wounded. People are decent!

In Orléans by the Cathedral of Sainte-Croix, a young couple makes the rounds.

They walk up to Papa's window with their empty gas can in hand.

"Monsieur, s'il vous plaît..."

"Sorry, I have none to spare," answers the man who last year at the onset of winter delivered to each of his workers one hundred kilos of coal and fifty pounds of potatoes. "So that the women and the children will have something to eat if the men booze their pay away."

From auto to auto the young couple pleads. "Monsieur..."

Horns honk.

They push their idled Renault unto the sidewalk.

"Papa, what about the metal cans filled with gasoline in the back of the truck, can't we share?" My adolescent outrage explodes.

The idealistic protest gets an unwelcome response. Behind the wheel, Papa breaks out into a dry stress-cough. Ghis's elbow pokes me in the ribs. "Ever heard of self-preservation?" she whispers with disdain. That's right, I'm an idiot. We need gas to escape from Hitler.

To save myself and Papa from further aggravations, I decide to internalize from now on the sights, sounds, and private feelings of war. I pocket my personal thoughts and start a diary.

"Tonight, we pull onto a side road, then into a farmyard somewhere in the chateaux region between Orléans and Blois…"

A stocky farmer clad in blue overalls and milking boots, his navy beret molding a debonair roundish head, walks out from the stable, lips ajar.

Through the rolled down window of the Ford, Papa asks:

"Monsieur, may we overnight in your barn without putting you out too much?"

"It's the least we can do, Monsieur," answers the native of the Touraine, and he comes over to the car.

"How is the situation, Monsieur?" Papa inquires at the foot of the ladder.

"Oh Monsieur, it's a national disaster!"

The farmer's pink face contorts in pain. Papa wipes a tear. A screw tightens in my throat. Oh, mon Dieu, it's not possible!

The following morning two men dressed in black leather jackets clamber down the rungs of the ladder from our hayloft. At once Aunt Martha pounces. "If I had daughters, they would sleep between Edouard and me! Two men by Marguerite's side, aren't you worried?" Maman and I wink at each other. They were stretched out more than ten feet away. Rape? They, and we, had "A*utres chats a fouetter*, other concerns."

Tin mug, soap, and toothbrush in hand, we brush our teeth, wash our faces in the farmyard. Cousin Jean, eleven, solemnly calls out: "The ladies are doing la toilette at the trough!" It is early morning, and already the sun inundates the horizon. I twist my neck, and scan the skies. Where is our Air Force? They must be winging through the clouds at any moment! Why aren't they engaging the Messerschmitts? We were told we have seven hundred fighters and bombers. They told us so! I believed them! I believed our government!

Alas, our government had failed to tell us that Hitler had destroyed our airplanes on the ground, and that the British had to withdraw their last squadrons to defend their own island.

Papa and I walk over to our host's farmhouse to thank him for letting us sleep in his barn.

It is the first time I am inside a French farmhouse. I look about. The doilies, the knickknacks, and the colorful hand-braided rugs fascinate me. Quickly, the dairy farmer fetches a white marble cheese tray under a cloche from a small table at the end of a dark hallway. "My own!" he says proudly, and he removes the cover.

Horror! Live maggots teem on the round *crotins.*

Maggots? The cheese-artisan smacks his lips at the sight of such ripeness. I stand there on the homemade rug uncertain what to do. Papa calmly scrapes off the rind with the maggots and eats the little round goat cheese. I do likewise. *"Pas mal!"* The proud proprietor exclaims, and he juts his chin forward in a gesture of approval. "Not bad!"

A moment later he returns with a bowl of fleshy Queen Anne cherries, their skins still pearly with dewdrops. "Picked this morning," he says with a grin. The dew hangs there. Papa and I taste the yellow-reddish Queen Anne's, worms and all. Delicious!

On the braided rug in the narrow corridor Papa queries: "Any news, Monsieur?"

"Oh, Monsieur, c'est la défaite!"

The French cultivator throws his arms up in the air, his good-natured face twitching.

DEFEAT!

On the back seat of the Ford, Aunt Martha and Jean play tic-tac-toe in silence.

These past few days the French High Command kept releasing a flow of victories. "We have won back Amiens." "The Weygand front is holding." "We are inflicting serious losses on the enemy who will soon reach the limits of his effort..." The Information and the War Ministry fabricated these deceptions.

Along the approaches to Blois on the National 152, British Tommies, clean and lean in crisp khaki uniforms, check identity cards. Papa produces *un Ordre de Repli,* an order to withdraw, issued by the French ministry of industry, to dismantle and reassemble his factory in the south.

The Tommies push the paper aside. They are not interested in an official order of withdrawal. All of northern France, Belgium and Holland are withdrawing. Instead, they thrust their heads inside the rolled-down window. Ghis and I sit on the back seat in white blouses and navy shorts. They flash a friendly "V" for-victory sign with two fingers. Excited, I raise my index and middle finger and return the salute with a wide smile.

The Tommies seem cocky and unbeaten. The idea that they already might hide a terrible foreboding, a sense that checking fleeing cars might be the last thing they will ever do for a while as free men, never occurs to me. I look at them as young gods.

"They are Ordinance," says Papa. "They man the British military stores in the Loire Valley, they search for la *cinquième colonne,* the fifth column," as we called the German spies.

The distance from Paris to Tours is 210 kilometers (130 miles). Normally it is covered in five to six hours. During the mass exodus, two days are needed.

Earlier during the "phony war" period (so-named because no military operations occurred on the Franco-German front from September 1939 to May 10, 1940), Papa and Maman had rented a first-floor two-room apartment in a country house in Tours with the help of a local client of Papa's, Monsieur Rivière. The French manufacturer of baby beds and dressers believed like my parents, me, and millions of others, that the Loire River represented the furthest line of imaginable penetration for German forces into France. The *Boches* will never cross the Loire River!

That summer, the Loire River was dry.

And the bridges were left intact.

It's here, on the first floor of a LOIRE VALLEY COUNTRY house — which we share with Uncle Edouard's family — that I hear on the radio: "Paris has been declared an Open City."

Impossible… They — us — the French army… they must fight for Paris…! Can't let them goose step under l'Arc de Triomphe!

34

Like stepping from shallow to deeper waters, wisdom comes progressively. Later I realize it's just as well the gates to the capital remained open. For Paris would have been reduced to rubble and taken anyhow.

JUNE 14. The radio announcer coins the word *Blitzkrieg* to describe Hitler's lightening war led by mobile Panzers. When Papa calls Savigny-sur-Orge, he learns from the switchboard operator that the town is in German hands.

JUNE 17. Premier Paul Reynaud broadcasts his desperate appeal on the radio to President Roosevelt: "When will the United States enter the war?" Monsieur Roosevelt, as the media calls the President of the United States, responds: "Congress alone has the power to declare war…"

Oh God, we are lost!

JUNE 18. Papa and Uncle Edouard stand on the lawn under a white beech beyond the open French doors. They speak in short chats. They turn their palms right, left, right; they look pensive. Frowns crease their foreheads. Through the embrasure I observe them making decisions out of earshot from their womenfolk. I would like to hear their thinking processes.

Past the weeping willows, at the edge of the manicured lawn, the waters of the Loire River flow by without a splash or wave. Mature sycamores give the landscape a balance of shade and light. Here lies the cradle of the French civilization about to be trampled by Hitler's hordes. I gaze at the peaceful Loire descending in the distance. I fight back tears.

Rumblings. German cannons belch.

The cans of salmon tumble back into their cardboard boxes. We are packing up.

Ever southbound.

At a roadside bistro, forlorn Frenchmen in blue overalls lean on their elbows against the shiny counter. They grumble, "*Nous sommes trahis*, we have been betrayed." Hunched over their glasses of vin ordinaire, they already point a mean atavistic finger at the perfidious Brits and the foreigners.

"They have to blame somebody," whispers Papa.

"Soon they will blame the Jews," Maman dispirited, says.

Rumors fly all over. Contradictory. "The government is continuing the fight in North Africa." *"Pas vrai!* Not so! Brittany is being turned into an impregnable fortress!" (Not another Ligne Maginot!) "The gold of the Banque de France was shipped yesterday by cruiser to Dakar." "Pas vrai! Pétain is suing for an armistice."

Yes! No! Every rumor contains a bit of truth:

Ministers and elected representatives leave for Morocco on board the *Massilia.*

Churchill proposes an Anglo-French union, "France to go on fighting with the British Empire, the fleet to join Great Britain's." That's the honorable thing to do! The French government rejects the idea. Charles de Gaulle speaks from London on the 18th: "Is our defeat final and irremediable...? No!" The BBC airs the broadcast at 2:30 in the afternoon. We were busy. In flight.

NOMADS, we travel along the southern roads.

Angoulême. In the newspaper we read the terms of the armistice forced on General Huntziger on June 22 in the same railway car near Compiègne in which Germany admitted defeat in 1918. **FRANCE DIVIDED — THE NORTHERN OCCUPIED ZONE** and **THE SOUTHERN FREE ZONE,** Germany occupies three-fifths of France. The cease-fire is to go into effect on June 25, 1940, at 00:35.

We read the papers; we look at maps. The family is in the Free Zone, so we think, and we go to sleep.

The next morning when we wake up in the downstairs of a small house Papa had rented, we see through the window pane a group of Wehrmacht working by the road. "Come, Marguerite. I want to go and speak to the Germans," Papa says to me.

Across the pasture, past the grazing cows and toward the stone-breaking Germans, my father and I walk.

"Was machen er do? What are you doing?" asks my red- haired Papa in the dialect of the Alsatian frontier.

"*Mir mache a sperr fer kontrol.* We erect a roadblock for control," answers a blond corporal in the same Alsatian idiom. And he raises his head: "*Da Krieg es fertig.* The war is over," he says, happy.

I tighten involuntarily. We woke up on the wrong side of the demarcation line.

Papa smiles. "As the war is over," he says, "I would like to go home with my family."

"*Yo.* Come early to-morrow morning, I'm on duty between 3:00 and 7:00; I'll lift the barrier for you. I'm First Cpl. Hans Schmidt."

At 3:05 AM, seven Lévys align at the check point in the dust-covered Ford and the truck. It's a dark moonless night. A silhouette approaches; a Wehrmacht soldier peeks through the window, then retreats.

A creaking sound breaks the silence of the darkness and the barrier rises.

Slowly the Ford and the two-ton roll into the Free Zone.

"*Uf wiedersehn!*" calls out Papa to his conscripted landsman from Alsace, and he waves Good-bye!

Maman sits very quietly in the front seat next to Papa. I see her lips move. Maman says a prayer. Why I don't feel frightened, I can't say, I sense triumph. The family made it!

To be on the right side of the demarcation line was a matter of life or death.

PÉRIGUEUX. Cousin Hélène, in her low-beamed kitchen, falls into Papa's arms. "Unkel Albert!"

When we tell her about our luck, she says: "Your First Cpl. Hans Schmidt is a real Alsatian *Dumkopf.* He doesn't know geography beyond his parish."

I can't argue with Hélène... but I know things are more complex than that. Since early childhood I have noticed my father throws off a strong aura to which people are attracted like paper clips to a magnet.

Hélène tells of her husband Julien and brothers Simon, Robert, and Louis. "They all are serving in the Maginot Line. I have no news," she says. "If I am lucky, they are among the two million prisoners of war the Germans have taken."

Two-million men! Five percent of France's population. That's how many young French male hostages the Germans have captured.

Cousin Hélène is the daughter of Papa's older sister, Suzanne. Suzanne died in Strasbourg during the influenza epidemic of 1919.

In September 1939, at the beginning of the hostilities, along with tens of thousands of Alsatians, Hélène had been relocated from Strasbourg to Périgueux (the capital of the Dordogne). Hélène has a permanent address. She is the family mailbox. Every member of the tribe checks in with Hélène.

High-spirited and plump, cousin Hélène tells us the tribal news: Uncle Louis has been nominated chaplain to the Czech brigade; Louis and Aunt Gretel are stranded in Sète. The ship never arrived to take the Czech brigade over to North Africa — they all are in the Free Zone and being demobilized.

The Kahns from Strasbourg and Nancy, Papa's maternal branch, have been evacuated to Roanne. Papa pulls out his stylo and a brown leather carnet from his breast pocket. With lips tight, forehead wrinkled, he jots down the information. Later it is to Roanne that we'll go. I learn how connections are preserved.

From the curb in front of their house Hélène and little Huguette call out merry good-byes as if they were taking leave from uncles, aunts, and cousins whom they will meet again the following Sunday. "See you!" Only these former dominant family members are now homeless.

And off to one of Géo Gignoux's lacquer and paints clients in the Corrèze. We travel the roadmap that Father and Uncle Edouard had decided on under the white beech tree in Tours: from client to client. Like immigrants do in the United States, we try to attach our upended rootlets to people we know.

So far the exodus meant: move from shelter to shelter, eat in the shadow of a tree by the edge of the road a daily picnic of sardines, bread and apples. And boil verveine tea on a collapsible stove.

The landscape of the central highlands closes us in. It is stark and lonely, made up of granite and limestone. I crane my neck out the car window; it's my first trip through le Massif Central. The craggy scenery fascinates me.

Aunt Martha, piqued, says: "When I was a young girl at home, my parents would never have let me go into an area like this." She feels uncomfortable in this savage nature. Ghis and I bite our laughter in the back seat.

I reflect that surely upheaval causes losses, death, and destruction, but the chaos offers opportunities for newness. I smile at the daily fresh sights, smells, tastes, and sounds. I like meeting new people, hearing their strange dialect and seeing exotic landscapes. The forested plateau is cut by deep, abrupt gorges. The dark chasms seem straight out of a Greek tragedy.

I note that the central highlands are sparsely populated. The soil is poor. In the fields, carts are pulled by mules instead of horses. But I can't share the excitement of my discoveries lest Papa, Maman, and Aunt Martha think of me as immature.

My memories of the outskirts of Brive-la-Gaillarde where Monsieur Chataigne's factory is located are vague. Inside his wood-paneled office, Monsieur Chataigne is not the least astonished at our arrival. He has the austere face of an old carpenter who has seen everything. He just says: "My dear Monsieur Lévy, every hut I know of is occupied by refugees!"

I would like to ask the furniture manufacturer what he thinks of the situation. The urge is on the tip of my tongue, but in the presence of Papa a youngster doesn't speak unless she is spoken to. I'm frustrated. Monsieur Chataigne — behind his chestnut bureau — refrains from any discussion about politics. He avoids all the polemics that the press uses to inflame the public: who is to blame for our collapse — the politicians, the military or the pleasure-seeking citizens? Instead, I watch him push his armchair away from his desk, lean backward a bit and, removing himself in space and in emotion, business-like, asks: "How Spartan are you willing to go?" He knows of a peasant who wants to rent out space in an old farmhouse. "The widower needs money for his drink."

"COMING!" calls a slurred voice from inside a dilapidated grey stone house at the end of an ocher-colored dirt road.

A moment later a stooped figure with the red-veined face of chronic cirrhosis of the liver sufferers stands on the threshold.

"Bonjour."

Whiffs of wine greet us.

The stooped figure makes an about-face and shuffles through empty ramshackle rooms. We tag along. In his broken down slippers, he grunts: "You can have that'n, the next, and the porch too." Maman pinches her lips. The sight of the crumbling plaster of paris walls and the broken hardwood floors drains the life out of her.

"Is there a bathroom?" Maman asks in a small voice.

"There!" he utters, and his chin juts in the general direction of a field.

In the middle of the room a bare bulb hangs at the end of a wire suspended from the ceiling.

"It works!" he says proudly and flips on the electricity.

The four women in tow, he drags his split slippers over the splintered floor boards to the kitchen.

"Cooking's done in the fireplace!"

I step out into the noon sun where I touch and smell a few struggling wild flowers in the parched soil. The wild flowers survive this summer heat, I observe to myself.

After weeks of wandering, a kitchen, a screened-in porch and a crude, bare room to sleep in seem romantic to me. I identify with *La Petite Fadette* stumbling on a mysterious old farmhouse.

Clean up! With a mop, a broom, a bucket, a piece of cardboard, Ghis and I form little mounds of dirt. We break cobwebs off the beams; we play at Lady and the Tramp and discreetly bump into each other. "Excuse me!" "Oh, but that's too bad!" Bump! bump! And another bump. Papa and Uncle Edouard work with their ties on. I'm not sure where Maman is.

There! She unloads the food.

That night, half-asleep, I itch and scratch. The following morning Ghis and I show each other where, bright with blood spots from our scratches, the fleas had feasted on our flesh. Aunt Martha, vexed, moans: "This is worse than the Paris métro!"

From then on, we wear long cotton stockings over our arms and feet at night. The family and I look like scarecrows. Aunt Martha, who decidedly possesses the gift to make us laugh, groans: "If only the fleas could see my appearance, they would be turned off."

The bloodsuckers avoid Papa and Uncle Edouard, but enjoy Ghis's and my young blood.

On the day of her oral baccalauréate exams in Brive, Ghis has to wear a long-sleeved winter wool dress in 90 degree heat to cover her flea bites and scabs.

The examinations, postponed on June 8 because of a national emergency have been rescheduled to July 18.

"Aren't you hot?" I ask Ghis.

"Do you think I want the examiner to see that I live in a flea hovel?" she retorts.

Within six weeks the entire educational system in France again functioned normally.

In Vignols-en-Corrèze, every morning, the women at their open bedroom windows beat their bedding with pretzel-shaped wicker contraptions on handles. Scarfs tied around their hair, they pounce with index and thumb and squash the fleas between their nails. One… two… three… six… my sister and I on our way to the bakery keep score. To Maman peeling carrots on the porch we report the day's tally.

Our drunken landlord staggers out of the house one hot night. "Sleep under them stars, too many fleas inside," he calls to Ghis and me on the screened-in porch and, cursing, drags his soiled pink coverlet along the dirt path yanking the old rag free when it gets entangled in the berry thickets. "Yep, sleeping under them stars in the vineyards is a good idea," we yell back. Giggles pour out of hearing.

IN THE CENTRAL HIGHLANDS (1940) the rats gnaw at our bread. Papa has to hang our round loaves of *pain de campagne* on a string from ceiling hooks. At night I hear the rodent's pad-padding on the wooden boards by my sleeping bag.

Once in broad daylight I see yellow eyes glare at me from behind a luggage. I fetch Papa. He grabs a broom. White shirt sleeves rolled up, he corners the huge black rodent. Crushes it. Maman, Aunt Martha, and Jean shriek. If they shriek, I'm going to be calm.

The latrine is a threesome creation. Uncle Edouard, Ghis, and I dig a hole in a field a way off from the house; then erect a two-by-two frame around it. We sisters sew together burlap lengths from empty potato bags, and Uncle Edouard nails the cloth to the structure. On a piece of cardboard he writes "*Libre*" on one side, "*Occupé*" on the other. Triumphant, he hangs the sign on the front entrance flap. "Well, how is this for a privy?"

We are in stitches.

At those moments I love the exodus.

After each use of our "toilet" we drop a small shovel of lime and a scoop of sawdust into the pit just like at Scout camp. Aunt Martha regales us for days with cryptic stories of near misses. "At least in Ruelsheim (her birthplace) we had seats on our water closet," she says.

I think quickly: smile, don't burst.

JULY 1940. A month ago, France asked Hitler for a separate armistice. Great Britain goes on fighting alone. The relations between Great Britain and France are strained. The French resent the Brits, a rivalry born at Hastings in 1066. The British distrust the French. In June 1940, the British beg the French soldiers they rescued at Dunkirk to enlist in the British army or marine. The Brits offer the Frenchmen the higher French military pay rate. *La guerre est finie pour nous,* the war is over for us, the Frenchmen reply, and they insist on being repatriated. Sad, I'm torn like a burning fever between two opposing loyalties.

JULY 3rd. The British fleet attacks the French naval base at Mers-el-Kebir (Algeria).

"The battleships *Bretagne, Provence, Mogador,* and a score of others are blown up. The French ships were sitting at anchor or with steam low. One thousand two hundred ninety seven French seamen are dead. The remaining fleet escapes to Toulon." La Radiodiffusion Française delivers the news.

French blood is being spilled. Ministers in Pétain's government want to declare war on Great Britain. I fear France is about to resume hostilities, but this time against our former ally.

The red sky is fading over the vineyards. The broken pebbles of the porch steps imprint themselves on my flesh through my shorts. I am frightened. It's a feeling that survives.

JULY 4th. The French announcer's voice cracks on the radio as he broadcasts: "Armed British troops in bedroom slippers stole aboard two hundred French destroyers, minesweepers, sloops, submarines, patrol craft at Plymouth, Falmouth and other ports in England. Sailors of the admiralty surprised or clubbed the sleeping deck watch and officers — men with whom they had fraternized in local pubs a few hours before. The dazed crew of the giant submarine Surcouf was overcome. In Alexandria, Egypt, one French battleship, four cruisers, three destroyers and a submarine were damaged. In Dakar the super cruiser Richelieu was attacked over and over again by torpedo planes from the British carrier Hermès."

I can't express my grief because I'm listening to Maman. She quotes an old proverb: "Rabble get along, rabble trade blows." Mother's anguish is turning to cynicism. Pain chokes me. These are my countrymen.

Papa clears his throat. He explains: "Churchill is up against a wall. He must prevent at all costs the French navy from falling into the hands of the Germans." Uncle Edouard (the younger brother) supports Papa. He adds: "From now on Churchill will fight to the death." Aunt Martha professes understanding nothing about politics, but she knows: If this continues we'll all die on land or at sea.

I sit on the porch step. I mourn for my country. Only I also wish for British victory. If Great Britain loses, we'll all be destroyed by Hitler. I go for long walks in the forests of juniper, oaks, and chestnut trees; in the hushed quiet of their bountiful leaves gently swaying in the breeze, I find that I'm many Marguerites. The French Marguerite. The pro-British Marguerite. So are there many different faces of France, and many different Great Britains. And after a war there are more conflicts.

SEPTEMBER 1940. I know that a huge German armada is being massed in French ports facing the Channel. I hear over the short wave radio the BBC broadcaster say: "The 14th is the last day in September on which the tides will be suitable for a German landing." On the Philips I listen to Churchill's voice booming from London: "We shall fight on the beaches, we shall fight on the landing grounds, we shall fight in the fields, we shall never surrender..." Every night I go to sleep thanking God for one more day without a Wehrmacht landing at Dover. Oh merci, mon Dieu!

September fifteenth arrives with no news. No silence could strengthen my hope more.

On the screened-in porch, the mothers prepare dumplings, shell peas, cut up apples for strudel. In the fireplace, they cook and bake. Until one day Maman tells me: "Don't talk to Martha, Edouard or Jean. We had a big spat. Aunt Martha took her marmalade jar away from Papa at breakfast. She also complains that we are eating her rice. While we share our canned salmon, noodles, and everything." Maman tells Ghis and me not to talk to our uncle, aunt, or cousin. In the house, we act as if we do not see them. We turn our heads away. We raise our noses. Thanks to the women, the two families are split in the middle. Martha, Edouard, and Jean on one side; Maman, Papa, Ghis and I on the other side of the demarcation line. Papa and Edouard go on taking their foot baths together in the same tub. Aunt Martha lets the fire go out. Then knocks on the wall that the kitchen is available for us. When our turn is first, Ghis and I tap-tap on the wall in Morse code "-.-----..-.-. ..." "Yours." I like signaling in dots and dashes.

At nearby farmhouses I go shopping for produce with Maman's black plastic bag. Carrots? Peas? Beans? "Let's see what's ripe in the garden!" answers the farmer's wife.

In the vegetable patch, she carefully digs the tubers out of the soil with her hoe so as not to split a spud into two. The clinging brown earth? Quickly, I remove the extra weight! Potatoes cost two francs per kilo.

My favorite people are a newlywed couple who live with the husband's parents. The young wife, pink-cheeked and robust, lifts heavy cast-iron kettles filled with soup onto the pothook in the fireplace as if they were toys. Always she wraps up a slice of pumpkin for me. "Here's to make une bonne soupe!" and her happy face smiles. Dressed in a sleeveless black frock, her good cheer gives me courage.

One day, as I enter her abode, her young husband comes in through the back door in the customary black vest, black peasant trousers with white shirt. He hangs his hunting gun on the wall rack and casts a side-glance at her. An intense current of love and desire passes between them. Their eyes lock. Yet he doesn't make a move to help her carry the heavy pots as Papa would have. The young Central Highlander considers cooking a woman's job. The intensity of their desire and the strangeness of THEIR CULTURE mesmerize me.

In the central highlands, milk is sold at farm stables at milking time. One evening I meet two girls queuing up, holding in their fingers like me an empty jug to be filled with fresh raw foaming milk. "Paris?" "Oui, oui!" "Lycée?" "Oui, Victor Hugo!" "Victor Duruy!" Introductions follow. They say: "We are Julie and Elaine Reich." "Marguerite Lévy," I say. We shake our free hands. They are staying at an aunt's estate on the outskirts of the village. "As soon as the trains run again, our mother will come and call for us," says Elaine.

Elaine and Julie, sixteen and seventeen, lighthearted gentry, save my life one day. Later.

At the stable in Vignols, Elaine and Julie say: "Our mother was born and raised here. And before her, our grandfather and his father." Their forebears have roots in this region of truffles and chestnut trees for hundreds of years. "Aunt Théa raises prized Charolais cattle," they laugh. "We, the young cousins (and do they laugh!) spend our summer vacation every year, here, at the family property, the *propriété familiale.*"

I can't return to Paris. I'm Jewish. I must remain in exile. Unlike Elaine and Julie, I can't go back to my lycée. They — they are bubbling teens, safe and secure. That's the way I'd like to be in this world. Although I put on a bright front, my roots are severed. I know that from Biblical times onward through the Inquisition to Hitler, a vile leader always arises who covets the possessions of the Jews and persecutes or kills them outright so that he can pay off his henchmen and finance his power-lusts. Marguerite, you are living through one of these periods of dispossession, I inwardly tell myself.

Sixteen, seventeen, and fifteen — I am fifteen. Elaine, Julie and I declaim our favorite poems in the dense woods around Vignols-en-Corrèze. I recite Racine's *Phèdre*:

... It's unimportant that with Antiope's mother-milk
I drank such pride as seems to surprise;
As myself I have matured,
I have become at ease with myself...

Exuberant, Elaine and Julie discuss Phèdre's notion of self-acceptance. "Ugh!" says Elaine, "I hate the color brown of my hair. See those horrible straight strings? They make me look dead!" and she rumples her nose. Julie admits to having grown too fast: "I am the tallest girl in my class. Oh, God, have mercy!" and she tips onto her heels in self-mockery. I cross my arms over my chest: No one is going to guess that I am embarrassed at my growing breasts. It's a personal matter and I dislike talking about personal matters. THE WAR, the DEFEAT — that's where my soul pinches.

One day Elaine, Julie, and I find ourselves walking along the edge of a wood. Beyond, in a field, we spot a tall thin girl in black. Stick in her hand, she stands clumsily in the middle of an open gate, urging a little brown cow to cross over from one pasture to the next.

"You are scaring the animal away. Move on!" shouts Julie in the direction of the girl in black.

Five minutes later the inept cowhand tells us why she makes sad work of her job: sent away by her parents from a poor neighborhood near the République quartier in Paris to an even poorer uncle's farm in the Corrèze, she has to work with pigs and cattle. "Why?" "Because I'm here," she answers. Her Vignol family defecates in the open pen with the grunting swine. "Why don't you dig a latrine?" I again ask innocently. "That's how they live here," the girl in black from the 11th arrondissement replies, and she shrugs her thin shoulders.

"Pigs!" snaps Julie of the Manor house and she walks away. I just stand there by the side of the thin girl in black, attracted by her loneliness.

WITHIN ONE MONTH after June 1940, our proud but weak Third French Republic gives way to a totalitarian regime. The democratically elected representatives — numbed, in disarray, and frightened — are semi-forced through manipulations, fear, and threats to vote in favor of granting full executive and legislative powers to Marshall Pétain as head of the French State. Marshal Pétain will rule by decree. Laval's gamble has paid off. He has persuaded Pétain to get parliament to scuttle itself. Pierre Laval is nominated prime minister, the heir apparent to Pétain.

Former members of the *Chambre des Députés,* the House of Representatives, as well as all prominent Jewish prewar political figures such as Georges Mandel, the former Interior minister; Jean Zay, the Education minister; and Léon Blum, the previous socialist Premier — are incarcerated.

I rejoice when General de Gaulle rallies the Hébrides, Cameroon, Equatorial Africa, Tahiti, and New Calédonia to Free France. Pétain fumes because whatever respect he can muster from Hitler lies in the power of the overseas territories and the French navy at large. On the BBC, de Gaulle calls his former commander-in-chief, Maréchal Henri Philippe Pétain, "The sultan of Vichy." Pétain has General de Gaulle court-martialled for desertion and condemned to death in absentia. Ghis and I refer to Pétain as "the old ga-ga." The former hero of Verdun is eighty-four years old and is vain and senile.

I am French, I am Jewish, and, although I am in denial, my mother is of German descent. Over the last six and a half years, I have become a proud Parisian. I live at 76 avenue de la Bourdonnais, Paris 7ème, the quartier of old money and strong military traditions where *Les Français de vieille souche* (old stock) reside.

In Vignols-en-Corrèze on that early fall afternoon, Maman sits on the porch steps shelling peas. I sit down by her side. "Marguerite, I am frightened," my mother says."There is a clause in the French-German armistice that obliges Vichy to hand over all German nationals to the Nazis on demand. What if they do not recognize my French citizenship by marriage?" Maman pinches her lips; she's pale. Her eyes look haunted.

I had spent all morning in the woods with the Reich sisters. My peers were refreshing in their casual trust in the future. Kneeling on a moss patch, Elaine had giggled. "I just flunked *Le Bac* (graduation exams). Next year I'll present myself again. In my family nobody succeeds on a first try."

Quickly my own pride of ancestry comes to the fore as it always does when I let it. To Maman I answer: "Of course we are French. We are as French as les pâtés de foie gras from Strasbourg." Below my flippant words I see the image of my grandmother Kahn. As a young girl she already had fled her native Nancy for Paris with her mother after the disastrous battle of Sedan in 1870 that Napoléon III lost to Prussia. Her mother chose to leave rather than live under the yoke of the Prussians. I see great-grandfather Félix Lévy born in Jungholtz, Haut-Rhin, on 10 Pluviose Year VI of the French Revolution and all the prior Lévy fathers born in Alsace... And there is Papa. We'll pull Maman along.

Absolument!

In Vignols, we wait for most of the 12 million refugees on the roads to return home to Holland, Belgium, and the occupied northern Zone of France. We wait if the armistice holds... We cook our food in the fireplace, shop for produce at nearby farms. We search our sleeping bags for fleas, and listen to the radio for news. The friendship with Elaine and Julie Reich enriches me. Together we three wander through the forests of tall chestnut trees reciting poetry.

Today, I can still hear Papa in his decisive voice say on the dilapidated screened-in porch of our ramshackle flea-infested farmhouse in Vignols-en-Corrèze: "For Rosh Hashanah and Yom Kippur, we'll be in Roanne." It's our culture. Jews celebrate the High Holy days en famille and with a congregation.

We pack up.

On the road to Roanne inside the Ford no one speaks. I peer out through the open window at the succession of black puys, the famed cone-shaped volcanoes in the Auvergne. They roll away before my eyes.

All I can do is imagine the view when the volcanoes were active ten thousand years ago. Papa doesn't stop in the Puy-de-Dôme. I meld with the brooding scenery.

Behind the wheel Papa clears his throat. He's about to inform us of his plans. "At first, we'll stay at a small hotel in Roanne. Then, as soon as possible, we must find an apartment."

"Why, Papa?"

"So that I can write to my customers where to remit their invoices to."

Papa glances sideways at his wife seated next to him. "As you know, I was unable to go back to Paris and withdraw any money from our Lévy account."

Father looks crestfallen. He has failed as a provider. "I will have to deed the factory over to Vitipon," he says.

Monsieur Vitipon — listening to Maman and Papa talk — lives in Èze, a walled-in city high above the Mediterranean on the Riviera. Vitipon is one of Papa's trusted clients, a toy manufacturer, a friend. Papa has decided to deed him the second largest paint corporation in France. Along with the buildings and the machinery go the bank accounts and the hundreds of drums of gasoline and pigments and precious oils. Much of the "lock, stock, and barrels" Papa had paid for with his own private monies.

In the Occupied Zone the Germans already had decreed that all Jewish businesses must be sold to, or taken over by non-Jews, as part of their Aryanisation policy.

Papa drives past the black lava. He glances into the rear view mirror, his facial muscles tight. Ghis and I are very still. "In Roanne I must see an attorney," he says, "and have him draw up the straw sale."

Papa admits to his children and wife that he lost the fief.

Now he addresses me in particular. "Marguerite, you will write the letters to my clients."

In the mirror above the steering wheel his eyes seek out mine. "Marguerite," he says reproachfully, "it's always such a struggle to work with you. I hardly recognize the letters I am signing as the ones I dictate to you."

The mirror reflects Papa's frowns; stress rattles in his throat. I look away at the bleak volcanoes. Of course he's right, Marguerite, and you know it. You can't stand taking orders. You can't stand writing boring business letters, over and over and the same. Always, you must inject your own thinking.

The stark volcanic landscape slowly ignites in me the notion that my years of green childhood, when nurture flowed one way without much return giving — are over.

The awareness that I am needed appeals to me. I straighten up in the back corner of the Ford. Bubbles of life arise from the defeat like small spirals of oxygen from a freshly discovered spring. All right Papa! I am looking forward to my war!

Chapter 3

Refugees

(1940-1942)

In Roanne, we stop in front of the Pension Les Platanes on cours de la République near the railroad station. In the dark vestibule Jean-Baptiste Troisgros, the burly proprietor, bald with rather an open face, proudly greets us. He says: "*La mère* and I are Burgundians," and he swells his chest as if he were a superior bottle of Clos de Vougeot from his Burgundy chateau. I notice he calls his wife "la mère" in the down-to-earth old provincial way.

Troisgros agrees to rent us a room without meals. "Usually I do demi-pension only, but I make an exception for refugees." His sons, Jean about fourteen and Pierre twelve, are playing "tag" up and down the staircase. "Donnez une main à ces gens, give a hand to these folks with the luggage!" he calls to the boys. Down the road of time tousled-haired Pierre invents la Nouvelle Cuisine and turns Troisgros into a Mobil Guide 3 Star restaurant.

In the night Maman falls ill.

The following morning Doctor LaRoche listens to Maman's heart, checks out her eyes. He carefully turns his back to Ghis and me. I overhear him whisper to Papa: *"Ah Monsieur, les temps sont trop douloureux.* The times are too painful."

My mother sick! Will she die?

"Maman will heal slowly," says Papa.

In our hotel room, Papa chops vegetables, cuts up meats for stews. He energetically kneads flour, yeast, and water into dough.

During World War I, Papa had been a cook in the army; now he feeds his family. Ghis and I daily go to the *boulanger* around the corner to have the food cooked.

On the way to the boulanger, I forget the somber atmosphere at home. My youthful joie de vivre takes over. I play a girl from the Martinique. Head high, back straight, I hold the baking tray on my cranium with one hand. At the bakery I plop my tray on the counter.

"*Voilà* Monsieur, how much will it cost?"

"Deux francs!"

Le boulanger in his flour-dusted blue denim apron shoves the cast-iron dish and our round loaves into his oven on a wooden paddle; a slight wiggle on the grate over the wood-burning fire and, with one clean jerk, he draws the flat shovel out, shuts the latch of the heavy black door shut. Snap! The scents of the warm bread baking seduce my nostrils.

The baker has a good round face over his white-floured denim apron and a not-so-slight plumpness.

"Come back in about an hour," he says, scarcely moving. There are other cast-iron casseroles and other oddly shaped boules browning alongside his straight baguettes. Thanks to the baker we refugees eat potatoes, leeks, turnips, and meat. Merci, Monsieur le boulanger!

At Troisgros, Papa nurses bedridden Maman in addition to bearing his other losses. The loss of his factory, the loss of his livelihood. The lost war. Yet he doesn't complain. He rolls up his shirt-sleeves and goes to work with a calm, determined energy. Almost with gusto. Later I realize how his strength and devotion percolated into me, unknowingly.

Papa is busy, Maman ill. We need a place to live. Go and find an apartment, Marguerite! A little voice orders inside me,

How does one find a furnished vacant apartment in a provincial beehive humming with refugees? I take up position at the main post office with Ghis about 3:00 PM when mail carriers leave for home at the end of their workday!

"Monsieur le facteur, s'il vous plait, mailman, please, would you know of a vacant dwelling for my family?" I approach any mailman willing to listen. My logic is — mail carriers know their territory. I'm not yet that familiar with Real Estate agents. My sixth prospect, short and stocky and slow-paced, dismounts from his bicycle.

"How many are you?"

"Four!"

"I have two rooms, a double bed in each," he says. "The second bed is in the kitchen. It's a large live-in kitchen with a coal stove, a table, six chairs, and a lavabo in the closet."

"Fine," I answer, eagerly willing to sacrifice privacy and comfort at a time of national emergency.

He quotes the price. It's very cheap, about twenty-five dollars monthly.

The address is 9 rue de la Chaise in Riorges, on the other side of the railroad tracks. "You can come with your parents and look at it tomorrow anytime. We live upstairs. The wife is there."

"Fine. Ten o'clock!"

The following morning Papa and I walk along the avenue de Mulsant. The main artery of Riorges is lined with haberdashers, cobblers, butchers, grocers, patisseries, and fabric and knit shops. I'm aware, in a general sense, that Papa has lost his factory. In my mind I think: we are poor, therefore we shall live in a poor neighborhood. I have not yet made out exactly what poverty means. I know that I'm not strongly attached to my privileges. I haven't earned them and I'm ready to slough them off. Out of the recesses of my collective memory arises an image of the famous letter King Francis I wrote to his mother after he was taken prisoner at the battle of Pavie on 25 February 1525: "Madame, to inform you of the rest of my misfortune, all is lost except honor and life…" Francis, if you can be a stoic, so can I!

I dip into that secret place in the human subconscious where selfishness, human comforts and judgment are seemingly banished, but sacrificial impulses reign. At the end, our tenement proves to be a good choice for different reasons.

At number 9 rue de la Chaise the door latch opens onto a passageway leading to a door on the left. Our two rooms are there on the ground floor. "You can wheel in your bicycle from the sidewalk without lifting your machine." I smile at Monsieur Massey's selling efforts for we have no bikes.

At rue de la Chaise I discover a world of two-story grey row houses where a W.C. consists of a wooden outhouse for "standing feet only." At number 9, our outhouse is located at the far end of a small inner green space. It serves the Masseys and their tenants.

My father hesitates.

"Let's take it, Papa!" With the impatience of youth, I think there won't be another chance.

The Masseys are a middle-aged couple of petits bourgeois, frugal and discreet. They appreciate their new tenants, the quiet Lévys, well-behaved and, most importantly, Papa pays the rent on time.

Monsieur Massey even builds a rough table under the lilac tree in the inner garden "for Mademoiselle Marguerite, so that she can read." Later the decent Masseys protect Aunt Jenny and Uncle Elias from police round-ups.

Unlike Vignols-en-Corrèze which was studded with old stone farmhouses surrounded by green vineyards and dark forests of chestnut trees, Roanne is a densely populated provincial city grown out of an old Gallo-Roman town located at a point where the Loire River turns into a navigable waterway after its exit from the central highlands' gorges. A sous-préfecture midway between Paris and the Mediterranean on the Nationale 7, Roanne is famous for its textiles. Here, we begin our lives as French refugees.

THE REFUGEES.

At the start, all refugees are treated alike in the Free Zone. Whether your name is Levoisier or Lévy, refugee families have to fill out the same forms. They must register. They get family-allocations. Refugees are a new strata of society. A ministry for Refugee Affairs is created.

When two refugees meet, the first question is: Where do you come from? What did your father do?

Thanks to the graduates of the Grandes Écoles, the venerable graduate schools in Paris which fill the society's upper echelons with top civil servants and engineers, the Vichy government functions rather well at the beginning. The elite administrators are technocrats, not politicians. We are lulled into acceptance. When --

on October 18, at the kitchen table, Papa is reading the <u>Journal de Roanne</u>. He coughs. Becomes very still. After Papa I read: "According to a law effective immediately, Jews are prohibited from holding public office. Specifically, Jews are banned from the judiciary, the military, banking, teaching, real estate and the media." The law is the first official statute against the Jews. Promulgated on October 3 and published on the 18th in the *Journal Officiel,* the National Registry printed by the State that discloses all laws, decrees, and executive orders of the government, the new exclusory law applies even to Jews decorated with the *Légion d'Honneur,* the highest Order of Merit in the land. "Is considered a Jew any person of the Jewish race with two grandparents of the same race, if married to a Jew, or..." I put the paper down.

We almost do not read a tiny paragraph at the end that states: *"Les préfets à leur seule discretion sont chargés d'appliquer toutes les lois..."* Anti-Semitism has become the Vichy regime's official policy, "but the prefects at their sole discretion are in charge of applying all laws..." Later we find out how important this fine loophole is.

French Jews overnight become salesmen from life insurance to kitchenware.

A day later, the law of October 4, 1940 authorizes the immediate internment of foreign Jews!

Then comes a time I remember only as a grey, formless, hazy succession of days and months. I still love the eternal France. I blame Hitler and our military defeat for the persecutions. I still can't admit to the treachery of my own countrymen; I feel this is "*une Heure Noire*," a black hour in my country's history when my government discriminates against us. Like children who cling to a bad mother because after all it is the only one they have ever known, we, the French Jews cling to France. To Marianne our mythical protector holding the flag.

So, when in November 1940, two hundred thousand Alsatian-Lorrainers are expelled from their towns and villages for refusing to become Germanic subjects, Ghis and I borrow a wheelbarrow from Monsieur Massey and up and down the avenue de Mulsant we go: "*Madame, s'il vous plait...*" We collect goods from store to store for the Christian Alsatian-Lorrainers.

That was in October-November.

In December a cyclist knocks on the kitchen door. With one hand he holds onto his bicycle, with the other he presents a yellow dispatch. "Hope the news isn't too bad," he says. Maman pales. Over her shoulder I read: "Jenny, Elias interned camp Gürs." Signed: Selma Wertheimer, Philadelphia.

Selma Wertheimer is Maman's older sister. She, her husband, and two sons emigrated from Mannheim to Philadelphia in 1938. Jenny must have sent a telegram from Gürs to Selma in the USA who in turn wired us in Roanne, France. Help!

Maman swiftly reaches for our two Hanukkah Stollen set out on the hutch in the kitchen that she had baked for *our* holidays. She wraps the cakes in newspaper and folds the ends under the loaves. "They go to Gürs!"

Zut alors! Darn it! I had been looking forward so much to a yummy slice of fruitcake.

It's Hanukkah without a cake.

On that first night of Hanukkah — when we had lost most of our possessions — Maman sets the eight-branched candlestick on the table (she must have packed the ritual object). Papa lights the *Schammes,* the candle that serves to light the others. In very low voices we four together sing "*Maos-zure j'-schu-a-ti...,* O fortress rock of my deliverance..." while Papa kindles the first candle of the *Menorah.*

Then my father gives me the finest possible lesson in family loyalty. He slips on his British wool overcoat, tucks his white silk scarf inside the collar, and turns the doorknob at 9 rue de la Chaise to take the night train for Toulouse at the foot of the Pyrénées Mountains in southwest France, then the bus for Gürs. Ghis and I send along two boxes of blue, pink, yellow and white baby booties, hats, little sweaters and blankets that we had collected for the Alsatian-Lorrainer refugees.

They go to camp Gürs!

Three days later Papa returns. A wide grin cuts across his hunger-hollowed cheeks. "Jenny and Elias will soon be here," he says. "I shook hands with a French gendarme under the table. The policeman promised they will be released within a few days."

Papa doesn't mention the dark windowless barracks at Gürs built in a hurry for the Spanish Republicans chased by Franco in 1938 and meant to last one short summer only. He doesn't mention that the wooden structures are damp, un-insulated and reek of latrines. The plight of the German Jews trapped in mud and filth, suffering from diarrhea is kept from Maman. Instead, my father reassures Maman that Jenny and Elias are both well, and should be with us n a few days.

On that fifth night of Hanukkah, my father appears to me like a messenger straight out of the Talmud: "He, who saves a single life, it is as if he had saved the entire world."

The Strausses need a home. I can't take the chance and return again to the post office lest Monsieur Massey gets suspicious and thinks *we* want to move. And we couldn't talk to him about the illegal Strausses who were technically stateless "enemy" Jews (expelled from Germany).

In a distant outlying suburb the main gate to a high-walled estate stands open. No one stops me. On the path up to the big house I encounter two elderly spinsters. "Excuse me, Mesdemoiselles, would you please know of a small lodging for two mature adults?" And I proceed to praise their two prospective tenants: "My aunt and uncle have no children, no pets, they are

57

refugees." I don't tell that Aunt Jenny and Uncle Elias are Jews from Germany who speak no French.

The two svelte demoiselles hesitate. They look me over. When they nod to each other and shyly point to the gatehouse by the entrance, I know I have won.

Fifteen dollars per month. I rent the one-room porter's lodge *inside* the high-walled domain. I have found a safe (albeit damp) home for Aunt Jenny and Uncle Elias. I am exultant.

Back home on rue de la Chaise I expect a hug. Instead Maman, busy, says: "The family does things for you, you do things for the family!" I hear her.

Gürs was horrible. Mannheim, terrifying. In Roanne, the Strausses have no ration coupons and no residence permits.

They eat and spend their days with us. We are six people in one kitchen/dayroom. Even the rutabagas get stretched.

We never talk about it. We are so proud. Aunt Jenny and Uncle Elias never once mention what it felt like to be shuttled for three days back and forth over the borders in sealed railroad cars because Vichy didn't want to accept Germany's Jews, and the Germans were determined to get rid of them. Instead, Aunt Jenny raves about the baby clothes Ghis and I sent to Gürs. She says: "Young mothers came over from other barracks. They were so happy with the little outfits, the booties and the blankets." Aunt Jenny is swell, I think. She gives credit to Ghis and me for our deeds. She told everybody that her nieces collected all the lovely things. In my adolescent state of mind I don't imagine what she herself endured and is hiding. Uncle Elias tells us that over 7,000 Jews from Baden and the Palatinate were expelled to Gürs. Within a few months, those who didn't die from disease in Gürs were sent in sealed trains to be exterminated in Auschwitz.

Aunt Jenny had such faith in Papa's power at rescue that she packed four lengths of material from her husband's fabric shop in Mannheim at the bottom of her one and only allowed piece of hand luggage — her gift to her nieces.

Family!

I can't see myself a burden to my parents, another mouth to feed, and I deeply question an academic future for a Jew in a Europe ruled by Hitler. At a street corner on avenue de Mulsant, waiting for the light to turn green, I tell Papa: "I wish to go and work for money." I'm recently sixteen and I want to pull my own weight.

Papa clears his throat. The man, who prided himself on being able to support his wife and children, struggles. He believes in educating his daughters. Ghis and I were supposed to go on to University. I always wanted to attend Science-po, the political Science Graduate school in Paris. I enjoy history and politics and I have a keen mind. Papa purses his lips. He coughs, he says: "Think carefully, Marguerite, before you drop out of school. You may regret it." He says it gravely, his advice is moving, but next day I enroll in an accounting course. I already know shorthand and typing.

Two months into accounting, I answer an ad in the *Journal de Roanne* for a secretary-bookkeeper. The CPA, Monsieur Cassain, interviews me on behalf of a client of his. He sits shivering in his winter overcoat in his unheated office. I shiver on a chair opposite his.

"You know how to type and take stenography? You know on which side of the ledger you enter the credits and the debits?"

I nod with a smile.

"Fine, you are hired!"

"When do I start?"

"Next Monday!"

He likes me! I'm going to get paid for my work! I see the gates of adulthood open before me. On the avenue de Mulsant, I skip on the way home.

On Monday morning, down by the river Loire in the industrial part of town — chimneys, block buildings, broken cement sidewalks — my employer's business sign reads **CHEZ JACQUES. Ready to Wear. Men, Women Apparel.**

I introduce myself: "I'm Marguerite Lévy, your accountant has hired me to be your secretary." Monsieur Jacques and I shake hands. My boss is dark-haired and fleshy-cheeked. He blushes and shows me to my office, a space paneled off the cutting room.

Jacques' new secretary is young, green-eyed, with chestnut curly hair. Fresh from two months at secretarial school, she dreams of being a Girl Friday weighed down with files and entrusted with responsibilities. A pillar of the business world.

I quickly learn that at Chez Jacques "the pillar" carries little weight. It merely abuts a desk.

Most mornings I sit at my silent typewriter and observe red-faced buyers furtively carrying bundles of tied sweaters through the exit door next to my office. *C'est ça!* I'm a front for legality. Jacques has hired me not because he needs me, but to accede to his CPA's wishes. Jacques sells most of his knitwear on the black market. Typed invoices are the least of his concerns. A shrewd businessman, Jacques takes advantage of the scarcities that war creates.

Within the week my boss hops onto the corner of my desk. He blushes profusely, oozes a great amount of animal charm, and shyly says:

"If my wife asks you whether I receive any visitors, please say 'No'."

I lower my eyelids. "Of course, Monsieur."

Exciting! I'm about to play a real life-role in *MÉNAGE À TROIS,* a play by Sacha Guitry I had seen performed in Paris at the Michodière theatre the year before the war — a comedy about a love-triangle between a husband, his wife, and her lover.

In Jacques' scenario, Nicole — Jacques' cute little mistress in a soft-tailored green suit, saunters in and out of his office most mornings, happy and giggling.

On Friday afternoon Jacques's dutiful wife dressed in black, demure, stops by my desk to do the payroll.

"Monsieur, has he many visitors?"

"Oh, non, Madame!" and I shake my head.

Pause.

The wife leaves. Lips pinched with the disappointed mien of a deceived spouse.

The kings do it... the bourgeois... Monsieur Jacques does it!

At home I don't broach a word about my life in the work place.

Jacques graciously grants me Thursday afternoons off to lead my Brownie meetings. *"Mais naturellement,* it's quite all right!"

In another gesture of generosity, Jacques sells me at wholesale price a burgundy wool sweater knit in the famed Roanne stitch decorated with three classical brass buttons. The garment wraps me in a fashion shield throughout the war.

Working at Chez Jacques is an enjoyable time in a stark world.

The war news is grim. Every night London is bombed. A firestorm destroys Coventry. German troops enter Romania. Bulgaria is forced to join the axis. The Wehrmacht attacks Yugoslavia and Greece. Yugoslavia capitulates. The British evacuate Greece. Rommel attacks in Cyrenaica. The Germans invade Crète. The HMS Hood is sunk. Convoys from America to England are attacked constantly by German U-boats in the Atlantic. In my diary I note, March 1941: "Last month 500,000 tons were sent to the bottom." Every loss stabs my heart. I personally feel the pain. The prospect of a thousand year-long rule of the Third Reich is a feared possibility.

Winston Churchill understands our dread. Nightly at 9:30 PM, he has the BBC broadcast to us: "Hello... Ici Radio Londres... The French speak to the French..." The BBC cheers us up with the ditty

"Ob Hitler, ob Goering,
Ob Himmler, ob Heydrich,
alles geht vorueber,
alles geht vorbei.
Whether Hitler or Goering,
Himmler or Heydrich,
everything's transient,
everything's temporary."

Reeling from defeat, bundles of misery, we listen to the announcer make light of German successes. In my world of 1940-

1941, I feel there is just Churchill holding out against Nazi Germany. "I have nothing to offer but blood, toil, tears and sweat." Churchill doesn't make false promises to his people. He doesn't lie as our French leaders did! I admire Winston Churchill's fighting spirit.

Inside metropolitan France queuing for edibles at dawn becomes a way for life. On many mornings, Papa rises at 3:00 AM and stands for hours in line at the butcher's for unrationed red tripe like spleen, stomach, liver, and pancreas.

Early SUNDAY MORNINGS at the farmers' market avenue de Mulsant there is a spot on the edge where a young shepherd sells little round goat cheeses without coupons. He stands next to his goat tied to a picket fence and plays the flute. The scene is out of a Ferdinand Bol canvas of rural life in the eighteenth century. I pet the goat and stare at the round wicker tray lined with large green leaves. I point to the biggest crotin. "S'il vous plait..." I purchase and wolf down the small round goat cheese greedily; I'm hungry. But in 1940 I am also ashamed. I feel I should have brought the cheese home for the family. I return to the flute-playing shepherd boy and guiltily count out a few more francs to bring *un petit crotin* home.

Every grocery store turns into a trading post. Maman barters wine for flour, sugar for oil, cheese for potatoes. Eggs cost thirty-six francs a dozen. The British navy embargoes French ports because imported goods are diverted to Germany. The Germans requisition our homegrown agricultural products for their homeland; France also must feed the occupation forces.

FROM JANUARY 1941 on, our rations are reduced. We get eight ounces of pasta per person per month. A ten ounce ration of fat includes butter, oil and margarine. Our family has a right to eight ounces of white tripe — kidneys and intestines. To make up for a shortage of chocolate rations, the German forces of occupation grant instead to category J-3, *jeunesse,* youth like me between 16 and 21 years, four liters of wine. Parents have but one thought: feed their young.

The WINTER OF 1940-1941 brings freezing temperatures for weeks on end. The thermometer dips to seventeen degrees Fahrenheit. Our household of four gets fifty kilos of coal per month, enough to heat and cook for two hours a day. The fire in the stove goes out. The cold breaks the skin on my fingers. Everyone wears bandages over suppurating frostbites. Bloody cold sores cover hands.

After a heavy snowfall, farmers can't get their produce to market.

OUR DAILY DIET consists mostly of rutabagas and Jerusalem artichokes. Papa cooks rutabagas in all shapes and ways — baked, pureed, sliced, and mixed with pancreas or leeks. A joke makes the rounds. It goes: "What is abundant under Vichy?" Answer: "Rutabagas!" After months on a rutabaga diet I bloat like a balloon.

Although deep down I love my parents, I'm hungry. I don't fail to let them know.

Around a sparse meal in the kitchen one night, I say: "But my 350 grams J3 bread ration is mine, why can't I have it?"

"We share."

"But I'm hungry!"

"Have you forgotten the Fifth Commandment?"

"Nothing counts in this house but the Fifth!" I snap.

I'm not forgetting to HONOR THY FATHER AND THY MOTHER, but am hungry. I can't sublimate my hunger pangs into joy of learning as I do later, for I have no privacy at rue de la Chaise. I share with Ghis the big bed in the kitchen.

We eat our rutabagas in silence at the same table.

Poor Papa — until now so solid, so powerful — is so miserable because he can't feed his family, that in order to salvage his self-respect, he must be tyrannical. Maman suffers in silence which is much worse. At her favorite corner grocery store on the avenue de Mulsant she frantically trades our wine coupons. When I recall Roanne, it's the darkness and my teenage hunger that come to mind.

63

Yet Maman slowly recovers her health with the help of the Demoiselles Joncour. The owners of the knit shop on avenue Mulsant listen to my mother's worries.

"Oh, Madame Lévy, the savages, they will get their due!" The Demoiselles Joncour reply to Maman who must have complained about our crammed quarters and Papa losing his fingernails due to a lack of calcium. When Maman voices her anguish about the decree of March 20, 1941 which appoints Xavier Vallat, a rabid anti-Semite, as commissioner for Jewish affairs, the Demoiselles Joncour at the knit shop answer: "Oh Madame Lévy, we are all in the same boat, Christians and Jews alike, we are French!"

"And they too suffer from arthritis," Maman reports at home, stressing yet another common bond.

You may be asking how Vichy was chosen as the seat of Pétain's regime. It had to do with housing. Ministers, a plethora of agencies, the embassies of the USA and the Vatican had to be housed. Where? Pétain was so afraid of Edouard Herriot, the powerful mayor of Lyon, that he dared not enter his town. There are few large cities in the NOZ. Clermont-Ferrand is too ugly. Vichy, a spa famous for healing the liver of the hard drinking colonial administrators, offered plenty of hotel space and villas. Voilà!

I don't go to school, but I go to work. The daily hardships weigh less heavy on me. Life is my own. About 7 AM, on summer mornings, I fold my clothes on the pebbled shores of the Loire River. My swimsuit underneath my dress, I pull my bathing cap on, and off I swim across the Loire River. I do several crossings, all breaststroke. At 5:00 PM, after work, I again head for the river. I enjoy swimming. Once or twice we swim en famille.

By 1941, I distrust PIERRE LAVAL: he's a snake. But even after the statutes of October and after the appointment of Xavier Vallat — I, a French Jew, do not separate myself from the destiny of France. It's my core being. Up to this point I have never personally suffered from anti-Semitism in France. Yes, we had to abandon everything in Paris and Maman lost her health, but deep down I still blamed our military collapse for the anti-Jewish laws in France. I am not yet cognizant that le Crédit Lyonnais and la Société Générale are collaborating with the Germans in the seizure of their Jewish clients' bank accounts. I do not know, yet, that the French State deducts the value of the Jewish properties and the Jewish cash assets confiscated by the Germans from the war tribute the French State must pay to Hitler.

I know that Papa, the founder and chief executive officer of Géo Gignoux, the second largest paint manufacturer in France after Ripolin, now sells paper goods to hotels and restaurants "while supplies last". Papa works for his nephew Robert who has relocated from Strasbourg to Périgueux. My father's ID reads: Albert Lévy, *représentant de Commerce,* salesman. Papa travels to Vichy, Clermont-Ferrand, Saint-Etienne and Lyon. No problem. Ghis is employed as a nurse's aide at Doctor LaRouche's clinic here in Roanne; later, she takes a position as governess to two children age five and seven in Lyon-Caluire. No problem. I work at Chez Jacques.

In July 1942, I attend a two-week non-denominational Scout leadership camp in Avignon. I am away when the mass arrests of French and foreign Jews occur in Paris on July 16-17. When I return, my parents are very quiet, but do not mention the catastrophe.

In Roanne, Jews divide themselves into French Jews and foreign Jews. As French provincial society is strictly stratified, Jews socialize with their own kind only. Amid their own kind, French Jews form sub-groups from orthodox to culturally assimilated. The latter stand on the top rung of the social ladder. A Brownie leader, I am involved with my Brownies' parents. They come from disparate walks of life. Some are wealthy, some poor, some are French, some Polish. I enter their worlds on a one-to-one basis. I relate to other Jewish refugees as well.

MADAME EPSTEIN lives with her family on rue de la Chaise, a few houses further up from number nine. The Epsteins are refugees from Belfort. In winter Madame Epstein wears a long black overcoat and her wizened top of thin white curls sticks out from her collar like an eagle's crown. In the street Madame Epstein stops Maman and in a shrill voice says: "Jeremiah predicted the events of 1940. It's all written in the Bible. God is punishing us because we have strayed." Tea leaf reading is another one of Madame Epstein's hobbies.

Maman, anxiety-prone, finds comfort in Madame Epstein's ideas of punishment and reward. Mother listens to the prophetess of doom and her ideas of pre-determination. For me, on the other side, "God willed it" means you refuse to take responsibility for your own life, and you abdicate your freedom of choice. If all you have to do is follow *His* Laws in order to get back into His good graces — and obedience saves you from the hangman — then you need not deal with the chaotic world around you. In my guts I know "God helps those who help themselves." So whenever Maman quotes Madame Epstein, I walk away.

ABIGAIL EPSTEIN is tall and strong-boned. She limps. The oldest daughter of the Epsteins works as a dental assistant. When I pass her on rue de la Chaise we never speak to each other. My senior by about ten years, Abigail looks aloof. I think that because of her mother's objectionable superstitions Abigail had to detach herself.

Then one day on rue de la Chaise, Abigail stops me. "Mlle Lévy, I am in love with a blind musician, a Jewish refugee, but he refuses to marry me out of concern for my own survival. He even forbids me to go and see him. I love him more than I love myself. If he gets deported, I wish to go with him."

I'm sixteen, still untouched by love. *If* he rejects her, why does she insist? Does she like martyrdom? I disapprove of her fatal attraction. Yet, I feel flattered that Abigail should confide in me. In normal times I would have had to wait much longer to gain an adult's trust. I discover that as social barriers and hierarchies crumble in the general upheaval of war, new bonds form.

Refugees from Strasbourg HENRI and DENISE LÉVI live on the third floor of a walk-up brick building in the center of Roanne. On summer days white voile curtains flutter in the breeze at their open bedroom window. Red roses bloom in a vase set on a blue embroidered tablecloth that covers the small ice cream table. Matisse might have painted their interior in any of his vivid, still-life oil canvasses.

Denise is twenty, and Henri just celebrated his twenty-fifth birthday. Both have their baccalauréate. They married before Henri was mobilized in 1939. Riri and Denise love each other more than any couple I have ever seen. Playful like children, in their presence my anguishes wash away like dirt under a shower. As long as I live I know I'll never forget their deep love.

Henri has been released from a POW camp for health reasons. I do not ask if he drank a lot of coffee like the other prisoners-of-war do to make their heartbeats flutter before their medical examinations or if it is his humped back. I do not ask why he has a humped back; it would be considered rude, and in France at that time, everyone cared about manners. Henri has chestnut-brown hair. His deep grey eyes twinkle with humor; when he plays the violin, he hums and sways along.

Henri Lévi is the Jewish Boy Scout leader in Roanne, a member of the National Committee of *les Eclaireurs Israélites de France*, the E.I.F. In France, at that time, Scouts are affiliated with their religion.

Denise is the Jewish Girl Scout leader.

I start a Brownie troop.

We affirm life and create a community.

Most evenings I stop by at Denise and Henri's third floor walk-up on my way home from Chez Jacques. We discuss scout meetings and exchange banter. Denise and Henri are my best friends in Roanne. Sometimes in their country kitchen I meet other interesting people like --

67

MONSIEUR HOLLAENDER, the downstairs tenant of Denise and Henri, is a Jewish professor of history barred from teaching at the Lycée Henri IV in Paris. Le professeur cuts an imposing figure. His high forehead dominates his face and he always dresses in conservative, three-piece suits and a tie. One Saturday morning, in Denise's kitchen, the Professor expounds to the three of us (mostly to Henri) his concept of modern warfare. He explains it like this: The socio-historic consequences of two clashing cultures meeting on the battlefields of Europe will have lasting universal repercussions for centuries to come as the savage elements contained in the Germanic character rise once again to the fore under the influence of multiple pressures... and, shaking his cold pipe at us as if it were a jabbing finger, he says: "This is only the beginning of many a great pitched battle to come."

I'm 16-17. I feel Le Prof. is a bit windy. Although I think I understand his theory of the convergence of historic pressures and national character, I know there is more to Hitler's rise to power. What about the Franco-British rivalry that let it happen? --

MADAME FEIST wears a reddish color wig because Orthodox Jewish law requires that all married women cover their hair so as to lessen their attractiveness. Her hairpiece is very pretty, albeit a bit stiff. You see it's a wig. Refugee from Paris, Madame Feist rents a house in a suburb of Roanne for her three boys, three girls, and two nieces. Monsieur Feist stayed in Paris because he studies at a Yeshiva. I met him once. It wasn't fun. He seemed not to notice me.

Madame Feist regularly visits Papa and Maman at 9 rue de la Chaise on Saturday afternoons. Orthodox, she strictly observes Exodus 20:10 "Thou shall not work on the Sabbath, neither you nor any of your servants." Forbidden by Halachic law to light a fire on the Sabbath, Madame Feist, "incidentally", warms her frostbitten fingers on our coals. After the recitation of a *Brocha*, blessing, over the fire and after the "Amen", she lifts the soft curve of her neck and, regularly, I notice an ecstatic smile brightening up her face. She glows with pure divine love. Always, my parents look forward to Madame Feist's company on Saturday afternoon.

One Sabbath I go to the Feists' cold home in search of daughter Judith, two years my elder. That day, around the dining table, Judith asks the younger children and me to translate prayers from the Hebrew text. I flunk miserably. Decide never to go back. On the following Saturday, alone, I attend a matinée of *La Bohème* at the Roanne Opera. Now that the memory surfaces I again feel all over my awkwardness in both situations. I'm the odd-girl-out, seeking self-fulfillment. Witnessing.

The members of the extended PIERRE DREYFUSS family are culturally assimilated French Jews. The family of my Brownie Isabelle and I are friends.

Refugees from the fashionable sixteenth arrondissement in Paris, they rent a free-standing house in upper Riorges. Their household includes the children's governess. Twice weekly after scout meetings Pierre Dreyfuss picks up Isabelle at rue de la Chaise. With little Isabelle tucked in the front basket of his bicycle, he cycles up the avenue de Mulsant. Pierre wears Lacoste shirts, sports pants, and tennis shoes. A graduate of the prestigious École Nationale d'Administration (the E.N.A. in Paris), an upper echelon civil servant, Pierre and I in our kitchen discuss Duhamel, Gide, Romain Rolland. Intelligent and sensitive, Pierre is in turn the son of a distinguished Ena graduate. His wife and his sister-in-law make the props for our Brownie plays. An older brother, Doctor Jean-Claude Dreyfuss, had been arrested in Paris and taken to Drancy; the family regularly sends food parcels to Dr. Dreyfuss at the transit camp for Jews. Whenever I ask Pierre for news about his brother, he answers cheerily: "So far so good, he's still in Drancy!" In Drancy, Dr. Dreyfuss practices medicine and delivers babies. In the Dreyfuss clan, no one gives in to doom. I admire their courage. Deep.

I must share with you the importance of a letter that I still have today dated "Vichy, 18 July 1941."

It was MID-SUMMER 1941, one Sunday morning, at the kitchen table. We had been half-reading the *Journal de Roanne* when Papa discovered on page three an article that said: "Several months ago, against the terms of the armistice agreement, Germany has appointed two Gauleiters (military governors) to rule Alsace and the Lorraine..."

The news hits like a bolt from the blue. For we can, as Alsatian Jews, fall under the jurisdiction of German laws.

At once Papa takes pen and paper and jots down a draft asking Vichy for clarification about the status governing Alsatian Jews. Tight-lipped, Father writes out the letter in longhand. I type his text without changing a comma, so serious I perceive the matter to be.

Within a fortnight, General Koeltz's reply arrived on official stationary of the French War Ministry.

ÉTAT FRANÇAIS

Vichy, 18 July 1941.
BN/2/GG
War Ministry
Section
Services of the Armistice

No 22.730   D.S.A./2

Sir,

In answer to your letter of July 3, I have the honor to let you know that no clause in the Armistice agreement stipulates a change in the nationality for the people of Alsace and the Lorraine.

The regime set up by the German authorities in Alsace-Lorraine — if it does not at the present time permit the French Government to enforce the rights of its citizens in those two provinces — in no way prevents the Alsatians and the Lorrainers from being French.

Please accept, Monsieur, the expression of my sincere esteem.

Général de Corps d'Armée KOELTZ.
Director of Armistice Services

to: Monsieur Albert Lévy
9, rue de la Chaise
Roanne (Loire)

Papa folds the letter carefully and sticks it into his jacket's breast pocket.

The situation of the French Jews is complex. On one side there are Pétain, Laval, Xavier Vallat, Raphael Alibert — all fascist collaborators, maréchalists, lusts of power, desires for revenge, report writers to the Nazi conquerors and their lackeys. On the other side are many decent hearts of individual men and women sobered by our losses who do not like to emulate the Nazis. Like General Koeltz, the Demoiselles Joncour, Monsieur Jacques, the Lejeune sisters, and the Masseys — so far, in the Non-occupied south, my family is unharmed but anxious about the future.

Our fate is deeply entwined with the wider War. Can Great Britain hold out? Everywhere in Europe and in North Africa, Hitler's forces are on the roll.

THEY have taken Brest-Litosk and Smolensk. The Russians are forced to blow up the Dnepropetrovsk dam. The Crimea is cut off. Kiev has fallen. The Soviet Government has left Moscow. Stalingrad is surrounded. On the seas, the *SS Reuben James* (an American destroyer) is sunk, the *Prince of Wales* is sunk. The BBC tells us that London is a nightly inferno.

Monday, Dec 8th, 1941. Seated around the kitchen table, we hear the news of America's entry into the war.

71

Papa gets up from his chair.

"Now we'll win."

The BBC broadcast evokes in my father images of Pershing and his Boys with the broad brim hats of 1917.

Alas, a long string of allied defeats follow in the Pacific and in North Africa. The *Repulse* and the *Prince of Wales* are sunk. We plunge into a dark long night. The raid on Dieppe fails. Pictures in the *Journal de Roanne* show the poor Canadian soldiers washed ashore on their backs, glassy-eyed. It's sad, so very sad. Hitler grants to the inhabitants of Dieppe 25 kilos of potatoes per family as a reward for not rising against the forces of occupation. At home, the silence weighs. Papa coughs his dry irritation; Maman doesn't talk. I escape into work at Chez Jacques and into scouting.

Time rolls. It is September 1942. I'm nearly eighteen.

Breakfast at the kitchen table on rue de la Chaise. I'm about to leave for work. Papa stands at the stove mashing the lunch rutabagas in the Moulinex while the embers last. Nails soft from a lack of calcium, lips tight, he concentrates on his task. When he hands me the wooden spoon for a lick, he bends his tall frame over me. His forehead furrows; I sense he is about to voice something of importance. "Marguerite," he says, "do you remember the story of the two frogs?"

I know the parable: Two frogs fell into a pail of milk. One frog gives up and drowns while the other paddles around until he finally churns up a ball of butter. Then he hops out.

Papa's sunken eyes sit deep in his hollowed cheeks. In his right hand he grips the handle of the coffeepot and pours some of the chicory brew into my cup. In Roanne our life is tenuous. The Nazis loom. Intuitively, I understand that my father wishes to pass on to his daughter a lesson in survival: I ought to be tenacious in holding out, churn through rough times like the strong frog, not give up like the weaker one. Papa sets his hand on my shoulder; I slide my fingers over his.

At that fragile moment in my existence, the fable's message penetrates my soul with a mythical meaning: This Lévy must survive!

Since, I have often dipped at the great mass and the depth of the feeling underlying the words. Whenever I am desperate or near the end of my tether, that little voice rises: "A Lévy survives."

OCTOBER 3, 1942, the BBC broadcasts: "A battle is raging at El Alamein in the North African desert near Alexandria in Egypt — all is going well."

I hope. I pray. "Dear God..."

Then the daily communiqué from the BBC stops altogether from mentioning El Alamein. For weeks there's a total news blackout about the fighting in the desert of Cyrenaica.

On rue de la chaise, Madame Epstein tugs at Maman's coat sleeve: "Rommel is at the door of Palestine. His Panzers are about to overrun Jerusalem..."

The news blackout lasts and lasts.

Gloom permeates our house. I can't pierce it. I can't shake it.

Finally the words pour out of the radio: "Rommel's Afrika Korps has been annihilated. The British Eighth Army and the Allies under the command of Field Marshall Bernard Montgomery have destroyed the German tanks." (The final tally is 440 crushed Panzers out of 450).

The battle of EL ALAMEIN has been won!

It is NOVEMBER 4, 1942.

Papa boils a pot of water on the stove. He crumples some dried mint leaves. We have no sugar. No milk. But something happy has happened, something important. We celebrate the first Allied win.

Within four days, on 7-8 November, General Eisenhower's forces land in North Africa. On avenue de Mulsant, I hum silently:

"Ob Hitler, ob Goering...

Everything's transient, everything's temporary..."

73

Chapter 4

Edict 108

IT'S NOVEMBER 11, 1942, along the avenue de Mulsant on my way to work I'm holding in my hand a thin volume of the Symbolist poets. As usual, I'm learning by heart four verses of poetry to develop my mind. On this particular morning, I memorize Baudelaire's "Albatross" out of *Les Fleurs du Mal*:

Exiled on the deck subject to derision,
Its giant wings prevent it from walking...

when I notice an eerie stillness around me that empties the streets. The 7:30 AM crowd — made up mostly of working girls and middle-aged men with their berets pulled down over one ear — is staring stony-faced at the approaches to the rail yard bridge. *Quoi?*

Wehrmacht soldiers, machine-guns on their shoulders deployed in fan-like formation around the overpass, here in the Free Zone?

Assault tanks painted with the black swastika guard the bridge. I retrieve some coins in my purse and purchase *Le Journal de Roanne,* a daily.

The headlines read: **"IN RETALIATION for the ANGLO-AMERICAN LANDINGS in NORTH AFRICA** the Führer orders his troops to invade the southern zone." It's Armistice Day.

In the layer of my mind where reason reigns, I'm cognizant that we are at his mercy: why should *he*, a ruthless conqueror, respect a demarcation line that no longer serves his Grand Design? Reason knows any pretext will do, but the actual event touches emotions

— the territorial imperative has been mauled. The Wehrmacht forces have overrun the Non-occupied Zone.

Past the Germans, through the Promenade toward the riverside industrial district where my sweater factory is located — I go on to work at Chez Jacques. It is late fall, the leafless trees bare their blackened barks; a low cumulus hangs over the power lines.

There isn't a sound in the cutting room. Only the scissors' steel blades clipping the fabric can be heard through the thin veneer wall next to my office. The usual chorus of clear girlish voices singing *Ma Normandie, À la Claire Fontaine, When Spring Returns* — which energizes production and stimulates patriotism — is dead silent.

When Mimi, a warehouse clerk, carries a bundle of ready-to-wear sweaters to my office for a packing slip, she just stands there next to my desk, her mouth opening and closing, unable to speak. Choked by sobs she simply extends her hand.

Later that morning, Madame Madeleine, the stodgy forelady surreptitiously wipes her nose with a white starched handkerchief when she enters my space.

Marshall Pétain's broadcast from Vichy is expected. Surely, the Head of State will tell us "the French Army and the Navy are fighting."

At 10 AM, a quivering voice appeals on the radio for calm, dignity and resignation. Pétain's meekness hurts. Once more he leads us down the surrender path. At my desk, I hang my head into my hands, depressed. Oh God!

Soon, the Vichy Defense minister, General Bridoux, a known collaborator, issues an order on the radio to our 100,000-man armistice army: "All officers and soldiers are to stay in their barracks." A second command to the troops orders: "Surrender your arms!"

Our army is gone. It's awful!

I grieve for the loss of our nationhood. I mourn for our trampled sovereignty. The fate of our fleet fills me with anxiety. The second most powerful in the world, within a few days it scuttles itself in Toulon rather than surrender. Oh God, what a calamity!

Now, the Jews in the former Non-occupied Zone fall directly under Hitler's jurisdiction! Now the Germans can arrest any French Jew in the NOZ, directly, without the French police! And tomorrow is Thursday, the mid-week meeting day when my Brownies assemble in the basement of the synagogue. What shall we do tomorrow? *Quoi faire?*

Denise and Henri are sitting side by side on the white chenille bedspread in their bedroom. I sit down on the straight ice-cream parlor chair by the small round table near the window. The voile curtains are drawn, a vase filled with red roses stands on the hand-embroidered blue table cloth.

I have stopped by at Denise and Henri's third floor walk-up downtown after work, expecting we will discuss the new circumstance.

There is a pause.

A diffuse silence.

Seated on their bed Denise and Henri appear just as usual — playful, in love, and joyously interacting. Denise, laughing, says: "Jean (Henri's twin brother) sleeps at night in our room on the floor in his sleeping bag (he recently was released from a POW stalag), and he snores terribly." And: "Two potatoes are all I have left in the house." And: "Riri made coffee this morning with chicory and ground acorns." Henri never tires of gazing at Denise. I listen, aware that the sense of urgency is here under the pleasantries as if everyone is waiting in their seats one more moment before facing the duress of reality.

When time comes for the serious discussion: disband or keep our regular schedule, we know we'll not give in to fear. We owe it to the children and to ourselves to stay connected. Our underlying strength has crystallized.

The following day about two o'clock, worried but brave fathers and mothers bring their little daughters — all twelve of them — to the basement of the synagogue rue Beaulieu. We shake hands, warmly. I think: perhaps it is best not to talk about it.

My program is tightly scripted: first we do the greeting ceremony, followed by "Show and Tell;" then I listen to their week's achievements, and in quick succession we play "Jump River," "Simon knows...," and the "Ferret runs..." I'm fiercely determined to provide normalcy --

Until in the street on that afternoon I lead the Thrushes, dressed in their scout uniforms and marching two abreast, into singing:

En passant par la Lorraine,
Avec mes sabots,
Rencontra trois capitaines,
Avec mes sabots dondaine,
Oh, Oh, Oh!
Avec mes sabots... —

"Walking through the Lorraine" is our favorite marching song, but it also is the song of the fighting Free French, de Gaulle's war song.

As we turn the corner, our troop comes face to face with a Wehrmacht officer. He stands on the curb in his grey-green uniform freshly pressed and shiny boots; in his hand he holds a slender crop. Blood rushes to my head. Quickly, in the middle of the refrain "Oh, oh, oh..." I switch to: "Maréchal, Maréchal, here we are..."

My Thrushes, children of their times, glance sideways at their leader and, without a tremor in their voices or a missed step, they sing all the silly words, since forgotten, of: "Here we are, Marshall, we, your lads swear before you, the savior of France, to serve and follow in your footsteps." In unison, they proclaim their readiness to serve Marshal Pétain.

We are near level with the Wehrmacht officer. He seems surprised. He plays with that slender looped whip in his hand. He taps the straps to and fro his left palm. My muscles tighten. What is on his mind? Did he understand the marked change in allegiance? Is he familiar with the hymn of the Resistance, or do these very young children (with Jewish features) affirming so

77

loudly their desire to follow Philippe Pétain of Vichy — remind him of the Hitlerjugend back home?

Back on rue Beaulieu, I am still trembling in my shoes, when wide-eyed Yolande asks:

"Cheftaine, we got you right away when you changed from 'La Lorraine' to 'le Maréchal'. Are we going to do that from now on every time...?'"

Yolande is seven.

"Hmm, we'll see...!" I answer, in the hope of gaining time.

Pas malin, Marguerite! The little inner voice scolds, not very smart what you did. You risked their lives to make your own personal teenager's statement.

For the first time I become aware of two opposite urges in me: one that protects, another that protests — both conflicting forces stay with me forever. That day I swallow hard and decide that from now on in the basement of the synagogue I'll practice survival skills with my Brownies rather than put their lives at risk — I want them to "Be Prepared."

BE PREPARED to pierce blisters. With a red pencil I trace circles on the heels of a doll to be punctured with a needle and thread. "Leave a length of white thread under the skin and let the 'blisters' drain...'" — If they must go on long marches —

Be PREPARED to carry an injured child on chain locked hands. I show each Brownie how to grip her left wrist with her right hand, and the wrist of her partner with the left fingers —

BE PREPARED to see blood. I prick the skin of my knee with a needle and ask each Brownie in turn to clean and dress the wound with gauze and tape. Cheftaine, it must hurt, says Isabelle, wincing. Never mind my knee, Isabelle. I'm determined to make hardened Scouts out of my tender Brownies.

In the courtyard at rue Beaulieu I instruct them how to keep a mess kit clean. We scrub the huge aluminum pot. Each one in turn carries a heavy-duty burlap pail filled with water without spilling. I drill them in memory games and scout knots. Seated in a circle we sing:

The kookaburra sits on the old gum tree,
Merry, merry king of the bush is he,
Laugh, kookaburra, laugh,
Kookaburra, gay your life must be —

I passionately wish to give the gift of life to my Brownies; impress their minds with happy memories so that they may bear up a bit better under the afflictions to come. The fate of my little Thrushes still scars my heart.

Many Jewish refugee families are poor. Imagine one Sunday the irate father of wide-eyed Yolande remonstrating with me: "Mademoiselle, you are too hard on shoes," he says. "I just bought Yolande a new pair and after the first outing, she returned home with uneven heels. You walk them too much, and all that rope jumping uses too much sole."

Poor lost Yolande, seven years old, just stands there in the synagogue basement like a brown-eyed unfathomable Picasso child: her father disapproves of her Cheftaine. Cheftaine is reckless. But I am resourceful.

At the Uniprix, the local Five and Dime store, I buy a metal foot and ersatz rubber pieces. Heels! Soles! soles! heels! I cut and hammer. I also repair my family's shoes. Maman, amused, looks at my cobbler's business set up on a kitchen chair. "You *Mamserbenitte*, you have the courage to try anything," she tells me with her elfin smile, using her favorite Hebrew term of endearment, "You little Devil."

God, what about a deal? If Thou let my Thrushes live, I'll pay for all the pastries I'm munching at the patisserie avenue de Mulsant on Sunday mornings. Fair? Whether God hears me or not, I can't tell. I make him participate in my life.

How many Jews are we in the former Non-occupied Zone? Monsieur Hollander on a Saturday morning in Denise's kitchen says that out of approximately 300,000 Jews in all of France before the war, only 180,000 are originally of French nationality, that number includes 30,000 Alsatian-Lorraine Jews. He says: "The former NOZ now holds 150,000 to 200,000 Jews, up from 5,000

79

before 1940." That number includes all the Jews who left Paris and the towns in the north, besides the 40,000 Jewish refugees from Belgium and Holland. Dressed in his three-piece suit and a tie, the professor of Modern History says he obtained the figures at the office of the Union Générale des Israélites de France, the U.G.I.F., where he works.

These reversals, losses and fears burned into me day by day until they seem to make sense, until they appear as if they constitute a new general order of life — actually only are a partial aspect of reality.

The other part is that the Wehrmacht in Roanne are thinly spread. It's strange how few grey-green uniforms you see on the streets. It is as if no Occupation happened. Every morning I go to work at Chez Jacques. No change there. I have a crush on Henri's brother, but cool down the desire. Mostly my Brownies are the recipients of my passions. A teenager, I give them everything I have.

SECOND HALF OF NOVEMBER 1942, Marc Hagueneau, a high-ranking commissaire of the E.I.F., visits Roanne. To our Scouts he teaches new songs, games, and cheers. Hip-hip-hurrah! Yea! Yea! Yea! Sparks of humor and intelligence just jump off Marc's skin.

He lifts our spirits with the latest joke that makes the rounds in Vichy: "A cabinet minister was heard exclaiming: Why do these idiots obey the decrees we make? Don't they know any better?" The joke allegedly originated in Laval's office. Denise, Henri, and I laugh.

At the same time my intuition tells me that the essence of jokes is to trivialize for a moment the most serious dreads, and that Marc's goal is to give us back a measure of self-esteem.

While eating his soup of rutabaga and leek in Denise's kitchen, Marc tells us: "Jacques Heilbronner, the president of the Consistoire Central des Israélites de France, is Cardinal Gerlier's former classmate from L'École Normale Supérieure (the elite administrative graduate school in Paris). Their relations are cordial." Also Monsignor Saliège, the archbishop of Toulouse and Pastor Boegner both, are protesting the inhumane treatment of the Jews in France. Mumbling: "I'm awake! I'm awake!" Marc falls asleep in his crumpled suit and tie, exhausted from a hard week of morale building. Denise, Henri, and I wink at each other. It's so good to have our high commissaire, Marc Hagueneau, visit with us in Roanne. We feel so isolated. He reassures us that we Jews have friends in France.

Friends in high places. These we seriously need, for we read in *Le Journal de Roanne* an article titled: "Jews Are Preparing a Trip East."

In the kitchen Papa's dry cough betrays his anguish. Maman pinches her lips. I can't believe that France has sunk that low. Around the table we read: "Judaism is a religion like Catholic and Protestant religions, but Jews believe in the Mosaic laws and therefore form a nation apart." The article further lists who should prepare: "You are considered Jewish if two grandparents belong to that faith." With flagrant hypocrisy the Vichy regime explains: "The government is not prejudiced against freedom of religion. It just considers the followers of the Mosaic Law as foreigners."

Foreigners! What nerve! It's a slap in my face. In Pluviose Year VI of the French Republic (1799) my great-grandfather Félix Lévy was born to Simon Lévy who was born to Nathan, who was begotten by Jacob, who was conceived by... a long line of Lévy ancestors who settled in Alsace on the Rhine River several hundred years ago and have lived there ever since in one uninterrupted succession. My lineage. And they consider us foreigners!

In my journal I note: "For Hitler, the Jews are a race; for Vichy: a religion. Which is it? Answer: our enemies use us for any purpose that suits them. We are their scapegoats."

At once rumors start circulating among the Jewish community that we, the French Jews, are being deported. Madame Epstein, in her long black overcoat and wizened hair, stops Maman on rue de la Chaise: "Trains are standing in the rail yard," she says. Monsieur Hollander affirms in Denise's kitchen: "The Germans

81

have raided the offices of the U.G.I.F., and made off with the card files."

I lend no credence to Madame Epstein the doomsday prophet, but I hear Mr. Hollander's facts. Although to myself I say: The French are different. France is not Poland. The French are not the Poles.

The rucksack period sets in unthinkingly. Every Jew in Roanne packs a backpack for his/her forthcoming deportation. I shove mine under the bed and go about my business as usual. Maman never talks about deportations, perhaps to keep the tears from flowing.

When I tell Denise: "I slipped two thin volumes of poems 'The Romantics' and 'The Symbolists' into the outer pocket of my rucksack" — she contentedly continues arranging the twelve long-stemmed red roses in her glass vase on the table by the window of her girlish bedroom, a gift from Henri. "That's the way to go. With poets!" she says.

Denise is equally imbued with idealism, I tell myself.

No one knows what the real world of the deportees is like. There is no news, no mail. No information. No one has ever witnessed and returned. There just is one big black hole somewhere far away in the east. Out there —

AND THEN, the black hole grows closer.

Soon, on a Saturday afternoon, Madame Feist pays a visit to Papa and Maman at rue de la Chaise, and, after the blessing over the fire, she sighs. Instead of cheerily chatting with my parents, she only briefly lifts her beatific eyes and with a heavy heart, says: "My two nieces have disappeared in Lyon."

Disappeared in Lyon?

"They failed to return home from the hospital where they both work as nurses"

Vanished!

Two French Jewish girls barely older than I have vanished in the streets of Lyon.

Suddenly in our kitchen fear grips Maman and Papa. Maman looks aghast as if she had bumped into a ghost. Papa's blood drains from his face. They both avoid my eyes. Our frail island of warmth has imploded.

The roundup of French Jews in the former Non-occupied Zone has begun.

Monday comes. As is his custom, Papa, in his blue denim apron makes breakfast for me at the stove. On the back coal burner, he toasts my bread; on the front burner he brews chicory coffee in the grey-and-white-speckled enamel pot.

The early morning is mine and Papa's private moment.

That day, when my father fills my cup with his steaming chicory brew, his eyes stay riveted on the coffee pot. "Marguerite, could you... would you, please... wear a scarf over your head like the peasant women do in Alsace?" He says. Papa is alarmed about his daughter. Oh Papa's alarm!

For several days I walk to and fro Chez Jacques through the Faubourg trying to look drab. I'm adjusting downward to the Occupation.

I don't like it.
I like my shiny curls.
The headdress goes.

IT IS EARLY DECEMBER 1942. The news from North Africa is exasperating. Darlan, Giraud, and Noguès are taking the Allies on a high-hopes-and-hellish-dips roller coaster. I'm sick to my stomach at the French political maneuvers in Morocco and Algeria. Why can't they join the Allies against our common foe? My guts wail when I hear on the BBC that Vichy's Admirals Esteva and Derrien have handed Bizerte and Tunis over to German Field Marshal Albert Kesselring, dealing the Allies a severe blow in Tunisia. They fired at the Allies. They killed hundreds of Americans and Brits. They sank dozens of Allied ships and didn't fire one cannon ball at the Germans arriving by air! I accuse the chieftains of treachery and indecision. It's — "Yes," in the morning. "No," at noon. "Perhaps," in the evening — waiting for orders from higher up... " They are nothing but a bunch of weather vanes oscillating with the atmospheric pressure!" I note in my diary. "Weak and cowardly, they debate on whose side lies their Honor. Disgusting! The whole world is watching their dillydallying between obedience to their superiors in Vichy, and responding to the appeal of the Allies. It is as if the French high brass is enjoying a recitation of Corneille's heroic passages in *Le Cid,* rather than mustering their courage and making a stand, unequivocally!"

My own personal dilemmas are shared by most French Jews. On the one hand, I am a product of French culture. France's past glories are deposited in me like the many alluvial strata in a delta. The French civilization has shaped me. Weren't we the envy of the world for centuries? On the other hand, my Jewish inheritance is also part of my self and, when one of my limbs is torn, the whole being feels wounded. At present, many French Jews suffer from this hurt.

A WEEK AGO I experienced this conflict acutely when the Protestant Girl Scout leader in Roanne chose both Denise and me to represent the Loire Department at the funeral in Vichy of a high Protestant Girl Scout dignitary who had passed on.

Walking in the cortege behind the coffin I broke out into hysterical laughter. I couldn't stop it. The absurdity of my situation hit me. Here were scores of people including Pétain's chief of staff, plus a minister or two, paying their respects to one Protestant Scout Commissaire who died of natural causes at a time when thousands of Jews are being deported and no one pays any heed to *them*. This is insane!

After the funeral I thought of the night of August 24, 1572 known as the MASSACRE of the SAINT BARTHÉLÉMY, when thousands of French Protestants were killed by order of King Charles IX under the influence of his mother Catherine de Médicis, and how similarities of our past histories cause this empathy between the Huguenots and the French Jews. Undeniably, both remember they are (or have been) at the mercy of French political vagaries.

As a courtesy, Denise and I go the following day and thank Arlette Trudot, the Protestant Scout leader in Roanne for selecting us as the two delegates for the Loire department.

"*Merci. C'était un Honneur!*"

Arlette Trudot, thin, tall and with a well defined chin, may well have been much more courageous than I had given her credit for at the time.

DECEMBER 11, 1942, Pierre Laval, the Vichy Prime Minister, publishes in the *Journal Official* his infamous law 1077 — quickly called Edict 108 within the Jewish community — ordering "All Jews in the former Free Zone to get their IDs stamped 'Juif' by January 11, 1943.'"

"Juif" stamped on my identity card means to me one thing: we, the French Jews, are being assembled for deportation east. "The trains are standing in the rail yard."

Cannot be! I am angry. I fume: we fought in every war; we contributed to France's glory. We upheld her laws. Sarah Bernhardt, Marcel Proust, Lévy-Brühl, Bergson, Darius Milhaud Jacques Offenbach, are just a few of our famous sons and daughters who brought universal acclaim to France. Our Jewish actresses, writers, sociologists, philosophers, musicians, and composers flowered her civilization, and now France is throwing us to the dogs! Not since the Revolution of 1789 have the French Jews been singled out as a distinct group with specially marked identity papers. My adrenaline flows. Laval, Pétain and his Vichy cohorts are traitors to our nation's traditions!

Wrath eliminates all ambivalence. You can't do that to me! I won't let you! I shall live and Papa and Maman and Ghis too! We shall not get our IDs stamped "J." We shall not be shipped east!

Deeply incensed, I burn with indignation. *Les Droits de l'Homme et du Citoyen* were the milk of my adolescence. Our teachers at the lycée inculcated into us the notion of Human Rights. They taught me that rebellion is a rightful defense against tyrannical masters. All throughout France's long history her citizens had rebelled against oppressors: the Gauls rose against

Caesar; the peasants against the nobility. The French brought about the Great Revolution of 1789. They gave the world the notions of Liberté, Egalité, and Fraternité. I inhaled the exalted air of the Dreyfus Affair, a cause célèbre, in which justice won over privileges. Weren't Esterhazy and his fiendish anti-Semitic friends punished, and Alfred Dreyfus reinstated? (I didn't know then that Emile Zola went to jail and into exile in Great Britain for the daring letter he printed in his newspaper *AURORE* under the title "J'ACCUSE!" in which he accused the French government of lying).

Aroused, furious, a cultural tail wind in my sail, I rebel: "We shall not comply!" I declare to Papa and Maman.

* * *

At Denise's third floor walk-up, Henri is alone in the apartment. He wears his habitual blue sweater; I notice his humped back and I look away through the open door at the roses in the bedroom. We both stand on the sienna tiles in the center of the kitchen. "Henri, the family and I are thinking about escaping Edict 108," I say.

America? Unless your name is Einstein, the doors are shut. The story of the "Saint-Louis" being turned away from an American port with 790 German Jewish refugees on board had been written up in the press. Switzerland is the only country, besides Spain, that incarcerates refugees in camps once they have successfully eluded the German patrols and the Swiss border guards. I do not know yet that this decision to evade "Edict 108" veers me into a course that changes my life forever, or that this rebellion is the start of a great adventure that opens new worlds and vistas.

By the window in his kitchen, Henri spontaneously answers: "Le passeur (the border smuggler) lives in Annemasse on the route de Genève... the house number is... tell him 'Paul sends regards...'"

I memorize the address and the password for our escape to Switzerland, but then Henri adds: "The E.I.F. is only organizing trips for Brownies and Cubs. You are on your own."

"Fine," I answer, quite happy at the challenge.

Later someone asks me: Why did Henri share top-secret information with you? Wasn't that dangerous? What if you had boasted or been caught? Wouldn't that have imperiled the entire network?

Yes, I suppose so, but Henri was a member of the national Council of the E.I.F. He thought about risks differently. He had sworn the oath "On my honor..." and he knew I'd obey the Promise as well. We had scouted together, worked alongside one another, and layers of trust had built up. He also was a good judge of character, I think. To this day I remember how he smiled: half mocking, half serious. On his lips — a dare.

Later Henri and Denise were caught at an SS-manned checkpoint in Lyon on the way to visiting Henri's parents hiding out at Tain L'Hermitage. Denise, Henri, and his father were sent to Drancy (the French-run internment camp for Jews only, near Paris). There Denise gave birth to a baby boy, Jean-Michel. All four were gassed on arrival in Auschwitz. My eyes still tear.

Meanwhile on rue de la Chaise, Papa and Maman agree that I should explore the border crossing into Switzerland.

After curfew, the following morning, I walk to the railway station in Roanne dressed in my Scout uniform with a string of merit badges on the jacket sleeve and board the train to Annemasse. The image I wish to project is that of an innocent Scout on a benign mission. Annemasse is a French border-crossing town into Switzerland.

Chapter 5

Escape

(December 1942)

It drizzles in Annemasse. At the railroad station, I go directly to a map of the city streets which is mounted on the wall behind the benches. I find the route de Genève in an easterly direction.

Like a gray mirror the pavement glistens in the street.

That green sign? On the right! Stucco homes on both sides of the route de Genève stare at me from behind hedges. Act self-confident. Read numbers. There! Your number is on a brass plate. I walk past the house, and then retrace my steps. The route de Genève is deserted under the rain.

Already he snakes along the narrow slate footpath. He must have seen me from behind a curtain. Suddenly he stands opposite me on the other side of the cast-iron outer gate; a *Gauloise* (French brand cigarette made of strong brown tobacco) dangles between his lips. Guarded, diffident — a typical Frenchman under the Occupation — his lowered lids are ready to deny any knowledge of the kind that might incriminate him.

"Vous cherchez? Are you looking for someone?" he asks, in a detached voice.

"Paul sends regards!" I say through the wrought iron bars.

He doesn't answer. Slowly, deliberately, he reaches into his sagging blue overalls and brings forth a cigarette lighter. After a long pause, he raises a head of curly dark hair.

"So Paul sent you, hmm? When did you see him last?"
"Yesterday."

"Yesterday, hmm? Where?"
"Roanne."

88

Now or never. "We wish to cross over into Switzerland," I whisper.

A quizzical look slips into his eyes. Head bent over his right forefinger, he taps the ashes from his cigarette; I notice the brown nicotine stains. My heart thumps. Without another word, he unlocks the gate and lets me in. In the garden, rain drips off the crushed chrysanthemum leaves; the wet rose stems glisten.

"Are you foreigners?" he asks on the welcome mat of the house porch and, facing me, takes me in from head to toe and back.

"We are French."

"Naturalized?"

"No, French-Alsatians."

He scratches his chin with his left hand.

"How many in the family?"

"Four."

"How do they look?" I sense that what he means is: Have *they* any Semitic features?

"Papa is red-haired!"

"And Maman?"

"Maman, my sister and I, we look alike," I quickly wrap Maman under the mantle of my high cheek bones, green eyes and straight nose.

A faint smile appears on his face. He takes another puff on his Gauloise and, once more, inspects me from scout beret to shoes. "I wouldn't go to Switzerland if I were you," he says under his breath.

"Why?"

"The situation in the camps is difficult. They separate the women from the men. Violence has erupted in the women's quarters."

"Why?"

"Because fenced-in females get hysterical and fight each other."

Won't do for Maman. Separated from Papa, she'll perish!

"What else can we do?"

Quietly stubborn, I dig my heels into the grey mopping cloth that covers the "good" outdoor welcome mat. He jingles the keys in his pocket. I wait...

Eventually in a barely audible tone of voice he says: "One can always live under an assumed name."

"Where?"

"*On n'est pas mal en Haute-Savoie.*"

"One isn't badly off in the Haute-Savoie" is uttered in a non-committal, impersonal sort of a way. He uses the non-specific French pronoun "*on*" which applies to anyone and to no one in particular, and which means: I didn't give you any advice.

A light goes on in my brain. The Haute-Savoie under an assumed name... Why not?

All around me, the chrysanthemums hang their purple, yellow and white heads, but in my heart joy explodes. The French Alps — Yes!

"Merci, Monsieur. Oh merci!"

Elated, I shake hands with the *passeur,* the man whom the Jewish Scouts use to smuggle Brownies and Cubs into Switzerland.

Going back to the railroad station on the wet asphalt under the rain, I see wild flowers bloom in a green meadow. Cowbells ring in my ears. Forests of pines and hazelnuts surround me. I smell rustling leaves in the wind. The grey road becomes a narrow green valley with a river flowing along the bottom, all hidden between high snowy peaks. The French Alps! A place to survive Hitler's deportations.

Calm down, Marguerite! Papa still has to accept the Plan. We will either go together, or not at all. Images of sun, fragrant flowers, and heavy cowbells tinkling in green meadows that so nicely had undulated under my head like in a Chagall escapist painting — are cut off.

Rue de la Chaise, Papa and Maman listen attentively. Papa left Germany at the very beginning of Hitler's rise to power, in March 1934, but the new plan involves illegality.

There's no telling what Papa thinks behind his furrowed forehead. The kitchen is very, very quiet.

"Sounds good!" he gravely says, after a tense pause.

Amazed at the speed of it all, I feel proud as a young eaglet. As inexperienced. Leave without a trace? False identity cards? Find a home? Live under an assumed name? All that!

It's mid-December.

Less than one month to January 11, the last day on which to get our IDs stamped *"Juif,"* "Jew."

Papa, Maman, and I work together as we have never done.

I'm no longer an adolescent prancing on the periphery. Until now I have been category J-3 (16 to 21), my parents: middle-aged (35 to 50); now our energies fuse. I find a used Michelin folding map of the Haute-Savoie at a downtown bookstore. Spread out on the kitchen table, the département shows a boundary with Lake Geneva and Switzerland to the north; Italy is to the south-east; the Savoy to the south, and l'Ain department to the east. Mont Blanc (the highest mountain in Europe) rises within the Haute-Savoie. Quick, think! Who has ever been in the Haute-Savoie?

Ghis!

Four winters ago at Christmas time 1938, my sister's baccalauréate class went skiing on Mont d'Arbois-Le Bettex, a high-mountain ski station above Saint-Gervais from where she sent back all those awful postcards: "Wish you were here," while I stayed behind in Paris green with envy, a sibling in the lower classes.

"Saint-Gervais looks good, Papa!"

Sibling rivalry isn't always the best source for wise decision-making. This time, it works. "Yes, and Robert went skiing in nearby Chamonix," says Papa.

"Isn't Saint-Gervais near Mégève where Alicel (Uncle Alphonse's daughter) learned French in a children's home?" Surprisingly, Maman voices a positive association as if she too were agreeing to set her family's course onto a distant fold in some far-away mountain because a passeur had suggested the move and a nephew by marriage once skied and a niece by marriage once

91

learned French there. The very next day, Papa travels by train to Saint-Gervais and looks for a place to stay.

January 11th looms. Six of the thirty days which Laval granted us have already passed. Madame Epstein, on rue de la Chaise, stops Maman. "I'm staying put. If your number's up, it's up. They will catch you anywhere."

Maman finds me unsympathetic.

"I don't care what Madame Epstein says. We are leaving!" I snap.

"Don't be a *Chochem* (a smart aleck), Marguerite," Maman sighs. "Madame Epstein knows of a family of four who was robbed and murdered in the Pyrénées while crossing over into Spain."

"Spain isn't where we are going!" I sass.

Poor Maman, usually so intelligent, now feels so anxious she doesn't see that Madame Epstein rationalizes her own tendency toward inaction.

"Madame Epstein doesn't want to assume the responsibility for her own future," I snarl.

We argue about the defeatist Madame Epstein and our responses to her passivity.

Two days later, Papa returns with an enigmatic smile.

Playfully, Father teases us. He gives a kiss to Maman, then to me; he hangs up his coat and hat; he slowly sets his gloves on a shelf, while we sit at the kitchen table on edge.

"So what is the news?" I pounce, tired of waiting.

With an ear-to-ear grin on his face, Papa, unhurriedly, takes a seat by Maman. He says:

"Saint-Gervais is a little hill-town surrounded by high mountains covered with snow. In the bus ride up from Sallanches I sat next to a local, clean cut and wiry. I talked to him and told him I am looking for a shelter for my family for the duration of the war. It so happens that he and his brother own a property at the foot of the Bionnassay glacier in Bionnay near Saint-Gervais and his half of the duplex is available. So far he has rented to summer people only, but the chalet has a wood burning stove and could be used year round."

"The name of the chalet?"

"CHEZ NOUS."

"Our Home" has two bedrooms, a full bath with hot and cold water, a modern kitchen, a pantry, a hay loft, and a gaily painted Savoyard wood-carved balcony.

"...Maman will again be able to climb with her Alpenstock..."

"...and our landlady, Madame Perroud, is a teacher at the elementary school..."

"...and our landlord, Monsieur Perroud, is a foreman at the hydro-electric power plant..."

Papa leased *Chez Nous* at a price of 3,500 francs for one year, with option to renew.

When I now remember our high spirits, I smile. There were less than two and a half weeks left to January 11. What name do we choose? How do we obtain IDs? The sheer size of the task seems daunting in retrospect, but we work happily. And limitlessly.

Papa sets rules: All luggage destined to the Haute-Savoie shall contain no Lévy documents, no religious amulets, and no Hebrew prayer books. Taboo items go into storage with all the other unneeded belongings at a rented garage where the truck and the Ford — under threat of fines — are sitting on blocks, the Germans having requisitioned all tires. Later I find out that Maman stuffed a Louach (a Hebrew calendar) into the bottom of a shoe inside her suitcase, "So that I know on which day fall Rosh Hashanah and Yom Kippour..."

Papa burns letters in the stove. "Our *Chometz*," he jokes, referring to the Jewish tradition of incinerating the last yeast-leavened crumbs of bread before the start of the week-long Passover festival.

For hours Maman works feverishly separating our belongings into a pile that stays behind and a pile we will take along or ship ahead by rail.

The minute the 9-to-6 curfew is lifted in the morning, my father quietly pushes cartons through the bedroom window into a cart he had parked flush against the wall on the sidewalk. At six, the street is still empty. No passers-by or neighbors should become suspicious.

ID cards? Blanks are issued by the préfecture directly to mayors and police chiefs only. Just like drivers licenses in the US, the blanks belong to the State. It's a monopoly. Professional forgers? I haven't heard of such craftsmen. Besides, we have no money to spare.

No time to spare either. After work (at chez Jacques) I directly go and see Henri Lévi. "Henri, where..."

The E.I.F. Scoutmaster in his sienna-tiled kitchen without hesitation says: "Here's the password... The current address is... It's on the top floor of the building, but the location changes..."

Fine. I understand: if the Gestapo gets wind...

That evening, my mother sews a secret pocket into a pleat of my Girl Scout skirt to hide the illegal blanks. "Be careful, Marguerite," Maman says, and she touches my arm.

In Lyon, the Wehrmacht struts everywhere. On Place Bellecour, a company of SS is goose-stepping under the beautiful plane trees, singing:

"*Wir sind die Herren der Welt,*
Die Koenige auf dem Meer..."
"We are the masters of the world,
The kings of the seas..."

Please go on strutting while I get my ID blanks.

Once upon a time, ladies and gents made social calls in horse-drawn carriages at Place Bellecour number nine. The elegant porte-cochère and the polished cobbles attest to the by-gone ways.

Today, I gaze intently at the carved Dionysian head above the lintel of the nineteenth-century, three-story classical stone house. I check for suspicious goings on to the right, to the left. Seeing no trench coats, I enter the spooky, dark and damp rear stairwell at the far end of the courtyard. I listen to noises; shadows move on the walls. Trap?

Near the top floor I make out the silhouette of an Eagle Scout, eyes fixed on the downstairs door. In my Brownie Cheftaine uniform, I emerge from the visible darkness, align next to him. I whisper the password, and: "I need seven cards for Roanne." Emotions (apprehension, excitement) heave in my chest.

A thin "Come back at four o'clock" escapes through his nervous lips and, lithe as a fawn, he bolts behind a double frosted glass door to the left of the landing. Alone under the skylight, I wonder where he gets his blanks.

I raise my eyes and peek through the skylight at the rooftops of Lyon. If the Gestapo comes up now, I will hoist myself through *that* window and escape over *these* rooftops.

They don't come up to the third floor, so I climb down to Place Bellecour, and the clang of Nazi boots. At a nearby café I buy a telephone token. Luckily Ghis answers. "I'm coming by in late afternoon," I tell her coolly.

While I wait, I don't stroll along the quays of the Saône or the Rhône River although they so much remind me of my beloved Ile de la Cité in Paris. Book in hand, ears pricked up, I stay at a small table in the rear of the café, close to the exit. If they come in through the front door, I'll flee through the back. If the Germans see "Lévy" on my ID, they will haul me away.

At 4 PM I climb the empty stone stairwell. The damp air conveys no information. Gloom cloaks. Intently, I peer into the semi-darkness. Is my Eagle Scout on the third floor? We are Lord Baden-Powell's Scouts with a risk here, defiance there, and without really believing in death.

In the dimness, a kerchief and lines of merit badges faintly glow on a torso leaning over the banister. When I finally stand next to him, he — all the while craning his neck toward the courtyard door below — without a word, pulls a pack of ID blanks out of his scout trouser-pocket and hands them to me.

He appears so slender, so shy, and so vulnerable. If only I had a present for him, a little round goat cheese and half a baguette.

I give him a heartfelt Girl Scout salute with the three right fingers and firmly shake his left hand with conviction.

"Merci!"

We both blush.

Emotions must quickly be squashed. Now I open the gate to: "Dear Eagle Scouts of the E.I.F., no one will ever know how many of you brave fighters were engaged in the struggle against extermination. 'Those also serve in combat that help others to escape.' You did a darn good job, ÉCLAIREURS ISRAÉLITES DE FRANCE, at organizing rescue operations for the Jews in France during World War II.'"

Impasse des Verchères. The apartment is the kind of high-ceilinged nineteenth-century dwelling where one tiptoes around on Old Persian rugs, admires the delicate mother-of-pearl inlaid desk that belonged to Louis XIV, and where you sit on the edge of a Louis XV chair in awe. I had never been inside such a home at once grandiose as a museum, intimate as a boudoir. Characteristically irreverence displaces awe in me. I wonder if these old sconces really work. In my fingers the brass knob turns and the opaque pear-shaped bulbs throw a pale yellow light on the deep red moiré curtains and on the Sèvres soup-tureen atop a gold-trimmed credenza framed by the silken curtains. Nice! The furniture and the accessories have seen centuries of human vagaries: war, peace, persecutions, and balls.

Ghis, says: "My employer gives me two kisses on each cheek every night. Remote as her antiques, not seeing my face, she wishes me "Une bonne nuit, Mademoiselle Lévy." On the piano a metronome stands ticking.

In the privacy of her room, I tell Ghis of our Plan: "The family is skipping 108. We won't get our ID cards stamped *J*. Our goal is to go and live in the Haute-Savoie under a false name and pose as Christians. Each one of us is going to fill out his/her own new false ID. Here is what you do..." and I hand my sister an ID blank.

"Oh," says Ghis, governess-like.

On a Louis XIV table I scribble "Lengel" on a piece of paper and show Ghis how to transform "Lévy" into our new, assumed name. I demonstrate how to change the "v" into an "n"; close the "y" into a "g" and, to the end of the "y' — graft on "el". "Like this... and here is how you stretch Mannheim into Markelsheim..." Voilà! "Your new identity card should read: LENGEL, Ghislaine, born in MARKELSHEIM, Bas-Rhin." I further instruct Ghis to use capital letters "And do away with the accent on the "E" in LÉVY, because LENGEL has no accent." I barely know how to curve, bend, and space the letters of my new identity. Ghis must obtain all the necessary official seals on her freshly filled-out blank at the mairie (city hall) and at the gendarmerie (police station), without the stamp "Juif". Then go home and make the alterations.

"Give two weeks' notice, leave on the best of terms, travel by night train with your new false papers, and join us in Saint-Gervais. We'll send you an unsigned telegram upon our arrival."

Ghis is completely won over. In matters of family security, we trust each other implicitly.

I take the late train back to Roanne. At 9 rue de la Chaise it's past midnight when I arrive. Maman sits at the kitchen table in her hand-embroidered pink nightgown with matching housecoat and pink leather slippers adorned with pompons. Her dainty Parisian sleep-wear is all she has. She is shivering.

"Thank God!" she exclaims when she sees me.

Annoyed that she stayed up, I say: "Why aren't you asleep, Maman? Nothing will happen to me!"

Maman takes offense. "I asleep, when my daughter is on the train transporting illegal papers in a pocket that I have sewn into her skirt? If anything had happened to you, I never would have forgiven myself."

Maman's mouth drops at the corners. I don't think how I would feel if I were in her slippers.

Voilà! There, mission accomplished! I say.

And I plunk six blanks in a neat pile on the yellow and white oilcloth.

97

My pack of trophies lifts me to the top of the world. The Germans looked the other way, not mine!

Maman rises from her chair and hides the incriminating evidence in a canister under the rolled oats.

Coils creak in my parents' bedroom on the other side of the wall. I hear Papa, half-asleep, say: "Marguerite is back. All's well that ends well!"

The next day I walk up to north-Riorges. I bring three blanks to the Dreyfusses, the family of my Brownie Isabelle. One each for her mother, her Uncle Pierre, and her Aunt Claudine. Six-year old children are listed on their mother's ID.

That night at rue de la Chaise, we three test our skills. Heads bent over sheets of paper spread out on the kitchen waterproof table cover, we try to shape our letters. Laboriously. At times I lean back in my chair and take a deep breath.

LENGEL...

MARKELSHEIM...

In my seat at the table I'm chewing through the cap of my fountain pen while attempting to stretch the eight-letter name of my birth place "Mannheim" (a German town) into an eleven-letter French Alsatian village "Markelsheim". This is easier said than done. Try it! I apply myself over and over like a first grader until, presto, I can do it, or so I think. When I review the documents for this book, I see that I spelled Markelsheim on my ID blank without the "s". The space must have been too tight. *Tant pis!* (Later I discover that there is no Markelsheim at all in Alsace, there is a small town named "MARCKOLSHEIM" on the Rhine River near Colmar).

Maman, another first grader, sits next to me.

"I can't... I'm frightened," she whimpers.

Tears roll down my mother's cheeks.

"I'll do it, Maman!"

And I fill out my mother's blank with her married name, nationality, place of birth, in a way that "Bas-Rhin" can be added next to GEMMINGEN later. "Née Oppenheimer" is too difficult to deal with. I delete it all together.

Do you shake your head wondering if someone that innocent in identity-forging skills can succeed? All I have to offer is defiance and a passion to live.

And Maman?

Seated by my side, she watches the pen. She squeezes my elbow. Her lips faintly smiling, my mother acknowledges that she, too, wishes to live. My index finger and thumb move the fountain pen.

Papa doesn't see all this. Mouth tight, head bent over his sheet of paper, he energetically traces LÉVY. He traces the V and the Y over and over again. Maman and I look at Papa. He's concentrating on his task. The ceiling lamp gives off light to his hand. All of a sudden he raises his eyes, "Marguerite..."

... and a third blank slides into my space.

Papa needs me. He accepts my skills! I'm good enough for Papa! I burst with pride of acceptance.

I make out the third ID to Albert Lévy, born 25 April 1885, Soultz, Haut-Rhin, French citizen, resident at 9 rue de la Chaise, Roanne. Profession: representative — all in a script that permits Lévy to be altered into Lengel tomorrow.

Although Papa built two substantial paint and lacquer companies, ALÉDY G.m.b.H. in Mannheim and Géo Gignoux near Paris — the second largest paint and varnish factory in France — he couldn't bring himself to forge identity papers even in order to escape hostile authorities. His sense of honor forbade it. Noblesse oblige!

At city hall, the following morning, things go only partly well. A meticulous clerk adds "Margot, Gerda," in parentheses after "Marguerite."

The same meticulous clerk writes "née Oppenheimer" next to Maman's married name. Oops! I blink. Not too good. "Born Oppenheimer" gives her Jewishness away. Papa presents his *Livret militaire* (French draft booklet) as proof of identity. No problem.

99

Papa is born on the right side of the Rhine River in Soultz, Alsace. He just needs a different surname.

The city hall clerk may be thorough, but she isn't vindictive. She treats us just like any other ordinary French citizen. "You have to go to the police station and get *their* seals and stamps as well," she says in a tone of neutral French bureaucratic efficiency.

At the Commissariat de Police (police station), the employee officially acknowledges the work done by her colleague at city hall. That's her job. She doesn't mention the law that goes into effect on January 11. She doesn't stamp our cards **Juif.** She kindly wishes us *"Une Bonne Année."* Papa, courteous, returns the greeting.

"A Happy New Year to you, Mademoiselle."

At least our gamble to get the official seals without the inked-on "J" stamp has succeeded. In the street I repress a grin, I think: "Nothing risked, nothing gained."

It's 2 January 1943.

On verra! We'll see!

That evening at our kitchen table, seated between my mother and my father, I make the changes on Papa's, Maman's, and my own ID in my teenager's tight hand. I carefully spell out our future. It's LENGEL. Tomorrow, tomorrow, we break away.

Although France had nothing remotely similar to the sinister Einsatzpolizei which immediately assembled and shot the Jews in Poland and in Eastern Europe, within two weeks the Gestapo in Annemasse set up checkpoints at the railroad station.

3 January 1943.

In the afternoon, Aunt Jenny and Uncle Elias arrive at 9 rue de la Chaise with their valises in hand. Our two-room apartment is a big improvement over their one-room moldy porter's lodge, and Papa thinks the decent Masseys will hide the Strausses if need be.

Aunt Jenny, Maman's oldest sister, the family's peacemaker, at once takes over. In her white starched apron she goes directly to the stove and brews a pot of chamomile tea.

Papa stands by the kitchen door. He is ready to go. Dressed in his good wool overcoat, felt hat, and with his white silk scarf tucked inside the collar, he turns around and tells us: "Edouard is the only one who knows our destination, address, and false name. He will send greetings every January first or write in case of emergency. Otherwise, there will be no mail, no phone calls, and no attempt at contact." Papa throws me a stern look which means: Marguerite, this goes for you too. My father knows that I'm independent and tend to go my own way. We cut the bridges. I feel infinitely eager and safe to disappear into oblivion. I guess Papa has provided for the Strausses. My father opens the latch at rue de la Chaise, and Maman and I slip through the door.

Good-bye occupied city! Good riddance cold water tenement! I'm on my way! It's January 3, 1943. Papa, Maman, and I are setting out in defiance of Vichy's Edict 108.

The three of us take the night train in Roanne with a change at midnight in Lyon.

The next morning at Le Fayet (Haute-Savoie), we change to a cogwheel train marked "Tramway to Mont Blanc". A blinding snowstorm rages in the French Alps. The signs along the tracks are covered with snow. Suddenly, the conductor calls out: "Saint-Gervais-Mont-Blanc." We scramble for our luggage, and descend from the TMB. There, by the gate, stands a one-horse drawn milk sleigh, the cart filled with five-gallon milk cans. A farmer wrapped in a brown woolen cape, scarf, gloves and cap takes a jump off the bench and walks toward us.

"I'm Joseph Barzat. Clovis Perroud ask'd me to come meet you," he says.

Papa and Monsieur Barzat shake hands.

"The... the Lengels... we are glad to be here," says my father, and he turns up the collar of his coat. I watch.

The Lengels are introduced with only a tiny hesitation.

The seam barely noticeable.

Thick flakes fall on our faces; a mantle of white powder covers the landscape. All about, the green pine trees glisten under the crystals.

101

Joseph Barzat climbs back up onto the driver's seat. "Giddap!" he calls to his horse and, reins in hands, the sleigh lurches forward with our luggage on top of the shiny cans.

Papa, Maman and I trek up-valley by the side of the brown mare. The packed snow crunches under our boots. The dense white fluff falling from the skies wipes out all tracks. We enter a virginal universe.

Energized by the crisp alpine air, Papa and I break out into song. We sing:

"My hat it has three corners,
Three corners has my hat,
And if it hadn't three corners,
It..."

Maman, playful, covers her ears with both hands. She conveys to us with an elfin smile that our off-key pitch splits her tympanum. Maman is happy.

Just as we reach Bionnay, the sun bursts out warm and generous through the thick white clouds. Barzat stops his mare by the bushes at the entrance of *Chez Nous* as a blue sky smiles on a fresh new world. It actually happened. Inside the chalet, a wood-burning fire crackles in the Salamander stove. The Clovis Perrouds are welcoming their new tenants, the Lengel family. It's early afternoon January 4, 1943.

The Bionnassay glacier is seen through the glass panes. In my old boots, I run from window to window and gaze at the snow-covered Alps. The wild beauty of the landscape fills me with a sense of wonderment. And isolation.

St. Gervais Region

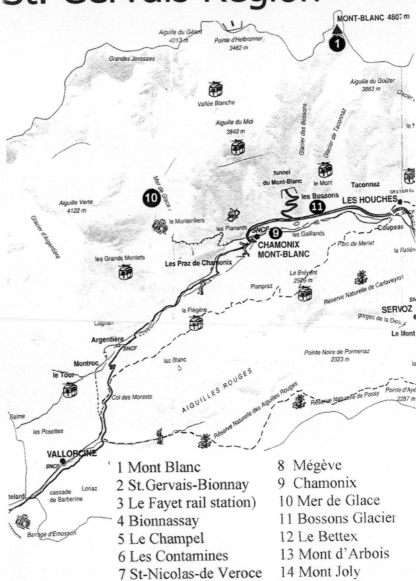

1 Mont Blanc
2 St. Gervais-Bionnay
3 Le Fayet rail station)
4 Bionnassay
5 Le Champel
6 Les Contamines
7 St-Nicolas-de Veroce

8 Mégève
9 Chamonix
10 Mer de Glace
11 Bossons Glacier
12 Le Bettex
13 Mont d'Arbois
14 Mont Joly

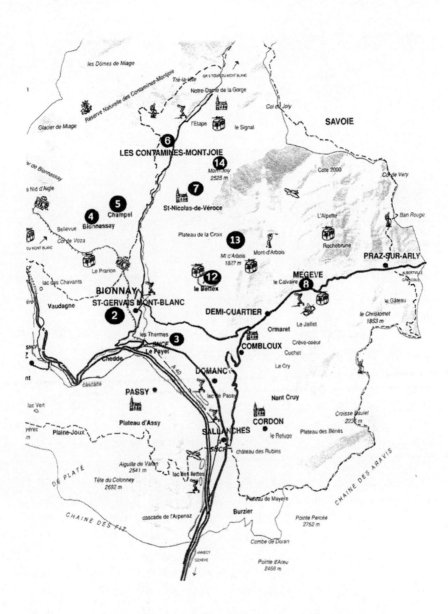

Chapter 6

Bionnay

(January 1943)

B'jour!"

Bridle secured, Joseph Barzat jumps down from his sleigh in front of Chez Nous the next morning. "Milk — how much?" he asks, lifting the lid off a shiny five-gallon metal can. And he dips a pewter mug into the creamy unpasteurized liquid with a slow motion of the wrist — the way farmer Ernst did in his stable next to my Grandmother Oppenheimer's house in Gemmingen.

None of us had tasted milk in two years because in the cities milk was rationed for babies and pregnant women only.

"Monthly pay's fine, you keep track," he says.

In his brown worn suit, brown hand-knit scarf, cap, and brown torn wool gloves, Joseph Barzat stands — all in threadbare brown — blowing on his knuckles like Shakespeare's Jack the Frostman on that eight o'clock cold morning by the curb of the road.

"A demain! See you tomorrow!"

Barzat rides off on the hard compacted snow seated atop his bench, his sleigh harnessed to his old horse. A trail of movement. I reverently carry the jug filled with milk to the chalet.

After we enter the kitchen, Papa says: "Tomorrow, I'll give him a home-rolled cigarette."

It's our first day in the French Alps under an assumed name, and already Papa starts weaving the threads of a local tapestry.

Mont Blanc from Bionnassay, Arbois from Joux — how do I tell the difference? The following morning Joe Barzat takes his whip in hand and points out the surrounding mountains to me. "That one is the Prarion; it resembles a buffalo's hump. The one on the other side of the valley is named Mont Joly; the locals think it resembles a Sphinx's head." The tip of his whip in the direction of the Vorassey and the Chardonnet (some of the smaller peaks surrounding Chez Nous), he quips: "Them is just a bunch of rocks!"

Tomorrow I'll ask him where he delivers his five-gallon milk cans set out along the curb, I think to myself as I watch him sleigh down the D 902 departmental road.

Dressed in my navy cloth ski outfit I explore Bionnay. The hamlet consists of about two dozen small stone houses and chalets strung out along both sides of a dead-end spur off the D 902 — the rue de Bionnay. The place has no shops or churches.

A local woman sweeping snow off her outdoor mat barely answers my eager greeting and my questions about the little stream that runs through the center under the wooden planks. "It's le Bon Nant, don't you know?" (The good little stream in old French), she reluctantly says, annoyed at my ignorance. I figure out by myself that le Bon Nant is one of many streams running down the mountainsides and draining into le Bonnant (spelled in one word). "Le Bonnant is our valley's main river. It flows along the whole valley floor," she says with a shrug and goes back into her house. I find out that Bionnay is the kind of alpine hamlet where peasants sleep in the winter in two-room stone houses with their cattle for warmth. At the same time Bionnay's location, at the foot of the Bionnassay glacier and surrounded by snow-covered high mountains, is picture-postcard pretty. Chamonix sits on the other side of the mountain in the adjacent Arly valley.

A hand-carved sign made of wood affixed to a tree by the wooden planks that cover le Bon Nant reads: "Le Champel" with an arrow pointed to the right. The second arrow indicates "Bionnassay-Col de Voza" to the left. And the fires of anticipation are kindled in me.

Two nights ago, my parents and I slept in a tenement in Roanne. Now I'm here in the French Alps at chalet CHEZ NOUS without my ID stamped "J." I read a date engraved into a grey stone lintel of the old school house: "École de Bionnay 1862." Thick cobwebs hang over the entrance.

Monsieur Dave, the owner of the tobacco shop across from Chalet Chez Nous, welcomes me warmly in his plaid bedroom slippers when Maman sends me over to buy a box of matches. "The Bureau de Tabac has the only telephone in Bionnay," he says with a jovial grin. "Please feel free to use it anytime." Ailène Dave, his wife, adds in a mocking tone of voice: "I guess you already have made the grand tour of Bionnay!"

On the way to Saint-Gervais, along the D 902, I notice a small hydroelectric power station behind a high mesh fence. It generates the electricity for the valley. Clovis Perroud, our landlord, works there as a foreman. Two tiny feeder communities, Les Bernards and Les Pratz, cluster downstream between Bionnay and Saint-Gervais.

I love the higher Alps from the moment of our arrival.

But I have arrived here as a package on a false bill of lading, and I must hide the sender — four thousand years of traditions, culture, religion, and upbringing. I must blend in with the locals who all are baptized Catholic. Marguerite, you can't mention that your father is the founder of Géo Gignoux Inc. or that your grandparents are Joseph and Josephine Lévy. You can't allude to your maternal Oppenheimer grandparents from Gemmingen (Baden). Your ancient roots going back to the times of Moses must be cut. Remember that you are born in Markelsheim (Alsace); that your name is Lengel, and that you are a Protestant Christian. You are starting anew. With a false identity.

A certain roguishness settles into me.

I might appear young, cheerful and carefree, but I'm not the person you think I am. I'm Protestant because everybody else here is a French Catholic. The secret makes me feel both inferior and superior. I'm different. I don't belong to a church, a temple, or a community. I am unaffiliated. I hope to encounter no other Jews. I must not. We must protect our secret.

I'm aware the enemy doesn't necessarily wear a German uniform. Informers dress in civilian clothes. If I or any member of my family should be careless we all die. Danger has entered my life. I find this stimulating. For the first time in my existence I feel that I'm the captain of my boat and I navigate in uncharted waters. Dressed in my navy cloth ski outfit and boots I go about discovering a white new world and, because living in the French Alps with false papers was all my idea, I feel responsible for Papa, Maman and Ghis. We have to make it!

Val Montjoie is a U-shaped secluded valley surrounded by high mountains — a natural fort backed against the Prarion and the Mont Blanc massif on one side, Mont Joly on the other side, and the high Bonhomme pass into Italy at the far end. Monsieur Dave told me that ten thousand years ago, three glaciers joined here in Bionnay. One of the three excavated Val Montjoie; the second, the steep Bionnassay ravine; and the third: leads to Le Champel. "All three glaciers descended from Mont Blanc, Dave had said." Chalet Chez Nous sits at the junction of the three.

From a comfort point of view CHEZ NOUS is a well-appointed rental property. Orange shutters frame the windows, and a wide slate roof ends in a broad overhang above the gaily painted Savoyard balcony. The modern interior is pleasing. Both the bathroom and the kitchen are equipped with hot and cold running water. In the right upper corner of the hand-carved wooden balcony is affixed a white-and-blue-ceramic plaque that reads: "CHEZ NOUS". OUR HOME.

The first movement of Beethoven's Fifth Symphony "Fate Knocks on the Door" enters our home nightly at 9:30, followed by "Ici Londres..." — the start of the French program on the BBC.

On the BBC we hear Hitler's declaration of total warfare against civilians; we hear of Rommel's defeat in Tunisia; of the hundreds of Lancasters setting Bremen ablaze. The news of B-17s bombing Berlin by day reaches us in my parents' bedroom on the Philips radio, heads under a quilt.

It is as if, here in this Mont Blanc isolation, we stand with one foot hors du monde and with the other (thanks to the BBC) inside the world at war. No one reads a newspaper here in Bionnay. Scarcely have we unpacked when our landlord arrives. "Is the

109

supply of kindling adequate? Is the new hot water heater in the bathroom working all right?" Maman and Papa assure Monsieur Clovis Perroud that CHALET CHEZ NOUS is most cozy. Merci. Comfort is not our problem!

About to close the kitchen door, Clovis Perroud adds as an afterthought: "The demoiselles surely wish to go skiing!"

Skiing? Ghis and I look at each other. From the corner of my eye I watch Papa. He purses his lips. What will he say?

Papa moves his head, right-left, left-right; he's weighing the offer. Then just like any other Christian father of two teenage daughters who leases "Chez Nous" for a season, my father nods and says: "Yes, of course!" Blend in! Don't stand out! For Ghis and me it's very nice to be treated like everyone else!

That afternoon, under blue skies in a fairy landscape of gleaming white powder, my sister and I trek on the D 902 down to the Fumex Sports shop in Saint-Gervais. We push into Kandahar bindings, measure ski boards to our wrist's length. Poles have little baskets at the end. We buy second-hand skis and used boots with our own savings — I'm happy, but soon I discover that my skis are warped and my boots leak. Later I hear that the dishonest shopkeeper and his family all are collaborators.

On the way home up-valley at Les Pratz around noon, Ghis and I ring the doorbell at the ski-instructor's chalet. No answer. I snoop around. Lo and behold through a window pane I see François, the ski-instructor, in bed atop a brunette, making love at noon!

Too bad, François!

Mischief enters my fingers. Back at the entrance I hit the bell at regular intervals, ding-dong, ding-dong, unwilling to let the moniteur off the hook at the cost of another three-mile round trip.

Fumbling with the zipper of his fly, tanned, athletic in his white shirt unbuttoned-at-the-neck, François opens the entrance door. "May I help you?"

"We would like lessons!" I answer, straight-faced.

He squints in the bright sun, a subtle ironic smile on his lips.

Lessons take place on the Bosse des Idiots, the Idiot's Hump, as the locals call the icy beginners' slope near the cable cars.

Ghis hurts her knee cap in a fall; I dislocate my right shoulder. My injury seems unheroic to me for it is not war-related. I feel guilty. Quietly, I fold a scarf into a sling and hide my pain. To my surprise, Maman teases Ghis-the-limper and Marguerite-the-one-armed-paper-hanger with her best pre-war humor. Mother again feels needed.

My wound mends poorly. Whenever I put pressure on the right humerus, it pops out. I have to push the joint back into the socket. Ouch!

Soon thereafter, as I return home, I see Clovis Perroud standing on the welcome mat holding papers in his hand. Papers, what for? Did they find out...?

In the kitchen Monsieur Perroud says: "Here are some forms to be filled out for your permits to reside," and he sets the forms on the kitchen table.

Silence.

"Oh yes, of course!" Papa quickly retorts with a forced smile. The Lengels hide their surprise as best they can.

"It's just a formality," our landlord casually remarks. "Le préfet est raisonable!"

Of course!

That night after dinner, Papa, Maman, Ghis, and I sit around the dining table. Papa slowly removes the cap of his fountain pen. The ceiling light shines on the print.

Name --
Religion --
Legal domicile --
Reason for application --
Length of stay --

I stare at officialdom. I remember the cause of our departure from Roanne... What is going on inside Papa I can't tell? His facial muscles tighten; he breaks out into a dry cough. My eyes are glued to the white paper, the black print. Surely permits to reside in the Haute-Savoie are never refused! Maman sucks in her lips. Papa mixes up Bas-Rhin and Loire, and something else too: he scratches

111

out a word on an official form, but he writes "Refugee from Alsace" after Soultz, Alsace.

The next morning as soon as the snowplow clears the road, Papa and I trek down to the gendarmerie, the local police station on the D 902. Dressed in his Paris-tailored winter coat, white silk scarf, and his beret cocked to the side, Papa wears an air of intense concentration. Earlier in the kitchen he carefully had tucked the four Lengel applications into his inner coat pocket. The forms instruct: "Attach a doctor's health certificate."

Papa is concentrating. His forehead frowns. I amuse myself reading off the names of the chalets: "Crystal de Roche" — "Edelweiss" — "Rhododendrons"... I yearn to explore Chamonix, Mégève, and the Mer de Glace, Mont Blanc. The wonders of the French Alps are almost within reach of my finger tips. THEY CAN'T DENY US A PERMIT TO RESIDE! WHERE ELSE CAN WE GO?

At the metal scraper outside the gendarmerie, Papa and I clean the snow off our boots. It's a crisp, sunny winter day, and the mountains beam.

Inside the gendarmerie my father states to a clerk the reason for his visit:

Permits to reside in Saint-Gervais.

I look around. The posters on the walls warn: Beware! Observe! Report the enemies of the Vichy State!

A stocky officer in a navy blue uniform with colored shoulder braids, leather belt and holster enters a glassed-in enclosure. I watch him through the panes as he bends over the first Lengel document. He picks it up. In quick succession a smile appears on his face, he dusts his jacket lapels with two rapid strokes, and he comes out to meet us. Oh, God!

"Hoffstaetter, vun Colmar," he says to Papa with genuine pleasure, and he extends his hand.

"Vun Soultz..." answers Papa, his face lighting up with joy.

Two Alsatians break out into the familiar Franco-German dialect of their birthplace in the Vosges, dozens of mountain ranges away from the French Alps.

The police chief says: "Jo, je vais signer vos demandes aujourd'hui, le préfet va les approuver —" as if the French police and the French préfecture were one huge benevolent system set up to protect the French Jews in Nazi-collaborating Vichy. Amazing, his calm confidence, when he says: "I'm going to sign your requests today, the prefect will approve them."

"How long will it take?" asks Papa.

"About ten days. Jo, don't worry, I'll call Dave in Bionnay!"

The police chief holds the door open for the illegal Lengels. His blue eyes twinkle with pleasure: "You and your family must come for Kaffee un Kugelhoph one Sunday real soon, the wife will be so happy!"

In the snow-covered parking lot, Papa's first words are: "Wait till Maman hears the good news."

The two previous Alsatian miracles had been: Private Schmidt who raised the barrier in Angoulême to let seven Lévys roll into the Free Zone, and General Koeltz's letter written on official stationary of the Vichy War Ministry to Albert Lévy. Now, Police Chief Jean Hoffstaetter from Colmar closes both eyes to the missing health certificates. Three Alsatian miracles. The individual citizen can thwart the central regime!

Trekking on the packed snow up to Bionnay, Papa's freckled face breaks into a boyish grin. "Marguerite, did I ever tell you the story about my first grade teacher?" I shake my head, although I know the story. I like to see Papa's mischievous grin when he tells of naughty childhood deeds. Hoffstaetter has made Papa happy. My father is about to tell me what happened when Miss Besser, his first grade teacher, slapped him because he talked in class.

Allegedly Miss Besser handed a note after school to the boy Albert and asked him to have it signed by his father. "I was frightened," recounts Papa. "At home I pretended I was ill and went to bed. Finally I had to confess. Your grandfather had one look at the note and said: 'Tell your Miss So-and-so school-teacher if she hits you once more, I'll pay her a visit, and she won't ever be a *Miss* again.'" "What happened, Papa?" I string along. "I repeated the message word for word to Miss Besser." "And?" "She blushed and bolted from the classroom."

Of course she never touched the cherub again!

I chuckle. What a grandfather I had! Joseph Lévy born in Soultz, Haut-Rhin, May 24, 1832 must have been a lusty fellow. Earthy? Sure! Sexist? I don't care! A worthy son of Félix born on 10 Pluviose Year VI of the French Republique. They all were cattle traders, one of only a handful of trades open to Jews. "Did you ever talk in class, again?" I ask Papa. "From the third grade on, they promoted me to teacher's helper," he says with a prankish freckled smile.

At Chez Nous the Bionnassay glacier brightens the kitchen with its noon glare. Maman refuses to count her blessings in advance.

"What if the préfet rejects our petitions?"

"Hoffstaetter knows his business," answers Papa.

"What if they inquire in Roanne?"

"The French aren't that thorough."

Papa was right on that score too.

Ten days later, Gisèle Dave, the tobacconist's young daughter, knocks on the side door at Chez Nous.

In her sing-song childish nursery-rhyme tone, she recites:

"The gendarmerie phoned to say you can pick up your permits to reside."

Residence in the frontier zone with Italy and Switzerland from which Jews and foreigners are specifically excluded — was granted to the four (Lévy) LENGELS for one month. Renewals will have to be validated after that semi-annually.

Maman's face relaxes.

I know I must blend in, obey the local conventions, not draw attention to myself, but in January 1943 I find myself at a town meeting convened on the third Sunday of the first month. Hoffstaetter personally invited Papa. Everybody comes on foot or on skis. Ten inches of fresh snow had fallen during the prior night. The slope behind the gendarmerie sparkles with white fluff. Tempting! A few minutes later I tie my seal skins to my skies and start the climb. For a moment I'm again a normal teenager, eager to be noticed: knees bent, skis apart, I ski in full view of the villagers assembled below. I tumble on my descent. For the next few days I hear a great deal from Papa about my lack of respect. "You have embarrassed me," he says.

So far: neither German soldiers nor Italian alpinis.

Jean Hoffstaetter, the local chief of police, makes good on his promise. He calls Papa at Chez Dave and invites the Lengels for Kaffee and Kugelhoph for the following Sunday at their private quarters above the gendarmerie.

SUNDAY --

Marguerite, this is your first social as a Christian! I'm excited.

From the welcome mat I fall with Alice straight into Wonderland. Dear me!

Chief Hoffstaetter!

He greets us at the door in civilian clothes. At once his wife springs onto the sill next to him. "Let's call each other by first name," she says.

"I'm Albert," replies Papa and he introduces Marthe, Ghis, and Marguerite — "my family."

"Mei Frau!" And the chief proudly points his square chin in the direction of his sturdy wife.

A pause.

What do we do after the introductions?

In the darkish living room, seated on the couch, the chief uncorks with a slow turning motion of his wrist, a precious bottle of Kirsch.

"Vun meim Kirshbaum! From my cherry tree!" he says with a broad smile as he wiggles the corkscrew in his fingers. "Jo, back home, a friend of mine owned a still in his backyard. I brought him my cherries... Jo, I took one bottle along for a special occasion..."

What? A precious bottle of Kirsch for us the illegal Lévys! I chuckle inside.

Mei Frau cuts in: "Those were the good old days, Martha." (She calls Maman: Martha, instead of Marthe).

115

Martha stops the brandy from flowing into Ghis's and my own separate snifters. "Just a taste for me and the children in one glass, please!" she says.

Why does my mother always interfere! I would have liked to get at least the customary French teenager's thimbleful in my own snifter.

"Oh, Martha, let's be happy, we have so much to tell each other!" Mei Frau hankers for a feel-good home party.

Maman turns white. I sit on my chair, stiff, waiting for... What, now? The Lengels are only two-three weeks old.

The chief quickly proposes a toast.

"To Alsace!"

"To Alsace!"

"Santé."

"Santé."

Papa and Hoffstaetter hold their snifters inside their large hands. For a long moment they warm the cold Kirsch into a full-bodied flavor; they sniff the pungent aroma. Slowly, they take a small swig in their mouths and, swish-swashing, they roll the liquor to and fro. Ah! Oh!

If it weren't for Maman I could participate in the ritual! And right there, the two Alsatians break out into the vernacular. The chief tells an anecdote about "De guter wine beholte mir fur die naechs administration..." The story allegedly happened at a banquet in Sessheim where sour wine was being served to visiting German dignitaries. They cough; they grimace, and ask the Sessheimers, "Don't you grow better Gewurtztraminer around here?" The locals are said to have answered: "Jo, but we keep the good wine for the next administration!" The time of the story is between 1871 and 1918 when Alsace had been annexed by Germany after Napoléon III lost the battle of Sedan to Prussia in 1870. The locals hoped for a French win the next time around. I understand the undertone: the chief is anti-German.

The Hoffstaetter boy, about twelve, and his younger sister join the adults in the living room. I forget their first names; but they represent all the uprooted children from Alsace and elsewhere, the

116

children between two cultures who — torn, confused, belonging nowhere — try to show off and gain attention.

"May I, Maman?" asks the girl, and she grips her skirt with both hands, and curtsies on the living room rug. With all her heart, recites for us the story of the Alsatian folk hero, "Hans im Schnogenloch" 'Was er hat dos will er net, un was er will dos hat er net...Hans doesn't want what he has, and can't have what he wants...'" The hero personifies the contradictory psyche of the Alsatian-Lorrainer frontier people tossed back and forth for generations according to the outcome of the latest armed conflict between France and Germany.

"Jo," nods the chief with a blush, "we used to say: "Alsatians do not like to be called Schwob" (from Schwaben, a district of south-west Bavaria, Germany). His meaning is clear: the Alsatians do not like to be Germans.

Mei Frau doesn't listen to her husband. She tells Maman about a specialty of Colmar: "la tarte flambée."

"Martha, I always add eight ounces of chopped bacon to my Flammenkuchen. I serve it real hot. Do you know that it only succeeds if cooked in a wood-fired oven? Martha, how I miss home!"

HOME... Better avoid that topic!

Unlike a cooling soufflé, Mei Frau refuses to settle. Recipes of dumpling soup, Coq au Riesling, Choucroute Garnie keep arising over the rim.

Recipes bore me stiff.

My mind wanders to — Caesar fought the Germanic tribes on the plain of Alsace, trying to check the Trans-Rhine migrations. The Teutons were barbarians believing in dark blood-bond forces and the demonic powers of life. They had a tendency to idealize violence, strength, and death for the Fatherland. While the Gallic character is independent, with an affinity for irony, wit and badinage ... —

Two seats away, I hear Mei Frau say: "Martha, I make my onion tarts with pure lard, and you?"

"I use margarine. Albert gains weight so easily."

Excuses. Excuses. No lard, please!

— Attila the Hun, in the middle of the 5th century, invaded the land between the Rhine and the Vosges mountains. Settlers along the banks of the Ill River, "the Ill-Sessers", took refuge in the highlands — henceforth, their name became Illsessers, pronounced Ellsasser, Alsatians —

"My baking sheets are that long Martha!" says Mei Frau, and she shows with both hands the size of her trays.

I feel like a cat at a dog show: It's not my species! Where is the exit? Only then comes: "Martha, how many sisters and brothers do you have?" Dear me!

Maman can't mention Selma, Gida, her brother Max, and their families who immigrated to the United States from Germany after Kristall-Nacht in 1938. And where are Maman's sister Bertha and her husband Isaac Hanauer from Heilbronn, deported east? Maman's face twitches.

Papa deflects the hit. He runs the ball back to Soultz. There, someone allegedly had toasted the newly elected mayor with the words "It's easier to find ten mayors than one good gooseherd." Papa covers the family. Not once does he mention Paris or Géo Gignoux or any of his energetic accomplishments since his precocious boyhood in the Rhine valley.

Mei Frau snuggles herself into the Lengel camp, not to hear them out — but to salivate with them.

"Albert, do you also like braised pigs trotters?"

Albert loves braised pigs trotters.

"Did your father also say, Leivele Du mush Rivele heisse?" His father also said: "Loaf, your name is crumbs!"

"Jo?"

"Jo!"

"Albert, I haven't met anyone familiar with that saying since we left in '39."

Little drops appear at the corners of Mei Frau's mouth. "Loaf, your name is crumbs" cruelly affects my diaphragm. I get the hiccups. I haven't yet read Marcel Proust's *Remembrance of Things Past*, so I don't know that the famous quest for his

118

Madeleine is actually nothing but a trip down the taste bud lane along the high road.

The rules: Don't break the social conventions, don't draw attention to yourself, observe, and blend in — are difficult to apply when close social contact betrays intimate body language.

The clove-adorned ham arrives on a platter decorated into a glaring enemy.

The boy, excited at the sight of the glistening pig moist with brown sugar and pan drippings, exclaims:

"Here comes Seigneur Cochon!"

"Martha, I told Jean I am ashamed to entertain you unless I have a whole ham," says Mei Frau to Mother.

At the time the weekly meat ration per person was four ounces, but extravagance is not the cause of Maman's pallor.

Maman was brought up in a strict kosher household and we kept kosher. Because ritually slaughtered meat was outlawed by the Germans and Vichy, Maman "kashered" or took out the blood from the tiniest piece of beef bought at the butcher by soaking and salting and washing it on all four sides under running water. Never in her life had Maman eaten ham. At a non-denominational Scout leadership camp in Avignon the previous year, I didn't bother to learn what I was eating; Ghis didn't check to see what she was eating in Lyon. I hold my breath.

Our host starts cutting the ham into three sections. He debones; he carves under the attentive eye of Mei Frau. Chin set, big-hearted, armed with a long-handled butcher's knife — Hoffstaetter serves copious portions. Mei Frau is excited. "More to Albert, more!"

Maman looks green. The taboo slice of ham on her plate desecrates her being.

The Almighty above must have whispered to my mother: "God helps those who help themselves," and she must have heard Him, because — swift as a feline, Maman pushes the unclean food with her fork over the plate's rim through a small space shielded by her elbow between her chest and the left arm onto the rug.

The Hoffstaetters can't see everything. He's in the kitchen fetching yet another yard of white baguette, and Mei Frau is busy piling Albert's plate with yet another hunk of home-baked ham.

My mother stoops under the table, blows her nose, and remains so for a long time...

I hear a shoe hit the leg of the table once... twice...

Her torso straight up again, Maman in a hollow voice says:

"Good... very, very good," in praise of the ham.

Pause.

Mother rises from her chair, purse in hand.

Tiens, I tell myself, she is limping...

A minute or two later, the toilet audibly flushes.

Back in the dining room Maman looks radiant...

I lower my head over my plate — while the pork in Maman's shoe is coursing down the plumbing.

Chief Hoffstaetter brings a Kugelhoph (a Bundt in a fluted tube pan) to the table and, proud, starts to slice the brown sugary Alsatian cake into eight parts. "One, two, three, four, five..." the children count aloud. As he is cutting the sixth, his <u>Frau</u> says: "Martha, when is your Saint's day? I will bake you a cake!"

Martha Lévy's Catholic patron day? We stiffen. No one knows the date of Saint Martha's feast day!

Quickly Hoffstaetter intones — what else? "Leivele Du musch Rivele heisse. Loaf, we'll eat you to the last crumb."

The children roll with laughter; the guests and the host feel relieved.

But the energy for crisis carries a long spin, "Never two without three." On the edge of my chair, I press my knees together. Mei Frau, seated next to Papa, her cheeks flushed with schnapps, abruptly says: "Jean sleeps like a log at night. When I nudge him under the cover, he just turns over and goes on sleeping. He's always tired." And her hand disappears under the table.

Marguerite, you can't, not now, not here — burst! My diaphragm contracts loudly. I lower my eyelids.

Papa once again astonishes me. His strong fingers set Mei Frau's errant hand back above board — calmly, firmly, and without a word.

Under the influence, wistful, Mei Frau leans across the table toward Maman. "I wish my husband was more like yours!" she says to my mother and she sighs.

You dummy, Papa's name is Albert Lévy, he's circumcised! You want to exchange a safe goy for a hunted Jew? I chew my lips until they hurt.

Papa weaves a fine phrase for Mei Frau. "An old well runs deep..." It's his response to her complaint about her husband.

Hoffstaetter smiles.

Mei Frau whines: "If only Jean talked to me that way!"

I think Hoffstaetter and Papa really understand each other.

By twos we step on the snow-covered road to help the digestion. The men ahead; a few paces behind, both wives; the offspring at the rear. We stroll through the village center, across the esplanade to Devil's Bridge, and back again to the Place de l'Eglise. We linger by the stone fountain for everyone to see the police chief extending in public his protection to the Lengels.

The sun is setting behind the buffalo hump-shaped Prarion. The two families shake hands in the parking lot of the gendarmerie. Papa and Hoffstaetter look like two Frankish chieftains about to take leave from each other after conclusion of a tribal alliance.

Crunching home on the snow-packed road, Ghis and I hum "Les Enfants s'ennuient le Dimanche, The Children are bored on Sunday..." a popular song by Charles Trenet which makes fun of the traditional Sunday afternoon promenade en famille. Frustrated, Ghis says: "I could have finished my sweater. All I have left to do is half a sleeve."

In the distance the Bionnassay glacier turns yellow, orange, and purple. On the D 902, Maman says: "Madame H. complained about her husband all the time. Apparently he doesn't share his thoughts with her; I refused to get involved." White evening clouds hang over the road up to Bionnay; Papa purses his lips, he's

121

pensive. After a while, he voices: "Hoffstaetter told me 'Albert, fear not. If I get an order to arrest you, I'll send the boy up at night to Bionnay.'"

Papa's freckled Frankish face cuts a complex smile as if he felt simultaneously the pride of being once again the effective protector of his family and, at the same time, the sobering thought that our special circumstance hadn't gone unnoticed. It's just as well the chief doesn't share his secrets with his Frau, I think. For Maman's birthplace on her residence application reads Gemmingen — a village in Baden, Germany. Besides, I later find in the telephone book at the post office that the correct spelling for "Lengel" is Lengyels. There are Lengyels in Colmar, but in all of Alsace there are no Lengels. Hoffstaetter, the former police chief of Colmar, must have been cognizant of this fact. When Papa in Roanne suggested LENGEL for our assumed surname, he must have remembered the phonetics of a classmate's name. All the better, because changing "Lévy" into "Lengel" had been hard enough. Then there is the non-existent Markelsheim.

* * *

In the kitchen at Chez Nous, Maman has to prod Ghis. "You can't let Marguerite go up to Bionnassay alone," she says. "Go with your sister!"

Climbing into the high country is one of the few challenges open to me. In the plains the Gestapo, the Sûreté Nationale (French police force), the G.M.R. (Gardes mobiles Republicaines), and the Wehrmacht — all check papers, but I know I can travel the vertical way safely.

I'm out of work. I have no occupation. I need an outlet for my pent-up energy or I will go crazy. My sister is less driven. She's more of a homebody; she likes to knit. Ghis is unwilling to come and identify wild animal spoor in the snow with me. Maman has to coax Ghis. "Please go!"

It's a sunny cold January afternoon, a day or two after the visit to the Hoffstaetters. Dressed in my navy wool ski outfit, hat and ski gloves, I am on my way with Ghis. Scout manual in hand, I study the page titled "HOW TO RECOGNIZE WILD ANIMAL TRACKS".

"Look!" I call out excited to Ghis behind me on the trail. "Five small footprints lead to that barn," and I point.

Ghis sulks. She's tired of walking ankle-deep in powdered snow.

"What do you expect? There are animals in the forest! There's even one donkey that will very soon return to the stable," she replies.

I go on enthusing.

"A fox slipped under the door through that hole. Here! Look! And there large hoof tracks go into the forest!"

Deer spoor on fresh snow? Ghis couldn't care less.

"I'm going home," she says.

"I'm staying!"

"Good luck!"

"Au-revoir!"

The call of the wild draws me deeper and deeper into the forest. The whiteness turns grey. The moon rises, the first stars appear. A lonely dog barks in the distance. Quiet descends on the alpine world. From atop a cliff I can make out the lights of my hamlet in the valley below, I stand on the edge, à pic; straight down is a precipice.

The night under the forest canopy is pitch-black. I pick up a dead branch, the length of a walking stick, and probe the ground around me. My cane encounters nothingness. "Darkness is over the face of the deep." **Stop**! My instinct warns. Don't go any further. Spend the night up here and at dawn, when the new day breaks, climb down.

I now have lived in the Alps for nearly three weeks. I prop my back against a two-forked limb and let my feet dangle in the void. With a full repertoire of "Ging Gang Gooli," "Alouette," "The Bear Went over the Mountain," and other scout songs, I loudly proclaim my presence to the wild animals around me. I look at the Big Dipper bright in the sky and make out the Milky Way. I hear a wild cat hunt. The victim's last screams tear up the stillness of the night. Branches crash to the forest floor with a dull thud while I go on declaiming Baudelaire, Rimbaud, and Verlaine. My muscles feel cramped, but this is one night only. Wild boars are not dangerous. The immense chandelier above twinkles.

When the first rays of dawn lift the ténèbres I see that I'm sitting astride a toppled giant tree, 180 degrees out over a sheer cliff, hundreds of feet above Bionnay. Gripping the rough bark with two hands, arms and knees tightly wrapped around the sides of the trunk similar to a rider riding backwards on her horse — I wiggle my way out. I know I must stay put on that horizontal trunk. Disentangling my wool cap from a branch nearly upsets my perilous balance. Eventually my buttocks touch the large root system of the old beech and I push off onto terra firma, fanny first, surprised to see I owe my life to a few tough roots (of a toppled giant tree) that cling to scarce topsoil inside a crack in a boulder. The night must have blindfolded nature's abhorrence of a vacuum in me, and the giant's branches reined me in.

I had not been afraid.

My return to Chez Nous is stormy.

Papa in city attire — suit, tie and starched shirt — stands in front of the hallway mirror about to slip his arm into his overcoat (a Frenchman always dresses with care before going out in public). My father turns around when he hears the kitchen door open. He takes one look at his disheveled, scratched, dirt-covered offspring, and he hisses "You idiot! You can't afford an accident, you have no birth certificate!"

Furious, Papa walks toward me.

Maman moves between Papa and me.

"Albert, she's back. Thank God!" and she hugs me.

"That such an idiot should have been fathered by me!" storms Papa beside himself with anger. He stops short in front of my face.

"Papa was ready to go to the police station and report you missing," Maman says. "We worried ourselves sick throughout the night," and Mother whisks me off to my room.

Ghis is all set to go to her skiing lesson with François, and I want to go too.

"To bed!" insists Maman.

"Why? I'm full of energy. It was great spending the night outdoors up there. I enjoyed it!"

Under the warm white feather cover, I mutter: So what? I made it back, safe and sound. NO BIRTH CERTIFICATE WAS NEEDED!

The adventure taught me two lessons in mountaineering: night falls quickly in the Alps and — there are different kinds of responsibility towards those you live with. Even though I liked to think of myself as being an independent young adult.

Ghis at dinner blurts out: "François said you were lucky the night was windless." I kick her under the table. The warring Alsatian temperament still smolders inside Papa. The folds of Maman's cheeks draw downward into a mournful pucker as if to say with silent lips: "How can you do this to me? Look at my grey hair! Don't I have enough *tzores* under Hitler? Do I need any additional worries?"

I'm angry, hurt. I don't say: Maman, I'm sorry for the trouble I caused you, because I feel my mother should have known that the spirit which led the family to safety into the French Alps is pulling me onward, beyond them.

Two days later, I decide it's time to go and seek employment in Saint-Gervais. With false papers and an assumed name.

Chapter 7

Something is Happening Here ...

(Winter-Spring 1943)

The headmistress, Mademoiselle Alain, opens the stained glass entrance door. It is Saturday 11:00 AM, we are expected.

Last Wednesday I had gone to see our landlady, Madame Perroud, at her apartment above the elementary school in Saint-Gervais and told her: I would like to work as a teacher-counselor. I explained that I had attended the lycée in Paris, liked children, and had been a Brownie leader for two years. Everything I had ever learned at school, and my love for the young — were converging.

In her burgundy upholstered armchair by the window overlooking Mont d'Arbois, Madame Perroud listens attentively. "Mademoiselle Lengel, we are in luck!" she says with a broad smile. "A friend of mine, Mademoiselle Alain, the headmistress at *Les Bruyères,* just mentioned to me yesterday that she's looking for a counselor-teacher for four children. They will be arriving next week from Paris. The home, *Les Bruyères* is located at the foot of Le Bettex on the route to Mégève near the cable cars." Our landlady assures me that she will get in touch with Mlle Alain at once, and send word up to Bionnay.

On Cloud 9, I climb down the stairs childishly thinking: if only I had a mother like Madame Perroud.

Quick, I check out *Les Bruyères*. Nestled at the foot of Le Bettex, the home looks similar to all the other alpine chalets in the area: built of wood and stone, with a pointed roof, a painted balcony, and painted wooden shutters framing the windows. Only

126

the Bruyères' is larger, and a swing set sits on the snow-covered lawn. Nice.

The following day, Madame Perroud's husband, Clovis, a foreman at the *Centrale d'Electricité* downstream from Bionnay delivers a hand-written note at Chez Nous. I read: "The owner, Monsieur Moreau, and Mademoiselle Alain the headmistress, would like to meet the demoiselles with their parents if possible on Saturday, at 11:00 o'clock." An R.S.V.P. is requested.

We are at the entrance door of the Bruyères.

Mademoiselle Alain's black-yellowish eyes pierce through us like two fiery coals. A Dickensian aura exudes from the head. Her pitch black shiny hair tied at the nape into a severe knot frame a bone-dry oval visage whose chilling whiteness stretches gauntly over a large nose and high cheekbones. Lucifer! Ouch! I say to myself.

We follow her tight steps on a mirror-like parquet floor along the hallway.

Inside the office, I think for an instant there must be some mistake. Someone in a purple silk housecoat with an ascot tucked inside his pajamas is sitting behind a huge mahogany desk. He has yellow pudgy cheeks, pale full lips, and he doesn't rise from his leather armchair to greet us. Instead, with a slow gesture of the open palm, he indicates four straight caned chairs grouped around the rug; a fifth in the rear.

"*S'il vous plait*... Please..."

Protruding eyes glance at Maman, Papa, Ghis, and me. Slowly, the heavy lids droop over the puffed face, and the body settles at ease into the black leather chair. Never before have I seen anyone receiving in his nightwear.

Curious, I take inventory of the room: a detailed topographic map of Val Montjoie hangs on the wall behind the desk. In the corner by the window stands a large metal globe. The two remaining walls are lined with books from floor to ceiling. Perhaps he is a harmless eccentric — a Balzac-like character, I tell myself. A naïve reflex for happiness inside me stares at the rows of books.

127

I'm in for further surprises. From his breast pocket Monsieur Moreau pulls out a nail file, and eyes fixated on his nails, he starts on a rambling monologue about the Bruyères having a contract with a Parisian industrialist to provide health care and education to his employees' ...children ill with TB, "because Saint-Gervais-Mont Blanc located at 2,600 feet above sea level is an ideal environment for healing diseases of the lungs." The climate here being mild and sunny.

I sit on the edge of my chair. I'm eager to learn about climate, TB, and the French Alps — my job and the wider environment. Columbus couldn't have been more enthralled when he heard about the New World from distant mariners.

From my land man I learn that the more serious cases of TB are sent to sanatoriums at Assy on the nearby Fiz range because the air is purer at 3600 feet, and the slopes offer a more southerly exposure than Saint-Gervais, therefore more sunshine.

My employer's voice descends to a barely audible drone when he starts to digress about the three girls and the one young boy. I strain my ears to hear: "The oldest, Michèle, sixteen, has been at the home twice before but she has suffered a relapse. All four youngsters have shadows on their lungs." He takes a breath and modulates in B minor that he doesn't think much of Michèle's mental abilities. "Michèle has reached a plateau. You might be able to put her through the eleventh grade paces, but basically she's a big dull daughter of a blue-collar family — limited." He warns Ghis and me not to expect too much of the others either: "They are children of the proletariat. Their files are being transferred. You will see for yourself."

In the well-appointed office I catch all the pejorative nuances of the class system then so prevalent in Europe. He must think that — although we are not worthy of his eye contact — we do appear upper-middle-class in clothes and manners. Therefore (he must think) we despise the working class just as much as he does. Not so! I'll help the children realize their full potential. Isn't that what I'm striving for myself in spite of the obstacles?

The prospect of teaching school excites me; his social disdain doesn't deter my resolve one bit. Hitler may have interrupted my formal education in 1939 when I was fifteen, but I have taken the equivalence of 10th grade algebra at the École Communale (the public school in Savigny), and all through my school years I have been an "A" student. Besides, I quite know how to read! I shall prepare the lessons for both Michèle and myself a day ahead. What better way to learn than by teaching!

The children will bring their own textbooks and homework assignments. I'll teach four levels. That's it! My classroom will be a one-room schoolhouse!

There will be daily walks, counseling, and individual lessons. The pay is lean. I'll make 650 francs plus room and board. A secretary in Paris earns 1,500 francs per month. I'm eighteen. I have neither money nor a job. I live with false papers. The work opportunities are few here in Saint-Gervais; this is my chance. My prospective employer offers daily free time from 1 to 3:00 PM, "Mademoiselle Alain will oversee the rest period." In addition I'm being granted one day off weekly, plus a half-day on Sunday. I'm eager to get this position as a live-in-teacher-counselor at the Bruyères.

A monologue can't last forever.

There's a pause.

Monsieur Moreau is about to reach a decision. The bulging eyes raise their heavy lids from filing ten fingernails. Their focus shifts toward the back of the room near the window. I turn around to his point of interest and there sits Mlle Alain straight as a fence pole, hands primly folded inside her lap. The fiery black eyes had sized us up all the while from behind; they had observed every inch of Maman's little felt hat, Papa's well-tailored topcoat with the white silk scarf. Ghis's immobility and my barely controlled impatience.

The Head nods.

The cue is caught.

"Which one of the two sisters would like to break away from the family?" Monsieur Moreau asks, and he turns on the Old World charm.

I! My finger shot up. If there's one only to be hired, I make sure it will be me.

With an ever so slight bow of the head, Monsieur Moreau acknowledges his new employee, Marguerite Lengel.

Flowery words follow. "I will try to open their hearts and their minds to the pleasures of learning..." I say. "Mademoiselle Alain and I feel confident..." he says. He consoles Ghis with: "When Paris-Billancourt sends all his workers' children to summer camp at the Bruyères in July and August, we'll employ Mademoiselle Ghislaine as well."

Mademoiselle Ghislaine on her chair acquiesces stiffly. I know my sister will not wait for his bon plaisir.

Mademoiselle Alain, like a dutiful proprietor, gives us the grand tour of Les Bruyères. My room and the furniture are built of local pine wood. The furnishings consist of a narrow bed, a dresser, one table, and one chair. And my lot is cast with the Bruyères. All FOREST SCENTS!

On the D 902 up to Bionnay, the sun dances on the snow with noon brightness. Maman wears her soft little grey felt hat with the wide blue velvet ribbon and the short veil. She always wears a short veil when she goes to St.-Gervais; the veil hides her Semitic features. Maman breaks the silence first. She says: "Mademoiselle Alain is the power behind the throne."

We agree. Mademoiselle Alain is no ordinary headmistress.

"She's Moreau's Pompadour (the Sun King's favorite concubine)," I joke.

Mother is concerned about sexual morality: the Pompadour might be a bad influence on Marguerite. She purses her lips.

The serious issue — that my false ID will have to be handed over to my employer once monthly to obtain my ration coupons at city hall — is a risk Papa doesn't like. He coughs and throws a side glance at his youngest. I'm determined to go out into the world, lead a productive life, and contribute to society even with false papers. I look the other way. A friend of our landlady can't... shan't... won't... turn me in. At the same time I caution myself: Marguerite, do your best work, keep your mouth shut, and use common sense. Socially connect in a thin way with your charges. This is no time for closeness anyhow. If you value your life.

Ghis, disappointed, mutters: I will look for a job elsewhere.

In the distance, the pointed white roofs of Bionnay stand out against the glacier of Bionnassay bathed in the noon sun.

I pinch my cheeks and make sure it's me, alive and free in Val Montjoie, walking on the snow-plowed D 902 facing the glistening Bionnassay about to become a teacher-counselor to four children. I have a job within a month of our arrival. Life in the Alps — not bad for an eighteen-year-old!

The first day is a packed day. I meet the children in the classroom at Les Bruyères.

"Bonjour les enfants." I say. They say:

"Bonjour!"

What heads! The little boy's shaven cranium is covered with bloody pustules.

"Impetigo!" Lisa says, pointing her finger at the contagious skull.

Lisa's own hair is wrapped in a white towel. Already she has undergone a skull treatment at the hands of Mademoiselle Alain.

La directrice isn't *chouette,"* French slang for "nice." "Why?" "She pulled and scraped my scalp and snarled that I am dirty. It's not my fault if I don't go to school in the 16ème (a fashionable arrondissement in Paris where well-off French children live). In Billancourt everybody has head lice." And she taps the white-turbaned towel bundled around her head with her fingers.

Michèle looks on sallow, indifferent.

"I'm fine," says Louise, the third girl, her pert little nose turned up. A short Peter Pan hairdo gives her a petite pixie-like look. Paris-Billancourt seems pale in the strong alpine sun.

Later that day, the headmistress calls me into the office. Tense, she adjusts the hairpins in her tight black bun. All business now, she needs to talk to me. I take a seat opposite the mahogany desk.

"Mademoiselle, we must beware…," she says with jaundiced eyes.

131

Of pus and head lice? (I secretly think).

Her pupils sparkle with a devilish glint. A pause.

Does she want me to instruct them,

or:

share her disdain of their lower socio-economic status, and perhaps their communist parents?

"Read these, Mademoiselle Lengel!" she says, and across the desk she pushes sheets of paper.

"*Il faut se méfier des enfants*, we must distrust the children!" she repeats.

The social worker's hand-written evaluations read: "... could do better... is distracted in class..." Lisa's father is a POW, her mother works third shift. Vincent's mother does factory work from 8 AM to 4 PM; his father is in a Stalag. "The boy is restless... doesn't apply himself..." The social worker found the apartment cold and empty of food.

My instinct warns me: return the letters without comment. The children are spending their days with me; I'll protect them from the headmistress. I feel sure I can make them happy.

I also know that if I take the first cable car up to the Bettex at 2:00 PM, immediately after lunch, I can complete one run and be in the classroom by 3:00 PM. To a passionate skier, one good run makes the day.

At the Bruyères, Mademoiselle Alain is all ears, all seeing, and always suspicious. She stares from face to face when she brings our meal trays to the classroom as if her yellowed eyes were trying to sniff out subversive activities.

Within a week I receive a second summons to the office.

What now?

Behind her desk Mlle Alain's eyes blaze like two coals.

"Mademoiselle Lengel, look at this!" and the headmistress hands me a picture postcard of Saint-Gervais that shows skiers frolicking in the snow. On the reverse side Lisa had scribbled to a friend: "I ski every day."

"Just so that you know with whom we are dealing, Mlle Lengel!"

132

The Head glows with delight. She has caught a white lie.

I know that all headmistresses read the mail, but this one informs on Lisa with perverse glee. I can't believe my ears; such a peccadillo! We have lost the battle of France, the Germans are occupying the country, and wages are controlled. Inflation reaches 50%. Fathers are in German POW camps. Deprivations ravage the health of the children, and she accuses a poor fourteen-year old from Paris-Billancourt who wishes to gain one inch of prestige with her classmates of skiing — on paper. A pretense that obviously springs from an inferiority feeling.

Lisa of course doesn't go anywhere close to a ski slope. Lisa daily walks between two points, A and B, which the headmistress shows with a ruler on the topography map behind her desk — to Mlle Lengel. The rest of the day Lisa is confined to the classroom or the dorm. Lisa wears slippers, and is asked to speak in a low voice. Lisa studies, does homework, reads, eats, rests and sleeps — under twenty-four-hour surveillance.

I hand the card back. By the door, Mlle Alain denounces the offender once again: "Lisa needs close supervision!"

At the same time she addresses me with much respect. Each sentence of hers is prefaced or ended with a formal: "Mademoiselle Lengel..." in the French custom of deference.

There are two possible explanations here, I tell myself: the first one is that both she and Monsieur Moreau are "Ancien Regime", a period in French history when the powers-that-be were vested in the nobility, the priests, and the teachers. Monsieur Moreau and Mlle Alain may be staunch Orléanists or followers of the Comte de Chambord both of whom consider World War II as an opportunity to wipe out the Republic and turn the pages back to a royal descendant of the last "Louis." My employers may belong to that layer of French society which is more or less actively anti-republican, anti-communist, anti-Jewish, and anti-Free Mason. The headmistress and Monsieur Moreau may wish to return to pre-1789 times.

The other explanation is that Moreau and Alain are just class-conscious bigots.

133

They intrigue me. But I'm also concerned about my personal safety. So far, when I hand Mlle Alain my false identity card on the first of each month to enable her to secure my ration coupons at the mairie, she keeps the ID exactly one day. Always she returns the paper in the evening saying: "Voilà, Mlle Lengel! Merci!" She doesn't suspect me, I tell myself. At the same time in the hallway, I could hear the voice of Radio Vichy drift down from the upstairs private apartment. "Last night, the Germans successfully blew up the old port of Marseilles with dynamite. They flushed out thousands of communists, Jews, resisters and other enemies of the state who hid in the narrow alleys. The French police, aided by the milice, immediately handed the 'criminals' over to the German authorities. All are to be deported.'" Our own police collaborating with the forces of Occupation!

Shutting out one of the many nightmares I carry inside my own depth, I close the door behind me. At least in my classroom I don't have to listen to Radio Vichy.

Whenever Mlle Alain brings the meal trays, unease grips the classroom. Over and over I notice that she is sly and manipulative; disobedience enrages her. She berates the young. That much I'm certain of: she enjoys informing. At the Bruyères I hear the silent roars of duplicity.

Edict 108 requires all Jews to register and have their identity cards stamped "Juif". My ID shows: "Marguerite (Margot Gerda) Lengel born in Markelheim (Bas-Rhin)" She may think I am one of the 200,000 Christian Alsatian-Lorrainers who sought refuge in the Non-occupied Zone in 1940 rather than give up their French citizenship and become German nationals.

On Sunday mornings, Mademoiselle Alain goes to church with Lisa, Michèle, Louise and the boy Vincent. Never once does she ask me about my religion.

In April, I see heads bobbing up behind a hedge opposite the Bruyères.

At first, I weave a rational explanation: It's men picking dandelions, the much-prized spring tonic of the French; but male heads pop up long after the dandelion season is over.

One morning, a visitor rings the doorbell. He asks to see Mademoiselle Alain. He's dressed in a non-descript garb; I don't know him. He gives me no message. He strikes me as being *louche,* a shady character. That night Mademoiselle Alain asks me not to answer the front door any longer when she's out.

What is she hiding? Where is she going dressed in her black coat, black shoes, black stockings, black hat and gloves — her black clutch purse tightly squeezed under the elbow?

Many things disturb me about my work place but I can't speak about it at Chez Nous. My parents would be alarmed and, besides, at eighteen, I'm accustomed to keeping my own counsel.

From the upstairs radio, news drifts down about SOL, the *Service d'Ordre Legionnaires,* the Vichy militia — and of the Resistance gunning down "innocent" SOL members.

If the dark forces in my environment hadn't already set me on edge, the Easter visit of nine-year-old Nicole, Monsieur Moreau's daughter, certainly would have done so.

"Our little one is coming tomorrow," Mlle Alain chirps coyly; the stern headmistress even appears skittish.

Next day I meet Nicole on the lawn. She wears a beautiful blue and white hand-smocked dress with white shoes and socks. A white bow ties her long dark brown pony tail. We shake hands. Nicole curtsies. Mlle Alain hurries along the front footpath with a hairbrush in hand. "What do you think of our little one?" she asks me in an almost lovesick voice while fussing with a wrinkle in Nicole's blue frock. She tugs here, pulls there, as if she were not quite pleased with Nicole's appearance. Yet Nicole's grooming is faultless.

The child scowls. "That's enough Nanna!"

"'We' don't want to look nice today?" retorts a sly Nanna, and she swiftly tries her hand at taming a rebellious strand of Nicole's brown hair.

Nicole bristles and takes off on the swing — into freedom.

I pay the expected compliment: "Nicole is charming... exquisitely dressed... so well behaved."

It is obvious that the child, a younger Nora out of Ibsen's *The Doll House*, lives under Mademoiselle Alain's tutelage. Nicole is her Thing. The "THING" is expected to live up to Mlle Alain's image of her perfect order.

"Nanna brought 'us' up,'" simpers Nanna.

Nanna had sent Nicole off to a convent at age seven, "So as to teach 'us' the triple virtues of discipline, obedience, and humility.'" Nanna's thin-lipped mouth speaks of the convent as a place where "we" are permitted to only talk in class.

On the swing, the wind blows through Nicole's long dark brown locks. The child laughs wildly at the speed, and the dizzying heights.

Such loose gaiety troubles Nanna who stands at the foot of the swing set, hair brush in hand, taunting:

"Matted hair... tz ... tz... tz... the brush is going to hurt 'our' little one.'" Hurt!

Fanatically, she brandishes the handled bristles into the air like a weapon.

Breezes waft down from the summits. Eventually, Nicole tired of swinging comes to a stop. Nanna's fiery black eyes flash with revenge. A short struggle ensues between Nicole and the brush.

"Oh Nanna!"

What would Mademoiselle Lengel think if she knew 'we' were punished for talking in class?'"

Nanna tries to shame Nicole into submission.

The top of Nicole's head barely reaches her tormentor's chest. "Cut it out, Nanna!" the child fights back.

"Perhaps we should INFORM Sister Beatrice about a little girl who talks back?"

INFORM! AGAIN?

First on Lisa, now on Nicole. Nanna uses a deceptively sweet voice, but sparks of cruelty and anger fly off her honey-tipped tongue. "Our little one tends to rebel; that's why 'we' were sent to a convent,'" she says, turning toward me.

Nicole grimaces and walks back to the house, evil following closely on her heels.

SOMETHING IS HAPPENING, HERE!
Our milkman, Joe Barzat, had told Papa:
"Mademoiselle Alain? *Pas du coin*! She's not from here."

Joe Barzat inferred: she's not bound by the local mores. Monsieur Moreau? Ah, he's a local son... wife died giving birth to a little girl...

On the last day of spring vacation Nicole visits the classroom. She looks at me with deep, softly confused blue eyes. "Good-bye, Mademoiselle," and she curtsies.

I imagine a Balzac-like illicit love story between a widower left with a newborn baby girl and a six year old boy, Michael. The widower hires a housekeeper-nursemaid. She takes control of home, hearth, and the widower; eventually she throws the sixteen year-old Michael out of the house — for rebellion. "Michael joined the Foreign Legion at a young age," Joe Barzat had told Papa. I see the headmistress capable of taking a soul into servitude or dispatching it with a vindictive toss.

The notion of collaboration with the enemy hasn't yet entered my head.

At the time, the country was polarized between pro-German and anti-German factions. Laval appointed himself president of the Milice and named Joseph Darnand his deputy Secretary-general. Darnand is a thug with a long history of violent behavior. First he belonged to the far-left, then to the far-right. Now he commands the Militia, a new parallel police force whose raison d'être is to torture and kill "the enemies" of the regime. The milice recruits from the ranks of the Service d'Ordre Legionnaire (SOL) whose forty-five thousand registered members swear to fight for French purity, against democracy, against Jewish leprosy, and against Gaullist dissent. The khaki-shirted SOL members wear a black beret and a black tie. Monsieur Moreau wears an ascot...

I'm not yet making a connection.

The SOL members take an oath to Maréchal Pétain on their knees after an all-night vigil. They promise to rid France of Gaullists, Bolshevists, Freemasons and Jews... Most (but not all) of the SOL volunteers are pro-Nazi diehards.

137

At the Bruyères, I breathe the highly charged atmosphere that sweeps the land. Laval had published a law in February that all French men born between January 1, 1920 and December 31, 1922 must report at once for forced labor in Germany. The BBC (which I catch sometimes at Chez Nous on my day off) is broadcasting: "Draftees say 'no' to Laval and Fritz Saukel, the former Gauleiter from Thuringe, Germany, the slave recruiter of occupied Europe... Escape to the *maquis*, the bush!'" Could she...? Would she...? I see her stealthy gait, the shifty eyes, and the pitch black hair tied in a severe knot at the nape...

In my locked diary I note in an elliptical script: "In the book I'm reading the main character is a sneer. The sneer is ambitious, and attaches the dark side of her soul to the highest maleficent authority in the realm..."

Letters of denunciation flood Gestapo headquarters. It's disgusting how widely the custom of anonymous accusations has penetrated French society. The BBC warns of the growing tide of informers. "They mostly are cruel, revengeful people."

At the Bruyères, in an effort to ward off gloom, I overreact. In the morning, I open the shutters in the girls' dorm, singing loudly:

"Row, row, row your boat
Gently down the stream
Merrily, merrily, merrily, merrily —
Life is but a dream."

Lisa snaps: "What's so good about waking up? Mademoiselle Alain here or the head lice in Paris?"

I come to a decision:
In the office, I give two weeks' notice to Monsieur Moreau. I say: "I wish to go and work with Ghis at **Bonne Maman**." Monsieur Moreau, robed in his purple silk dressing gown, ascot tucked inside his pajamas, accepts my resignation "With regrets." He compliments me on my work with the children. He says: "Mademoiselle Alain mentioned their progress." This time he rises

and sees me out of the room. Obviously I had earned his respect. I take away a last impression of a receding chin, flabby cheeks, and sick opaque eyes expressing secret quarrels. We both hide behind a mask of politeness.

"Best wishes!" he says.

"Thank you for giving me a chance!" I say.

Within a fortnight, I join Ghis at Bonne Maman as a junior counselor-teacher. Bonne Maman is a private home for children located on the Mont Paccard slope above Saint-Gervais. I feel as if I have entered a different world where children laugh and play. At Bonne Maman, children make funny faces at people taking their pictures, and parents visit.

In the spring in 1944 at the boulangerie, I pick up a whisper by the cash register: "Mademoiselle Arlette Alain, the headmistress of Les Bruyères, was killed yesterday at the Le Fayet-Saint-Gervais-south rail station in a train about to leave for Annecy."

"Eh, oui! A fatal robbery..." shrugs the baker's wife with a little doubtful glint in her eye.

A few weeks later *Le Petit Dauphinois,* the regional paper, prints a notice saying: "The police closed their file on Mademoiselle Alain's death as an unresolved murder."

Murder: yes. Unresolved? No. In June 1944, I learn at the secret headquarters of the Resistance that Mademoiselle Alain had been dispatched by so and so... with a bullet to the head through the open window of the train waiting at the Le Fayet-Saint-Gervais-south station. So and so snatched her purse and ran into the bush. Made it look like a robbery... The black pouch had contained a map showing the exact locations of the chalets and huts where the maquisards were hiding out in the forests around Saint-Gervais.

Mademoiselle Alain was on her way to the Gestapo in Annecy about to betray the young "rebels," the fugitives from the compulsory Work Service in Germany.

What about Monsieur Moreau?

139

One of the district's founders of the Service d'Ordre Legionnaires, the far-right SOL, Monsieur Moreau comes to heel when the Allies win.

Chapter 8

Inside the Forbidden Alpensperrzone

Mosaics of Life

Teenage tensions rumble in me. Extinction looms, yet every cell in me strives for fulfillment. I'm eighteen going on four thousand. It is 1943. My instincts sharpened by circumstance acutely observe all the minute details of daily existence inside the forbidden Alpine frontier zone. I live in a state of psychological revelations.

* * *

Six life-sized stone statues surround the far-end altar of the Lombard rococo church in Saint-Gervais. One represents Moses holding the tablets inscribed with the Ten Commandments. I imperceptibly wink at him. Bonjour, ancestor of my Levite Tribe!

Except for Moses, everything else is different. Two oaken confessionals with carved latticework stand against the wall to the left; along the right wall, steps lead to a hand-carved oak pulpit. The same sort of rough local pine boards that I see at the sawmill on the D 902 cover the floor. The Soldate brothers built the church in 1822. The soft pink stucco columns that support the ceiling in the Italianate architectural style and the gilded ornamentation, give the house of worship a feeling of warmth.

It's Sunday morning. In two straight lines the children dressed in their best holiday clothes and I march down the hillside asphalt road from Bonne Maman, blaring at the top of our lungs *Alouette, Je Te Plumerai; Napoléon Had 500 Brave Soldiers; Malb'rough Goes to War, and Frère Jacques.*

141

By the ornate portal of the church, we join the throng of mountain folks clutching their prayer books in sinewy hands more accustomed to splitting wood than holding a delicate breviary.

Past the heavy wood-carved door, my charges genuflect, dip a finger into the holy water, and quietly move to the front where they can see well. I slip into the last row.

"Mademoiselle, come and sit in front with us!" says 12-year-old Henri.

"But I'm Protestant!" I reply spontaneously.

I write my dissertation at mass on the pros and cons of Jean Jacques Rousseau's *Noble Savage*. To myself I say: Péguy and Claudel compose their best work inside a church, why not I? No one stares at me; the St.Gervolains respect my privacy.

After church lets out, the children and I assemble Place de l'Eglise by the fountain for the climb up to Bonne Maman. We sing loudly our songs of yesteryear. A visiting parent who witnesses the scene says with Gallic humor: "I am sure your voices reached the heavens. They sounded generous, round and crusty like a handful of mountain hazelnuts."

* * *

At Chez Nous, the electric lights are still off. It's evening, time for me to return to Bonne Maman.

"Good-by!" I call out to Maman. No reply.

I go and search for her. In the darkness of the hallway a line of unsteady light filters under the pantry door. Maman's head appears in the opening and at once withdraws, but not before I detect a flicker of two candles.

"Maman!"

It's Friday.

"Sh-sh!"

Index finger to her lips, Mother says in a hush: "Marguerite, the candles must always burn to the end, they can't be snuffed out; their flame is sacred."

Cheeks flushed, a look of anguish over her face, Maman instructs me in the practices of the Jewish religion.

142

"Yes," she whispers, "I welcome the Sabbath, just as my mother of blessed memory taught me and before her my grandmother — your great-grandmother whose name was Gidel and for whose soul I bestowed the middle name Gerda on you!

Maman, clad in her best wool dress with a matching grey shawl, stands in the windowless cellar-like room amidst brown earthenware pots filled with sauerkraut and jars of home-canned green beans, similar to a Marrano under the Spanish Inquisition when Queen Isabella and King Ferdinand of Spain worried that the Jews would contaminate the Catholics newly liberated from the Moors.

Later I say to myself: "History repeats itself with a weird twist every five hundred years."

* * *

Last week, Maman said, "It's terrible, how we have to hide our past." The dangerous memories, I call them. Whenever they pop up, they must be repressed. For instance, the picture of Grandma Oppenheimer as she sat at her dining table after a meal in Gemmingen, head bowed over her white faience plate, reciting her blessing: "G-d, thank you for our food, and may all the children of Israel have as bountiful a meal as we do. Amen." The grace warmed my child's heart. Now, I must have nothing to do with ancestral Jewish prayers. I wall them up [in my soul] as if they were ships in a frozen Arctic bay.

* * *

It is in the higher Alps that I begin seriously to doubt my childhood God who revealed himself on Mt. Sinai and proclaimed HIS TEN COMMANDMENTS to Moses: "I am the Lord your G-d who took you out of the land of Egypt... You shall have no other Gods... Do not take the name of the Lord your G-d in vain... Remember the Sabbath day, and keep it holy... Honor your father and mother..." After four tumultuous years of wartime adolescence, I realize I have been fed too many myths.

One foot in front of the other, body bent into the Mont d'Arbois slope, I take Him to task: "G-d, you don't seem to care much. You didn't save France. You don't strike Hitler with a deadly blow. You haven't punished me for neglecting you."

In the vastness of the Alpine universe, I reflect:

G-d if you are the CREATOR OF THE UNIVERSE, make your power known.

Man, whom you allegedly created in your image — he constantly wages war.

Men!

Men didn't save my Brownies. False identity cards or a host family in Switzerland saved a few of my Thrushes.

Cowbells tingle in stables.

Men lust for power and control.

In the Bible, you, G-d, give the women all the duty roles. Rebecca draws water at the well; Ruth follows her mother-in-law Naomi, "Wherever you go I go." Queen Esther saves her people in the King's chamber. Eve is born out of Adam's rib. This inequality of the sexes hurts. The way it is, I have to hide my intellect which is often sharper than that of the men I encounter. Are you really the G-d of *justice?* Perhaps justice is a fantasy of the excluded.

In sight of the Voza Pass, a second argument: Do you G-d, know at all what is happening on earth? Do you know that men and women suffer equally from the defeat? Equally, they fear arrest, deportation, torture and hunger. You may not know this, G-d.

And G-d, did you know that hunger is a social leveler?

All around me, small apples fall off trees not pruned since the war.

Above the Contamines in the open fields, I walk like ancient shepherds did in the Middle East desert under unlimited horizons.

The mountains rise epic and immense. A vital force flows everywhere. In the wind, in the sun, in the streams cascading down the steep cliffs.

Nature's vitality *IS* — THEREFORE *I AM*!

I logically establish my being on the premise that there is one common *élan vital.* Henri Bergson's original "chiquenaude." All right, I am part of the evolutionary push toward a more complex life.

But a week or so later on my day off trekking through the forests of pines, oaks, birches to Mégève for my regular lesson in philosophy, I question my new found belief: if we are an evolutionary phenomena, then we are not "His" Chosen people.

That thought unsettles me.

For weeks, while setting one foot in front of the other, I unravel the systems of thought I am studying for the baccalauréate: Stoicism, empiricism, hedonism, and determinism.

Methodically, I peel off layers of absolutes as I would strip an onion, with salty tears.

Down to the center.

But as soon as I shed one unsatisfactory premise for the next, I feel the pain of the loss. For days, weeks, and months I am defenseless — spiritually naked. I find that the search for Truth is a vulnerable journey.

So far all I know for certain are that the earth rotates around the sun, therefore the "sun sets and the sun rises;" the gravity of the moon attracts the oceans, thus causing tides. In the atmosphere, cold air turns water to snow.

In Saint-Nicolas-de-Véroce, without warning, the clouds part and Mont Blanc appears with a dozen glaciers hanging down its flanks. "God, what beauty!" I exclaim spontaneously. I put my hand to my eyes to shelter them from the brightness of the sun.

In the meadows of multicolored wild flowers spread all about Le Bettex in view of Mont Blanc shining its white glacial splendor under an infinite blue sky, a sudden light explodes within me: I see Rebecca, Ruth, and Sarah, and I reject the matriarchs as my sole role models — I'm aware that my pantheon is populated with Eve Curie (a scientist), Joan of Arc (a courageous warrior), and George Sand (a novelist).

Here in the Alps I outgrow the story of creation inculcated into me since childhood: the myths of the six days, of women created out of Adam's rib, and the belief in the original Garden of Eden. Surely knowledge is bliss, and not a sin!

145

Poundings of my heart acknowledge each discovery.
I am trekking towards an unknown future.

* * *

Every night at Bonne Maman, I sublimate hunger pangs into learning. After the children are tucked in at 8:00 PM, at my table under a forty-watt bulb, I drink cups of knowledge sweet as ambrosia.

I delight in history, philosophy, and anatomy (subjects required for my exams. One day I discover the secrets of chlorophyll — how the green coloring matter contained in plants converts carbon dioxide and water into carbohydrates in the presence of sunlight. Although my body lacks fats, carbohydrates and proteins, my brain ingests unending free data about bones, tendons, marrow and cells. I become the best-fed person at Bonne Maman.

I escape not only hunger but Vichy and Hitler and the dread of the hunt and the hunters. In the morning, accustomed to the finer light of my inner illuminations, I squint at the raw sun over chicory brew and toasted brown bread.

Did Plato write his *Ideal Republic* because things were too rotten at home in Athens?

* * *

Eric, a little five-year-old golden boy with the face of a cherub, is one of my charges at Bonne Maman. In the dormitory one morning, while putting on his clothes, he says, *"Mon papa est un voleur."*

"A what?" I ask.

In French, the verb "voler" means both to steal and to fly. The noun "voleur", however, has one only correct meaning: thief.

Which trade does his papa ply?

In a voice as clear as a bell, Eric chimes: "Papa flies high up in the sky on the other side of the Mediterranean sea."

His father is a pilot with the Free French in liberated North Africa. A dangerous career to admit to in Nazi-occupied France.

Eric's mother hand-embroidered *Eric C.* on every brief, every pajama as if she wanted to set a bit of herself on the yarn that touches her son's tender skin. Most mothers use indelible ink.

146

In the distant alpine valley to which little Eric was sent to heal his lungs, he kneels at bedtime by his bunk, and quietly prays: "Our Father who art in heaven...." Followed by, "Little Jesus, please embrace Maman, Maria, and bring my Daddy safely home from the skies. And thank you for healing my lungs. Amen."

He makes the sign of the cross, rises, and slides between the dry white sheets of his narrow bunk bed.

At night he quietly wets his bed.

* * *

Ghis is a knitter. Seated in the parlor by the lamp, my sister whiles evenings away knitting yarn into sweaters.

Fresh wool being unobtainable, Ghis unravels a sweater after a few weeks' wear, and then starts knitting a new one. With each sweater, she goes through the tedious process of winding the yarn around the four legs of an upturned chair, tying the strands, and washing the bundles. After that she hangs the wool on a clothesline, and lengthens out the wrinkles. She needs me to transfer the wrinkle-free strands to my outstretched arms so that she can start balling the yarn.

* * *

Seventeen, a lycéenne from Paris, Arlette is one year younger than I am. Tall, thin, she wears her permed blond hair pulled back by two combs, one on each side of her wide forehead. At Bonne Maman, Arlette follows her own independent treatment to heal TB under Doctor Tissot's supervision. In the course of submitting to a strict regimen, Arlette had acquired a quiet poise, the kind TB patients often do. Her self-discipline impresses me.

I invite her to come with me on my day off to the Mer de Glace, above Chamonix.

"I'll be happy to go with you to the Ice Sea," she answers calmly.

Jumping crevasses as blue as the sky one hundred feet deep, doesn't seem especially hazardous to me. Hadn't I, last week, hopped across the Bossons glacier near Les Houches and back, alone? It will be fun to share a similar experience with someone I like.

147

We forget TB.

From Chamonix at 3,422 feet above sea level, we climb to Montenvers at an altitude of 6,276 feet. There, the glaciers of Tacul, Leschaux, Talèdre join and form the famed Mer de Glace that stretches 3,900 feet across. The crossing involves jumping deep chasms.

Perched on the edge of a crevasse, Arlette seems as sure as a gull about to take off.

From then on whenever I turn around and look at her, I see Arlette totally at ease with the whole ice world. She's a natural. She enjoys it.

After the crossing, it makes sense (to me) to descend directly to Chamonix along the rocky tracks of the Montenvers cog rail instead of climbing down through the winding forest trail.

We meet a guide who does the same.

Why not join his long strides?

"We just traversed the Mer de Glace!" I tell him.

Silence.

"We climbed to Montenvers on foot (I never had enough money for transportation). We didn't take the cograil."

(Silence).

"It's a 2,800 foot height differential!"

He throws me a "big deal" look.

The rest of the descent, our boots roll on the pebbles as we try to keep up with the pace of a cocky member of "the Company," the famous *Compagnie des Guides* of Chamonix.

At a bend, and without breaking his cadence, he points his chin at la Verte. That's where he came from, from atop the 13,900-foot jagged free-standing needle.

A thousand feet above Chamonix, where the glaciers' melt tumbles into a white-crested torrent that feeds the Arve River, our guide forks off.

"R'voir!"

"Au-revoir!"

By the falls, elbows set on the railing, Arlette and I throw sticks into the whirling white waters and watch them go under and reappear in the foam.

Half an hour later, she and I make our way out. We flag down a small Citroen camionnette, the name of a dairy printed on the side.

* * *

On the esplanade by the kiosk, Claire stops me one early afternoon, distressed. Her fingers play with a tiny gold cross around her neck.

"They came at 3:00 AM and took my father away," she whispers without an introduction. "My mother and I are worried. If they keep him, they'll torture him to make him talk; if they send him home, the Resistance will shun him, thinking he has compromised the network. In any case, my father's role in the Resistance is over." She holds back tears. Her father is General Magnin. The family resides temporarily here in Saint-Gervais. Like most war-displaced people, they come from elsewhere. "His cell is sprung," she says.

"His two contacts, the one above him and the one below, will have to go into hiding," she adds concerned.

It was the first time I heard about the cell system.

After a deep breath, she looks at her watch. "It's almost two o'clock. I have to go and read to my blind man," she says, again composed. "He lives up on La Vignette."

Why has she decided to confide in me? Because she had to tell somebody her own age whom she doesn't know, someone whose face is familiar to her from having seen it for over a year in town; and because trust is a visceral decision.

I feel sympathy for her but little surprise. By then arrests and people cracking under torture and becoming double agents were part of social fabric. I never met Claire again. The family must have left Saint-Gervais in a hurry to go into hiding elsewhere.

* * *

Géraldine, one year my senior and a student, lives with her parents on the Mont Packard slope. I visit to borrow an anatomy textbook.

The visit takes a bizarre turn.

In the kitchen, Géraldine says, "Keep *Anatomy I* as long as you wish; I'm done," and she pushes the book across the oilcloth. Leisurely I flip through pages of bones, tendons and veins when all of a sudden the garden gate creaks.

A minute later, Géraldine's father stands in front of us with a shopping net full of rutabagas weighing down each arm.

Medium-short with a narrow bird face, he's clad in a thick overcoat and a navy beret; between his teeth he clenches an unlit pipe.

Géraldine and I had been discussing exams — the type of questions asked, the grading.

Without warning, the narrow bird-eyes rip through *Anatomy I*, through Géraldine, and through me. A storm breaks loose. He thunders:

"France's place in Germany's new Order is to return to the land. Agriculture is our future. A woman's role is to bear children. You better clear your heads of fancy ideas!"

"Papa!" moans Géraldine.

"Be quiet when I speak!"

I bite my lips while he rages on: "Hard work and discipline will do the French a lot of good!" It's mid-morning and Philippe Pétain's slogan of the moral revolution that Vichy is brain-washing us with since the defeat is unleashed. "Work, Family, Country."

"Papa, please!" pleads Géraldine.

"France must collaborate with Germany to establish a lasting world order! All the *vauriens* (good for nothings) should be deported!"

Does he mean me? Has he a sixth sense?

He sets down his bags of rutabagas.

I have no choice but to listen to: "France's duty is to submit to German rule like an obedient older daughter'" and other bleak Nazi advice.

"Pay no attention to him," whispers Géraldine under her breath in a barely audible voice through the corners of her mouth as prisoners do without moving their lips. "He's a colonel in the French army; he owes allegiance to his Marshal!"

A few minutes later in her room, Géraldine rummages through a drawer. Suddenly she cries out, "I detest this town. There's no place to escape to."

I stand ill at ease by her dresser. Why am I here in this hostile house? The sooner I get out, the better! I know I should support her, but enough is enough.

Through the window I see a cumulus of snowy white clouds floating high over the valley.

While I am walking toward the door, Géraldine pulls a hollowed head of curly blond hair from under her lingerie. "My wig!" she exclaims.

Up to the light she holds on her right fist her get-away fantasy. "I can't wait for this war to end so I can run off to Paris," she says, and she kicks the drawer shut with her ersatz leather shoe.

Outside, the heavy clouds are hitting the summits and bursting open. The dues for Anatomy 101 have been paid.

In the hallway in the direction of the pantry, I coo, oh so sweetly at the little colonel who, on his knees, is busily stacking away his rutabagas compliments of Herr Hitler.

"Au-revoir, Monsieur!" *Cocu,* you don't know Marguerite Lévy was in your home. ("Cocu" is a French insult meaning "cuckold." My generation dispensed the pejorative term freely.)

At the front door, Géraldine taps a forefinger on her temple in the age-old gesture signifying, he's crazy.

The garden gate closes behind me. I stand on rue de la Vignette under the fresh thick snow swirls. My knees, I hate to admit it, "No, yes, I am afraid..." they shake.

* * *

Chez Nous, on the border of the D 902, behind the hedge, Papa, from seeds, plants a vegetable garden. He plants rows of carrots, cabbages, onions, potatoes, lettuce and climbing peas. In the early summer, after he makes breakfast for himself and Maman, he goes to the shed, takes out his long-handled hoe and sets to work for a couple hours. Before noon, he stops his bending, digging, and planting, stands up straight and admires his rows dug along a string attached to two sticks. Then he puts his tools away in the shed in such a way that he can, the following day, identify them at a glance and without much light. He arranges the long-handled rake against the back wall, the hoe and the shorter spade in front. With an energetic step, navy shirt-sleeves rolled up, his bare arms ready for a wash; Papa enters the house through the rear kitchen door wearing his satisfaction on his face.

Before the war Papa whistled while gardening. Now, he doesn't draw attention to himself.

Papa waters his plants with two large metal watering cans, the two-gallon size, one in each hand for balance. The weight of the cans travels up his stiffly held arms and intersects at his compressed lips. Papa walks straight as an arrow although he suffers from a hernia.

The Bionnassay glacier in the background, he turns, seeds, weeds his garden, wearing a blue denim apron over his slacks. Under the apron, he wears shirt and tie. At home (before the war) he sported Victorian-style three-piece striped suits. Now, in the evenings, at Chez Nous, he uses the coat minus the vest for warmth. Deleting the vest is his concession to comfort.

When his chores are finished, and only then, does he allow himself the leisure of reading by the window or the stove. Weekly, he walks the four-mile round-trip to Saint-Gervais, knapsack on his back. In town he goes to the butcher, pays the utility bills, buys razor blades, pumice stone soap, and whatever other few basics Maman and he need. His longest stop is at the library. Like other CEOs, Papa had little time to read. In Saint-Gervais he selects biographies, novels and books on European history. His preferred authors are André Maurois, Thomas Mann, and Stefan Zweig.

After having read the biography of a certain king, Papa says to me, "That ruler bankrupted a whole nation, as he would have bankrupted a business." Papa is still amazed at his own audacity to enjoy leisure.

He admires the sunsets and the sunrises over the Bionnassay glacier with his binoculars. Beauty, books and one thin home-rolled cigarette daily are his pleasures.

Mother is not domestic, so at Chez Nous, Papa cooks, does the laundry, washes the dishes and tends the fire in the sitting room.

* * *

On Friday nights in Mannheim, my Papa blessed me or, if I had been naughty, acted "hesitant" before dispensing the benediction. After the *Brocha* (the blessing), he gave me a kiss on the forehead.

His stature was immense. After a bloody fight with Ghis during which she badly scratched the skin off my hands when I was seven years old, Papa ordered both of us to his library — the winner and the loser stood before his Chippendale desk, two culprits, head bowed, expecting the worst.

My father calmly ruled, "From now on, Marguerite has the power to say, 'Stop!' or you, Ghis, will have to deal with me!"

Seated on his striped brown and black velvet chair, Papa, to me, loomed as large as Abraham Lincoln on the Mall in Washington D.C.

Ghis tested her first-born strength once more, but the newly anointed referee shouted her magic word —

And Ghis's fingers froze in mid-air.

Papa, I wrapped myself in the feeling of your protection throughout my life — like in a respected umpire's uniform.

* * *

If —

Rudyard Kipling's poem hung in a pine frame on the wall above my bed at Bonne Maman. *IF* — is my soul's companion. I still know by heart:

"If you can keep your head when all about you
Are losing theirs and blaming it on you,
If you can trust yourself when all men doubt you,
But make allowance for their doubting too;
.....
Or being hated don't give way to hating,

153

And yet don't look too good, nor talk too wise:
.....
Yours is the Earth and everything that's in it,
And – which is more – you'll be a Man, my son.

Unconsciously I modified the last line and read "... you'll be a Mensch, my daughter!" I felt Kipling spoke to me.

* * *

Chapter 9

Without Anesthesia

Part I

(Summer 1943)

Life at Bonne Maman seems on the surface civil, and ordered. I teach class from 9 AM to noon. After lunch and a two-hour rest period in the heated solarium, I actively play with my charges or organize outings into the mountains. I meet with visiting parents. In the evenings, the children choose their own entertainment. At night I study for Le Bac.

One July evening I see Henri, Gaston and François scratch with bare hands the soil in Raymond's garden.

"What are you doing?"

"We are digging up potatoes!"

They laugh and gag and wash the tubers at an outside spigot — and eat them raw. They get too sick to walk to bed.

In the kitchen Raymond laments: "My potatoes, they weren't even ripe!"

What do you expect? They are hungry!" comments Marie, Raymond's wife standing at the stove.

Marie senses that the tenet of French culture, MODERATION, cracks when the guts growl: reason works when life is gentle but now it's wartime and the basic needs erupt under pressure.

Alleviation in the garden they found none, but the following day in the dining room at lunchtime cheerful Henri — from sun-drenched Nice and well-to-do happy parents — rises to his feet, something up his sleeve. Grinning, he calls out: "Hey guys! Let's dance around the tables singing, 'We want food! We want food!'"

155

On the parquet floor, hands set on the shoulders of the child ahead; they break into a farandole and chant "Food! Food!" to the rhythm of Georges Bizet's six-eight allegro of the Arlésienne. *L'Arlésienne*!

Madame Vachette hears the cadence of Provence and, she who comes from le Midi, is touchée. Touched.

That night the portions of rice are plumper. Afterwards, the portly directrice nobly sets a sweet on each child's plate. "*Tenez!*" she says with a sort of subtle distant contempt as a duchess would who tries to appease her subjects whose rations she had hoarded for months in her pantry.

Madame Vachette doesn't like the parents of her paying guests to read about hunger in the weekly letters home.

My own repressed cravings erupt in a different fashion. For months I haven't tasted a morsel of my J3 (youth 16 to 21), chocolate ration. Madame Vachette has right to my food coupons, and I lack the leverage the children possess. I wake up at night repeatedly from a nightmare in which I see blue and gold-wrapped SUCHARD bars streak before my eyes. They disappear just as I'm about to touch one. So, under the influence of my lust, I "borrow" Madame Vachette's keys from her desk and let myself into the pantry.

Quick! I scan labels: "Rice", "Sugar", "Beans", "Candy", "Coffee", "Pâtes" (pasta)… What else is stored on the top shelf? Flimsy, unmarked, rectangular grey cardboard boxes! I lift up on my toes and pull off a lid. My fingers tremble. Blindly I grab one — two — three — four — and more — red-brown tubes of ersatz-chocolate wrapped around white gooey sugar paste. I swallow one entire pound box. What starts as delicious ends as disgustingly sickening. I wipe my sticky fingers clean on my white petticoat. For two days I have to keep myself from walking bent over with stomach pain in order not to give myself away. My mother would have said: "You are meshugge!" Crazy. Had Madame Vachette found me inside her pantry, she could have fired me or reported me to the police. For days I feel isolated in my guilt.

The wartime food shortages and the avarice of Madame Vachette constrain Marie's best efforts to adequately feed the children and staff. She resorts to fillers. One day, I watch her from the kitchen threshold grind up livers, hearts, spleen, and sweetbreads in the Moulinex, stuff the mixture of organ meats into limp pork gut casings, and divide the grit with a tight knot into four-inch wigglies.

At lunch Marie serves her Wigglies on top of Raymond's potatoes mixed with rutabagas. After the meal, she enters the dining room and, hands rolled into her white apron, her pert little nose upward-turned in a self-congratulatory lift, she asks the children, "Did you enjoy my sausages?"

On Sundays, she molds the innards in gelatin and calls her creation: "À la mode de Caen."

My right arm begins to swell. For days it has felt strange. A slight touch of the fingertips leaves a deep watery dip in the flesh — white, yellow, red. It'll go away, I tell myself. But the swelling spreads all the way to the shoulder. My arm throbs and hangs by my side like a pendulum.

Quoi faire? I'm a teenager *sans asssurances et sans argent,* without insurance and without money. At the hospital, if I talk under anesthesia, I might reveal my real name.

A snapshot of Papa in his World War I uniform that I have seen many times appears in my mind. He once told me the story of suffering from blood poisoning, and I had asked him:

"Why, Papa, didn't you go to an infirmary?"

"Because you didn't know when you entered a field hospital if you would get out alive. Contagious diseases ran rampant."

And Papa made his own incision in his arm.

Ruck zuck! Get on with it!

Through the open balcony door in Ghis's room a fresh breeze is drifting down from the Prarion Mountain. My nostrils breathe in scents of earth, rocks, pine and wild flowers. In the mirror I see my elephantine arm hanging by my side. I cannot comb my hair. Two overlapping images arise in my mind: the first one of Papa's in

World War I — the second: Marguerite's swollen arm in World War II. Ruck zuck, right now! Let the pus spurt out! Cut into your flesh.

At the basin in Ghis's bathroom, I wash my hands, strike a match, and sear the large blade of my Swiss army pocket-knife Maman had offered me for my 12th birthday.

"Watch!" I call out to Ghis.

"Tu es folle! You are crazy!"

My fingers probe for a soft spot between the two small bones on top of the right wrist. The blade's point cuts through the epidermis, crosswise.

The pus streams out like toothpaste from a metal tube. At first it is yellowish and thick; then thinner and whitish. I press the right arm with my left hand from the shoulder downward until the plasma appears liquid and clear. It doesn't hurt. Quick! A piece of gauze, adhesive tape, and the wound is dressed.

Ghis isn't impressed. She says: "I would have gone and seen Doctor Tissot." The mark on top of my right wrist is a small souvenir of wartime home surgery.

Pleased with myself, I clean up the mess, re-sterilize the four blades of the red Swiss army knife with a match, and skip down the stairs to the boys' dorm.

"Bonjour, les enfants!"

Part II

(Winter 1943)

WINTER ARRIVES: a damp chill spreads from the mountains into the houses, and I catch a cold. The virus settles in my ears. This time I really need a doctor. I feel reluctant to go and see Doctor Tissot to whose office I often escort the children because I fear he might ask personal questions. What is that name etched into that brass plaque on the door of that chalet by the road further down on Mont Pacard, Doctor...?

Paillot!

I go to the post office during the rest period and call him. "Doctor, a lot of mucus is running down my nose, my ears hurt, I have difficulty breathing, and I have a fever. Could it be...?"

"Let's have a look," he answers in a gruff voice. At the appointed time I push into my Kandahar bindings and ski down to his chalet.

The doctor himself opens the door. In his residence on the first floor inside his dark pine paneled office, I sit down in a black barber-like reclining chair with arm rests. Doctor Paillot probes my nose.

"Polyps!" he says tersely.

"Polyps. Can I cure it myself?"

In his white coat, and with a square set country chin, he suggests *he* should perform the operation for the removal of the infected growth. "Your nasal passages are obstructed. It's a serious infection."

Already I had tried salt water sniffed out of my hollowed palm and Vicks-medicated steam inhaled from a cooking pot.

In the barber chair the light shines directly into my reclining face. To my right, four neatly arranged tools sparkle on a tray. The doctor wears rimless glasses on the tip of his nose.

"Bend your head all the way!" Doctor Paillot orders, and he picks up the nasal speculum.

AH, ANALYSIS! I say to myself, according to the latest acquired knowledge straight out of my *Philosophy 101* textbook Chapter One.

He sets the speculum down. Again he runs his fingers over the outside of the swollen nose bridge; he presses here, presses there...

AH, INDUCTION!

I follow the surgical procedure through the familiar principles of logic applied to the art of surgery. But invasive surgery involves live human cells.

The doctor spreads the blades of his scalpel.

Ouch!

His stubby fingers tug hard. Cells crack. Tissues tear.

159

Blood and pain run everywhere. Doctor Paillot curses.

"*Merde!* I can't see anything. Too much blood. Fuck!"

A click on the glass tray — an instrument plunked down.

Rough fingers push up two thick gauze packings into my bleeding nose. Too thick!

With my head bent backwards, I eye the white coat walking over to a massive dark country table; on it lays a heavy book bound in thick, brown leather that looks like a 14th century hand-lettered Bible. Dr. Paillot pulls a chair, sits down, and pores over the pages, face close to the script. In his white coat, rounded back, he resembles an alchemist out of the Middle Ages learning the secrets of a new formula. The doctor reads. While in an effort to overcome the pain, my brutalized brains dissociate and rise into a pure intellectual mode. I review the performance:

He felt, he sensed; he analyzed his perceptions. He inferred that the reddish lumps are polyps — good as far as analysis and induction go. The problem is in the execution — his rheumatic fingers can't hold the soft growth in his instrument's grip.

Dr. Paillot like many people in Saint-Gervais suffers from the rains, the winds, and the snows. "It's the weather" as the locals refer to arthritis. I know that, but I didn't know that my pain lessened because the nervous system can only handle one awareness at a time. My brain, engaged in the mental process of the operation, shut out the pain receptors.

Eye-glasses perched on the tip of his nose, the Doctor slowly walks over beside me. Fiercely he pulls his stool close. He picks up the curved scissors in one hand, the suction instrument in the other — and action begins.

Inside my nasal cavities, it's crr-pff-crr-pff. The sharp blades cut and the mini-Hoover sucks up cells and blood. My nose turns into a crick-crack torture-chamber. According to Chapter One, I expect a synthesis.

The smell of seared flesh enters my nostrils. AH, SYNTHESIS!

Doctor Paillot wipes the sweat off his brow with his left sleeve. "Done!" he exclaims. The wound is cauterized.

I follow the bloody white coat to a side-room. The shutters are closed, the greenish curtains frayed. There isn't even one old magazine on the low table. The doctor motions me to a couch. "Rest here in the waiting room for a while before you go home."

I sit on a threadbare brown and black plaid sofa where the cushions sag and the springs popped years ago. Maybe he told me what to do if the cotton wadding gets too bloody... I vaguely hear "Keep swelling down..." In the dimness, he apologizes for a lack of something... "Unavailable...!"

I remember thinking, "Don't worry about me, I'll be all right!" And I lost touch with it all.

An hour or so later I come to, stretched out on the uneven springs. Dazed, I try to rise to my feet. Papa and Maman will offer me shelter for the night at Chez Nous.

Thick, dry snowflakes whirl in the air and prickle my face. I set my poles into a V and shoulder my boards for the two-mile-trek up to Bionnay on the snow-compacted D 902.

At Chez Nous, I lean my skis and poles against the wall by the side entrance. Low clouds fog in the Bionnassay. Papa is at the sink scrubbing the laundry on an old fashioned metal washboard.

"Papa, where's Maman?"

"Up at Le Champel trading wine tickets for flour," he says, and he winks an eye.

"I'm going to sleep here tonight," Papa.

My father looks at my face. He sees the bloody wadding.

"Remove the pillow from the mattress and lie flat, there's a fine icicle hanging down from the shed's roof!" Papa says with a twinkle. I don't tell him I went to a country doctor and had polyps removed without the benefit of anesthesia "because morphine is unavailable." Papa knows, and he really isn't interested in details. He believes that, at eighteen, nature heals itself if given a chance. And it's wartime. *C'est la guerre!*

Standing tall over his scrubbing board, my father can't help blurt out what is dearest to his heart.

"The German lines have broken in the Ukraine."

Fact.

161

I break off the icicle and wrap the pieces in a towel. In my bed, I mold the ice pack to my face and pull the down quilt up to just below my chin.

Fact.

At dawn, after curfew, I walk down to Saint-Gervais.

I can't really eat my parents' scarce rations; I eat breakfast at Bonne Maman where Madame Vachette has right to my bread coupons.

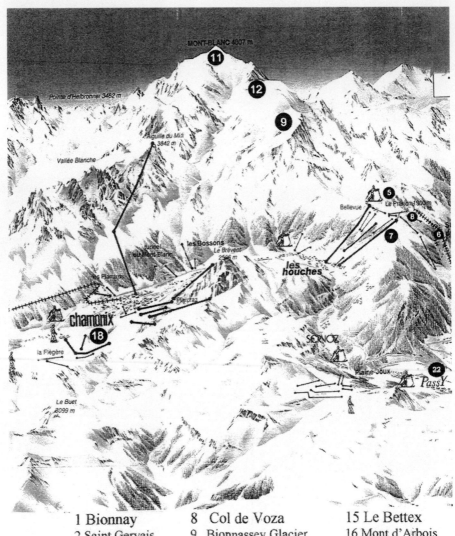

1 Bionnay	8 Col de Voza	15 Le Bettex
2 Saint Gervais	9 Bionnassey Glacier	16 Mont d'Arbois
3 Les Pratz	10 Dômes de Miage	17 Mégève
4 Le Fayet	11 Mont Blanc	18 Chamonix
5 Le Prarion	12 L'Aiguille du Goûter	19 Mer de Glace
6 Le Champel	13 Saint Nicolas de Veroce	20 Mont-Joly
7 Bionnassay	14 Les Contamines	21 Sallanches
		22 Passy

164

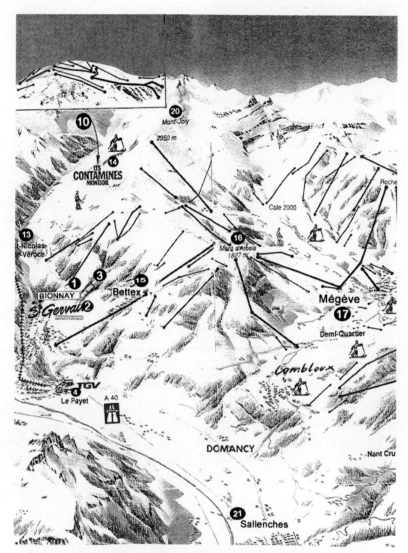

Au Pays du Mont-Blanc

Chapter 10

To the Summit of Mont Blanc

(August 18, 1943)

W hen summer finally arrived and storms at the higher altitudes were fewer, you could see in downtown Saint-Gervais two or three mountaineers walking in rhythmic cadence — each carrying a rucksack from which dangled an ice ax, crampons, and a carefully folded rope; sometimes a native son, nonchalantly balancing his piolet under the arm, led a trio. The sureness of their gait and the upward tilt of their heads set off in me a call for the wild.

Mont Blanc, 15,782-ft. high is the tallest mountain in Europe. I have seen the magnetic cupola shine in a golden blaze from the opposite slope of our valley, from atop Le Bettex. Its glacial mass and the beauty of its rounded shape are bewitching. To myself I say: 4,810-meter high Mont Blanc rises in the very same massif I live in, 10 miles away; there are no Nazi checkpoints in the higher regions. It's safe.

The locals affirm that there are only twenty climbing days in all of late July, August, and early September. "It depends on the *météo*, the meteorology."

The problem is my parents. Papa and Maman would forbid me to attempt the summit. Papa would say: "You have no birth certificate!" followed by a dry cough, the "No" being final and without appeal. Mother would pucker her lips and say: "Look at my white hair. You are a girl, a Jew under Hitler..." while I see myself scaling Mont Blanc. Now. This year. If others can do it, so can I! It is my opportunity. Mont Blanc is here. Prove your mettle. Measure yourself against the mountain!

166

So in secret I enroll Madame Perroud (our landlady), Madame Vachette (my employer), and the staff at Bonne Maman (Raymond and Marie) as accomplices.

Madame Perroud seated in her burgundy armchair by the window overlooking Mont d'Arbois calmly says: "I would entrust myself to Louis Viallet. Louis hasn't lost a client to the mountain, he'll bring you back." Graciously she offers to go and talk to Louis personally and, accustomed to seeing the young reach for one peak or another, she adds as an afterthought: "If I meet your parents in town, I won't broach the subject."

On Cloud 9 I float down the stairs of her apartment.

The following day on the red-tiled entrance of his farm rue la Toile, Louis Viallet — medium tall with brown hair — stands, legs apart.

"How fit are you?" he asks. And he looks me over from ankles to head.

On my fingers I count: Mont Joly (8,130), Arbois (6,000), the Prarion (6,045 feet), the Voza Pass, Le Bettex — "I climb up and down a goat path most days," I say. "On my day off I sometimes hop across a glacier."

I hold my back very straight.

I am eighteen.

"C'est bon!" he says. He has a client waiting in Saint-Nicolas-de-Véroce. "That will make a cordée of three."

Louis mentions the going rate and, in a black spiral notebook, writes down my name: Marguerite Lengel, Bonne Maman.

We shake hands.

"As soon as the météo is favorable, I will get in touch with you," he says pointing his chin in the direction of Mont Blanc: "We need at least two days of good weather. No wooly clouds over the peaks."

I didn't know then that I was about to climb Mont Blanc with a hero of the Resistance whose black spiral notebook contained much compromising information. Neither did I know that the Gestapo had the Viallet farm under surveillance nor that Louis

167

slept at night in a barn away from home. Daily I pass by the Bureau des Guides to see if Louis Viallet had left word for me.

On August 18 at 6:30 AM at the TMB, the Tramway to Mont Blanc station, I check one last time the contents of my rucksack while awaiting the arrival of my two *compagnons de cordée*.

I touch the mess kit, two pairs of wool socks, wool scarf, long underwear, two sweaters, extra mittens, soap, wash cloth, toothbrush, and the food. All are there. In the outer pockets are suntan lotion, sunglasses, first aid kit, Velpeau bandages, and toilet paper. From the rings of my belt dangle the Swiss Army knife and the ski mittens. Ice ax, cleats, and a metal drinking cup hang from the outer flaps of my backpack. I am wearing my ski outfit and boots.

Madame Vachette had granted me two days off work and promised not to leak a word to "Mlle Ghislaine..." My employer gave me precious foodstuff: twenty sugar cubes, a few pinches of tea, two chicken legs, an egg, prunes, carrots, half a boule of bread, a hunk of Tomme de Savoy cheese, and one entire pack of biscuits LULU! "Here Mademoiselle Lengel, you need strength up there," she had said. Later I reflect that perhaps the essence of helpfulness is ultimately to be responsible for someone else's life, bring a small measure of comfort, and assist in making a dream come true.

I check my watch. In thirty minutes or so, we'll be on our way. The TMB (the highest cogwheel train in Europe) takes us to Eagle's Nest at 7,350 feet.

Jean Marie Dix arrives trim and fit; he wears heavy horn-rim glasses over a fine oval face. Professorial. Louis Viallet is clad in full alpine regalia of green wool socks and knickers; a plaid flannel shirt rolled up at the sleeves shows off his tanned muscular arms.

It's 7:28 AM, the TMB rattles around the last bend. It can't come too soon. We grab our backpacks by the shoulder straps, the conductor blows his whistle, the TMB jerks into motion, when at the end of the platform I see a silhouette running... The female yells and waves an urgent arm...

"Missed, too bad!" exclaims Dix with Gallic humor. I freeze. I know the figure.

As the engine cogs into the pine and hemlock forest, I swallow hard and join Dix singing "La Haut sur la Montagne..."— a popular French folk song. "Up there on the mountain..."—

In thirty minutes the TMB stops at the 5,450 feet high Voza Pass where the wide expanse lets us see the Swiss Valais Oberland in the distance.

At Bellevue, a couple of climbing parties from Chamonix board the train with ice axes, crampons, and rope attached to heavy backpacks. We hang onto the overhead leather straps.

On the left, the TMB is scraping the mountainside; on the right, an abyss plummets straight down.

Past 5,700 feet, we enter a region of stark rocks and scrawny juniper trees. Dix points to a low cement structure on barren Mont Lachat.

"*Tiens*, a blockhouse up here!" Dix says to Louis.

Louis looks elsewhere, as if he had not heard.

Dix repeats "What's a cement–like structure doing up here?"

Silence.

The secret of Mont Lachat is revealed one year later in chapter 18.

Seated on a wooden bench, face glued to the window, I watch the snow melts rage into the narrow Gorge de la Gruvaz as patches of blue poke through the dissipating mists.

Further along, the broad cirque of Bionnassay opens up bathed in an early morning alpenglow; red, yellow, and orange. Topsy-turvy blocks of unstable ice lie all about.

At Eagle's Nest, the Tramway du Mont Blanc discharges its mountaineers.

"Where is Mont Blanc?"

"There!"

"Where?"

"Behind Tacul! Behind the Goûter!" My legs quiver like a filly's about to be released for a run.

From the start, I love this mineral wilderness. It spills eternity.

In the valley one believes a glacier is quiet. Up here, one hears a continuous rumble of cracking ice breaking off and crashing.

I rub my face with snow. The cold flakes burn my skin. Delicious! Small finches twitter happily on narrow patches of ice found between two boulders. Twick, twick. Beyond, an alpine chouca cries its plaintive screech. Hrafn, Hrafn.

Louis outlines the plan for the ascent: "Today, we'll climb via the Cabine Forestière, the refuge de Tête Rousse (10,292 ft.), and up the Dôme du Goûter. We'll spend the night at the 12,554 ft. high refuge." Atop his boulder, he looks at Dix, at me and, plaid-shirted sleeves rolled up to his elbows, he says with a dare in his voice:

"Tomorrow, the summit!"

"En route! Let's go!"

At a bend, our guide turns about and sets down the rules of the climb. "No hurrying, no falling back, keep a steady pace. No slowing to admire the blue sky or the shapes of the clouds. Set your foot into my tracks. Do not stop to drink. Water makes you thirsty. In the mountains we conserve energy!" He says all this very authoritatively.

The order of the file is Louis, I, and Dix at the rear. Knees bent in rhythmic cadence we round narrow ledges.

I follow the rules until my curiosity breaks loose and admires the blue, purple, pink lights playing on an ice mass. "Mademoiselle pay attention to my footprints," is the immediate rebuke.

After about three hours of serious trekking on rock, shale and slate below the layer of permanent ice, Louis calls, "Casse-croûte!"

Near Tête Rousse under limpid blue skies, we break bread against the backdrop of Mont Blanc. The noon sun seems to stand still above in an azure firmament. Yellow rays shine on what looks like a vast three-dimensional topographic full-scale model of the Alps in relief seen from above. All about, an infinite expanse is filled with jagged needles and ice-covered domes.

Seated on a rock to the left of Dix's boulder, I look up and see him cut slices of salami with his pocket knife. He tells us he is a professor of geology at the Lycée Saint-Louis in Paris. He's taking a leave of absence to be with his wife who has a bladder problem. A bladder problem? That young!

170

Louis is taciturn.

Dix says, "The ice cap is life-giving. The Alps are a watershed for the Rhine, the Rhône, the Pô, the Danube, the..." No one is paying attention to an 18-year-old girl climber. I bond with Les Drus, la Blanche, les Grandes Jorasses and a dozen other jutting peaks all bathed in a vivid light. La Verte points her rocky needles straight into the sky. Though the highest of all the peaks, Mont Blanc's glaciated rounded head is less dramatic.

Dix eats his salami. Louis salts his egg. I examine some shiny specks of quartz, feldspar, and mica encrusted in a piece of granite.

Dix points to les Aiguilles Rouges, L'Aiguille du Midi, and says, "Results of the collision! When the tectonic plates collided, the crust of the earth lifted northeasterly upward into a series of folds. It all happened about forty-million years ago."

Dix calls it the Alpine-Himalayan upheaval. "The great upheaval stretched from the Rif Mountains of Morocco to beyond the Himalayas."

"The field of slate we crossed?"

"Once a sea covered the entire area leaving deep layers of sediments. Shale turns into slate under heat and pressure. Slate is nothing but compressed and compacted seashells with well defined cleavage lines."

In the whole geological chain of events, the element I am most knowledgeable about is the hot magma cooking with minerals. When hot magma erupts and cools, it turns into quartz. In the Alps, quartz is pink, transparent, and prism- shaped. You see Alpine Crystal de Roche for sale in Saint-Gervais' gift shop windows.

Louis leaves and returns with a bunch of edelweiss in his hand. Edelweiss! I want to go and find my own rare, white woolly-prism-shaped-small-yellow-flower-heads near a boulder.

"Don't start looking!"

We pick up the garbage. I adjust the straps of my rucksack, and put some precious lumps of sugar into the pockets of my jacket. Louis takes his ice ax in hand.

"En route!"

The wind tousles my hair, the sun warms my face.

At a couloir, Louis orders: "Make a dash for it!" First he, then I, race across the corridor. Dix barely reaches the opposite side when an avalanche of loose rocks comes crashing down. Our guide winces. "En route!"

Louis probes for snow bridges with his piolet.

"Step exactly into the little round holes I make in front of you!" He points his ice ax at his footprints.

I'm aware that the physical challenges I'm meeting exceed my needs. Yet up here I'm experiencing the freest moments of my existence.

In the afternoon sun, the snow takes a hard pink tinge. I put on my hat, scarf, sweater, and mittens. The rope binds us together at midriff. I seek out the little round holes ahead of me, the little round holes... I'm exhausted. Mechanically, I step into the little round holes...

The endless slope of the Dôme du Goûter devours my energy. Gravity pulls me downward while I struggle, for how many hours? Upward a steep, endless sheet of ice! The weight of my body, the rucksack, and the lack of oxygen drain me. Louis must have sensed my fatigue, for he gestures with his piolet in the direction of something stuck to the side of the Aiguille du Goûter. "*On y est!*" he calls out. "We are there!"

One hour later!

One-Two, one two...

"Salut à tous!

"Salut!" answers a voice from within the darkness.

Louis, Dix and I hang our ice picks on nails by the door. Inside the smoke-filled room I make straight for a wooden bench by the table; head on arm, I plop down. Vaguely, I see our guide melting small amounts of snow on his Bunsen burner. Vaguely I hear: "On mange! Let's eat!" Without appetite I force myself to chew on a drumstick. I sip sugared tea. Seated on the bench, Louis, Dix and I and the others eat and drink in a worn out-silence.

"Fatiguée? Tired?" inquires an older, more benevolent guide.

I blink.

Louis and his peers talk shop. "Powder's fresh above 13,400...
Ice lies below six inches of snow..." In the sudden heat inside the
refuge, the clipped language of the guides comes and fades away
as a soothing hum.

Dreamlike I listen to the noises of soup spoons hitting metal
plates. Tumblers clank. The scrape of steel-rimmed shoes against
the wooden floor resonates in my rib cage. The stretcher fastened
to the ceiling sways its long shadows against the walls; an all-
weather lamp weakly lights the interior. The cabin creaks in the
wind.

A second mug of hot sugared tea.

After dinner, seated on the bench, back against the wooden
wall, I tear a length of thread and match-flame a needle by the
glow of the lamp. I leave a length of thread under the collapsed
skin of the blisters for drainage and slip on clean white socks for
the night. The Scout tends to her feet.

Where do we go to the toilet? Brush teeth? Wash face? Decades
later, I can't say. In 1943 the refuge du Goûter consists of a one-
room dormitory-kitchen fastened to the granite of the Aiguille du
Goûter with copper cables. The shelter built of wood
accommodates maximum twenty climbers overnight. Each body
occupies a two foot wide space on the sleeping platforms set up on
the floor.

In the forties, backpacks have no frames. My crêpe soled,
leather-upper, ski–walking boots are porous. In winter, down in the
valley, I normally wrap my feet in newspaper — on the climb to
Mont Blanc, the paper freezes. In Saint-Gervais, I regularly stuff
paper under my sweaters to keep my lungs warm. *C'est la guerre!*

Our cordée sleeps on straw-filled burlap sacks set on the lower
planks. Fully clothed, rolled up in a blanket like a mummy, I
stretch out between Louis and Dix. The wind batters against the
shutters. Through a small window the stars twinkle in the black
sky.

Suddenly curses fill the cabin. Spats of *merdes* (fucks)... and
damn it... spew out on the upper bunks. A cordée of four bad-
mouthed females spit out their attention-getting wrath. For a

moment they succeed in waking us up. On the lower planks the tension crackles, but the men hold their tongues. Louis stretched out next to me, snickers. I'm furious at the odious women.

It's 3:00 AM. The alarm clock rings. Get up! Put on two pairs of socks. Pull the second sock tight over the first one to avoid creases. Remove the wet paper from your boots and wrap your feet in dry newspaper. I lace up my stiff, frozen boots.

We fold blankets, check ice picks and cleats. Steel-edged shoes jar the wooden floor. Louis goes outside to get fresh snow. By the light of a miner's lamp, we drink hot sugared tea, and eat bread with Tomme de Savoie. I put the last sugar lumps into my jacket pocket. Louis folds his Bunsen.

Dix and I, seated on a bench, fasten the steel spiked crampons to our shoes. Louis stands over us and watches his clients cinch the cleats as tight as they will go. "Pull the leather straps all the way! I am not going to freeze my fingers out there if they come loose," he gruffs.

Off and on, I'm still at the one-room refuge du Goûter suspended over a two-mile-high void. Vitality and joie de vivre, curses and adventure, freedom, anticipation — oozed out of the climbers amidst some of nature's most hostile elements.

Louis by the door casually lifts his backpack onto his shoulders, grabs his ice ax off the hook and, holding a flickering miner's lamp in his mittened hand, calls out:

"R'voir à tous!"

Outside, the 4:00 AM glacial night is pitch black. The exposed skin on my face pricks. In his left hand the light from the miner's lamp flutters. The translucent chips spark and fly as Louis cuts steps into the ice.

We are three tiny ants crawling up the glaciated, steep Dome of Goûter; twenty feet ahead, Louis is barely visible. The wind snarls.

One-two! One-two! Breathe! Blow! In the frigid temperatures of the unpolluted nitrogen and rare oxygen, I listen to the clear crystalline cracks of my cleats piercing the ice.

After three hours, a sudden blast of wind brings me to my knees. The fine dry crystals of a northern gale, *la couce,* strike my

174

goggles. Stiff ski mittens try to clear the glasses and instead smear the lenses. I wipe them with a clean spot from the underside of my jacket sleeve. To combat the numbness in my hands and feet, I move my fingers inside my mittens and wiggle my toes.

The sun's early rays shimmer cold on Mont Blanc.

Louis passes his flask of hot sugared tea around. I'd never tasted tea before in my life! Quickly he retrieves and closes the canteen.

"En route!" (Standing in the cold stiffens limbs).

Breathe deeper and faster than in the valley below. Deeper... faster... I repeat to myself.

Air! Air!

Crossing a saddle, Louis is sucked waist deep. He plants his piolet on the far side and, propping himself up against the wind, he pulls me then Dix roped together — through.

When I get to the spot where Mont Blanc stood, it's not there. The wind whistles sharply. But I saw the summit! It was there! I even tried to quicken my step! I am sure.

Later I learn that the magic trick of the disappearing summit is the same as the mirage travelers experience in the desserts. The phenomenon is caused by alternate layers of hot and cool air distorting the light.

The horizon is getting lower and lower.

After the next turn we trek on a narrow spine less than fifteen feet wide swept clean of snow.

Air. Air.

Louis disappears. Did he fall? Yet the rope around my waist tugs gently. Where is he? There! in the fog trekking in slow cadence on a narrow ledge around another bend. Curiously, the wind loses its sharp whistle.

Abruptly, my head and my body stick out. Nothing to the right, nothing to the left, and nothing behind; in front: a void.

Louis is here!

I align next to him. Dix steps up by my side.

We three are standing on the roof top of Europe.

Icicles hang from Dix's brows, a fluff of frozen frost glistens around his mouth. In a halting voice he says: "Wh...ere... ees Switzer...land...? I...ta...ly?" Louis points in the direction of an imaginary Jungfrau, Monte Rosa, and the Matterhorn — all are fogged in!

The last thought that enters my mind as I gently slide into the snow remains with me. *Oh God, please let me sleep for just one minute.*

"Oh, no you don't!" And someone yanks me up to my feet.

Thus, arms around each other's waist, we stand, Louis (the covert resister) and I (the secret Jewish girl), on August 19, 1943 about 11:00 AM on the summit of Mont Blanc at 15,782 ft.

We stay a minute or two. Then Louis moves to the rear ready to break his cordée for the descent.

At the refuge du Goûter, the caretaker teases: "Oxygen's rare up there!"

My high spirits had returned (with air in my lungs). I tease him back:

"No problem. I made it."

"Any view?"

"Clear. All the way to the Jungfrau!"

Past the Dome of Goûter, free, unroped, I cast my eyes back at Mont Blanc glistening in the light. I linger.

"En route!" calls Louis.

Swift clouds pass the sun and skirt Mont Blanc's icy flanks.

At the upper edge of a steep snow field Louis grips the long handle of his piolet with both hands. He sets the steel pick between his legs and, body bent backwards on a one seat T-bar, he speed-sleds downhill in a whirl of fresh snow. The powder might have been three feet deep; it spits above his head. My turn. In a white backlit spray, I sled downhill. I exult awash in speed, golden light, and backlit snow.

Rucksacks bouncing on our backs, wind filling the open flaps of our anoraks, Louis and Dix and I schuss over fields of slippery slate all the way past the Cabine Forestière.

"Winged Victory!" exclaims, Dix.

At Nid d'Aigle, the orange and white TMB sits on the tracks awaiting the 6:30 PM departure. Our cordée is early.

Elated, exhausted, I sprawl out on the flat-topped granite boulder. Trails of vapor propelled by hot, late afternoon updrafts undulate along the base of the Bionnassay.

Head against my backpack, I close my eyes. I realize that my lungs had met the challenge of sparse oxygen, and the weight of my body had defied gravity.

Erect on the granite boulder next to me, Dix declaims poetry. The image of the last line: "When chaos dies and resurrects for the night," reminds me of the Germans below. Up here, for two days, irrelevant had been Hitler and Vichy. For the first time in years, gone was the war. — Mont Blanc is a fort stronger than any army.

When Louis, Dix, and I finally sit on a wooden bench of the TMB for our trip down to the valley, small talk is unthinkable.

On the hard pounded dirt platform at the station in Saint-Gervais, I shake hands with Louis and Dix.

"R'voir."

"R'voir, Louis. Merci."

With reluctance I leave my cordée.

Back at Bonne Maman, Ghis, seated on my bed in my room on my yellow blanket told me she had found out my trip's destination was not Chambéry (the capital of the Savoy) — when she had inspected my closet and seen that my sweaters and ski outfit were missing in August. "I arrived at the station to take you off the tram just as the TMB left."

I shrugged.

The next morning, Madame Vachette and I meet by chance Papa and Maman on the cobbles downtown in front of Le Café du Mont Blanc. Papa is carrying a small knapsack on his shoulders, Maman is wearing her chic little gray felt hat. The four of us stand on the uneven pavement. Maman puckers her mouth; she slightly shakes her head at me. Papa cuts a stiff upper lip. They speak to

Madame V. as if I didn't exist. My employer defends the culprit. "Oh, Madame Lengel, you must forgive her. It's a great feat," then excuses herself. The Lombard baroque church at my back, the old stone fountain to my right, I face le Dôme du Miage aglow in the sun. It hides "my" Mont Blanc.

I feel I have wrestled with the big One, with myself, and won. No one can take my victory away.

"Well, if you disapprove, I don't care, I'm not coming to see you at Chez Nous for six weeks," I say. And I walk away.

That night I write into my diary: "My achievements are obtained more and more against the will of my parents." The awareness astonishes me: the image of the separate being.

The locals tell you that from Chamonix via the Grands Mulets the climb to the summit is easier; from Saint-Gervais by way of the Dome of Goûter more interesting. The attempt from the Italian side is more perilous. Whichever, every year the Great White One claims several victims. Louis Viallet lost his oldest son to the mountain.

Chapter 11

Identity Card 00736

(Winter 1943)

I keep my resolve. After seven weeks: I will just push the rear door open to the kitchen at Chez Nous as if nothing unusual had happened, and say, Bonjour! I tell myself in secret, my independence firmly established.

The wildly high Glacier of Bionnassay and the Dome of Miage glisten that morning in the sun's rays, yellow, orange and red. When, all of a sudden by the wire fence at the *Centrale d'Eléctricité* on the D 902 downstream from chalet "Chez Nous", I see four uniforms.

What Wehrmacht soldiers?

They seem to be summit-gazing. They pay scant attention to a girl with a rucksack on her shoulders and wooden-soled shoes passing them by on the way to Bionnay. I nonchalantly think: they are here. It's all part of the Occupation. So far we had seen no Germans in our "petit coin." In Saint Gervais, two miles away, I had spotted none. No one had mentioned at the boulangerie that the entire Italian garrison in Sallanches had been taken prisoner in their barracks and put to work for the Third Reich. No one knows anything outside their little corner, or dares speak about it. Too dangerous.

In Bionnay, with butterflies in my stomach, I push the kitchen door at Chez Nous open. Maman stands by the stove; she looks ashen. Without a preamble, she blurts out "Marguerite, THEY moved in by night. In the morning they were here."

In the same intimate tone as if she had seen me just yesterday, Mother says: "Papa heard on the BBC that because of a secret armistice signed between Marshall Badoglio and General

179

Eisenhower after the Allies landed at Salerno in Italy on September 3, the Germans at once occupied — besides Rome and the North of Italy — the Haute-Savoie and seven French frontier departments bordering Switzerland and Italy."(All eight departments had been under an — to us — invisible Italian administration.) Maman ads: "Clovis Perroud (a foreman at the plant) thinks the Germans fear sabotage; they are guarding all the power plants." *They* granted Clovis Perroud a business pass to visit at Chez Nous, but refused one to his brother who doesn't rent out his half of the chalet.

The Germans now effectively control the access to the entire region upstream from the dam, the forbidden Alpine Frontier Zone with Switzerland and Italy that includes "Chez Nous."

Although the location of chalet Chez Nous is INSIDE the restricted *Alpensperrzone* and thus confers de facto resident status on its inhabitants — Jews and foreigners are specifically barred from taking up residence therein.

So far, during our nine months stay in Bionnay, the Italians had not enforced the exclusion rule. Rising in the morning, we knew we were quasi-safe if we act "normal" according to the local code of behavior, and if we keep our identity secret: no one had checked papers.

Bad news.

After the first flurry of excitement, the daily rhythm of village life takes back over: Monsieur Dave keeps on selling cigarettes, matches and stamps in his Bureau de Tabac on the first floor of his grey stucco house opposite Chez Nous. In the evening, Chapellan drives his cows from the pasture to his home on the rue de Bionnay around the bend of our chalet; always his long stick comes down hard on their backs. Waoh! Waoh! Early morning, Joe Barzat collects the five-gallon shiny milk cans set out along the D 902 by the curb in Bionnay, Les-Bernards, and Les Pratz. He hauls the milk from the feeder hamlets to the co-operative by Devil's Bridge in Saint-Gervais. To Papa, Barzat mostly talks about the weather.

At Chez Nous, Papa tends to his chores. He does housework in his blue denim apron. Once a week, my red-haired Alsatian father energetically treks on the departmental road down to Saint-Gervais, knapsack on his shoulders, navy beret set at a jaunty angle. In town he visits the library, pays utility bills and, at the boucherie, buys his and Maman's weekly rations of eight combined ounces of meat. Emile Delachat, the friendly butcher, regularly says: "Here's for *une bonne soupe,* a good soup," while he wraps a piece of marrow-bone in a crumpled paper for his loyal customer, Monsieur Lengel. At home Papa unpacks the hacked piece of marrow-bone, proudly shows it to Maman, and reports Monsieur Delachat's kind words. As always, after dinner, Papa smokes a cigarette. I continue to carry around with me the image of Papa's tobacco pleasure.

After his work is done, and the dishes are put away, my father sits down at the dining table in a relaxed mood, his tobacco pouch to the right, the pack of white cigarette paper to the left. He tears a thin sheet off, sets it flat before him on the table top, takes a pinch from the pouch of tobacco that to me looks like sawdust, and spreads the bits delicately on the paper. He rolls the limp stick between finger and thumb, and then wets the length of the sheet with the tip of his tongue. I think: There is more paper than *tabac* in this cigarette. Even so, Papa saves a few shreds of tobacco and rolls a weekly *Gauloise* for Monsieur Barzat. "Tomorrow morning, I'll give it to him," he says. Papa always looks content and happy as he sets the milkman's "cigarette" on the buffet. My father exhales slowly like a king.

Our non-threatening coexistence with the Germans comes abruptly to an end in the second week of November.

Whereas previously the sentinels stood guard down the road at the Centrale d'Eléctricité, one night they seek shelter under the balcony at Chez Nous because of the cold rains mixed with snow and the blustering gusts sweeping down the alpine peaks.

On my weekly Thursday visit, Maman, white as a bed sheet, says: "Marguerite, they spent the night under our roof!"

"Where Maman?"

"There!"

181

And Mother points her chin at her bedroom window fronting on the D 902. "I found cigarette butts and two candy wrappers this morning in the flower bed."

Enters Papa.

Facing the same danger, Papa and Maman, here in their bedroom before their offspring — bare the mainsprings of their opposite temperaments in a memorable duet.

Maman, anxiety dripping down her face, voices her alarm. "Papa listens to the BBC every night at nine-thirty."

Papa, in the middle of his Savoyard room — as if the Wehrmacht's presence under his roof were unthreatening — cuts a boyish grin from ear to ear. "They, too, should hear the truth!"

"Albert!" exclaims Maman horrified.

Albert, mischief in his voice, teases his mate about the benefits of enlightenment. "How else will they know of the Allied victory in Sicily and southern Italy?"

"Albert!" remonstrates Maman.

"Do you think their papers tell them that the Russians have recaptured Kiev?"

Maman makes another attempt at seriousness. "Albert, how can you make fun of them? They are dangerous!"

"I bet they don't know that the Free French have liberated Corsica and captured the entire German garrison."

Albert gloats; he enjoys the attention. Maman looks out their bedroom window and shakes her head, but a tiny smile appears at the corners of her mouth. Papa always knows how to make Maman smile. I am the audience. I listen to Papa and Maman's verbal exchange. I hear his vivacissimo answer her trembling phrase, and I think: If I have an optimistic streak in me, it's that I'm Albert's daughter.

But beneath the humor, common sense and practical prudence are deeply ingrained in Papa's character. From the second night on of harboring Wehrmacht soldiers under his roof, Papa listens to the BBC's 9:30 PM program: *"Ici Radio Londres..."* with his head tucked under two blankets instead of one.

The weather worsens. The fierce alpine gales arrive. The Germans seek shelter from the snow drifts under the balcony at Chez Nous by day and by night. To enter or exit our chalet, we must pass them by.

Mother's collective Jewish memory tries to inculcate subservience into me. "Marguerite, you must greet Erika," she says.
"Erika?"
Erika is a big chunk of a girl who lives with old André Chapellan in the center of the hamlet in a two-room stone house along with their cattle for warmth. Erika is German. She takes in and washes laundry at the public lavoir in the village. I see her shuffle about Bionnay in wooden clogs under a long, dirty denim apron. En famille, Maman, who is rather strict when it comes to sex, bestows the German pejorative *"Hur"* on Erika. It's "Erika-die-Hur!"
"Me, greet that slut? *Jamais!"* I reply.
"Marguerite, please do it for my sake."
"Why?"
"German soldiers visit her!"
"How do you know?"
"I have seen them go off singly in direction of her house on the rue de Bionnay with that certain look...Yesterday, one of them marched by our garden, the fly of his pants open." Mother blushes.
I try to keep a serious mien, not laugh at my mother, but the image of Aryan warriors marching in single file, the flap of their pants open, makes me burst.
"Don't be haughty, Marguerite," pleads Maman. "Erika might inform on us if she feels slighted. Please, greet her."
Never! Absolutely!
That evening, upstream from the power station on the D 902, heavy set Erika-with-the-large-feet-and-the-shuffling-gait trudges up to Bionnay, a basket of dirty laundry balanced on her hip. I am walking downstream back to Bonne Maman. We cross paths. Past

Erika-the-Whore I march, straight ahead like the heron in LaFontaine's fable scoffing at the minnows: Better fare is due me!

Within a month I wish I had greeted Erika. Because —

Thursday afternoon on the D 902, returning to work from a visit to my parents, I noticed that the weight of the rucksack on my shoulders felt lighter. Much lighter. What did I leave out? You didn't! Forget the homework of your pupils? Go and get it, Marguerite!

On the footpath around the chalet I pass the four Wehrmacht. They slack off under our roof. One leans against the wall on a leg, his second foot folded under his long coat, his bored eyes yawning at the summits; the other three seem equally relaxed. Although they are not the blue-eyed Aryan zealot type — they are smaller, thinner, you can detect flat feet; boots and clothing several sizes too large — in spite of their seemingly harmless state, the ill-fitted ones do their duty.

They hunt down Jews. And I, for one instant, forgot that they are the hunters, and I, the hunted.

Just as I'm about level with them, the first one says to his companions with dry humor in his voice: *"Was man nicht im Kopf hat, hat man in den Füssen!"*

Off-guard, focused on nothing in particular, "What one hasn't in the head, one has in the feet" makes me laugh. Oh terror! They stare at me. Fear travels down my spine.

At Chez Nous, Papa and Maman sit peacefully at the dining table. Awful, Marguerite, awful! My blood throbs through my ears. Dear God in Heaven, what have I done? Marguerite, you gave your parents away!

Outside, on the snow-covered slate path, I walk past the Germans, head high, chin set, and looking straight at Mont d'Arbois in the distance. No one is going to sense that I'm afraid!

If ever I had had too high an opinion of myself since climbing Mont Blanc, I quickly lost my hubris. Here, on the D 902, I reproach myself: how could you lose control? I prick the soft fold between thumb and index with my nails — the sharp sting brings tears to my eyes, but I don't wince. Look, Marguerite, you can withstand pain... I harden myself not to talk under torture. One didn't really know how one would behave under torture. One heard rumors... I want to be able to withhold that my name is Lévy. I can train myself!

In dire need of help on the road between Bionnay and Saint-Gervais, I imagine the soldiers asking Erika (during sex, of course) "Do you know the people who live in that chalet at the corner?" And Erica answering, they are nice folks, don't touch them! If only I had greeted Erica!

At Bonne Maman, time goes by slowly. Whenever the doorbell rings I peek through the curtains. Are they coming for me?

A week or two later at the tobacco shop, Marcel Dave breaks out into a jovial grin. "By the way, Mademoiselle Marguerite, the Krauts came to inquire why you understood German. I told them you are from Alsace. They seemed satisfied." Marcel Dave's face expressed the self-pride of a man who had covered for a friend.

Inside the dim tobacco concession, amidst the smells of Gauloises (the national brand of French cigarettes) and sulfur tipped match boxes, a weight lifted off my shoulders as if someone had removed a block of granite. Thank you, Monsieur Dave! Thank you for my family's lives.

I don't say one word to my parents.

Sometimes I clamber into the hayloft at Chez Nous, and look out through the half-moon shaped window at the downstream valley road all the way to the hydro-electric station and see what I can see. On that day I saw Jacques Ibert, the famed composer of *Divertissement* and *Persée,* a recipient of the Prix de Rome, out with his Schnauzer on their constitutional. *Tiens,* he is being stopped by the Wehrmacht at the mesh fence. They are asking for his papers. They are shaking their heads, and the composer is turning on his heels. I don't need to be told they are checking papers of people entering the FORBIDDEN ALPINE FRONTIER ZONE. What if they stop Maman and see "née Oppenheimer, Gemmingen, Germany" on her ID card, what then?

That evening, we three clandestines sit around the dining table. We are thinking, *quoi faire?* What can we do? Née Oppenheimer born in Gemmingen, Baden, has to go. But how? My connections with the Scout movement are cut. We know of no other link to false papers. I reflect, What would an ordinary St.Gervolaine do if she needed a new ID? She would go and see her *Monsieur le maire*, but no one of us has ever met — What is his name...? My mother is afraid. "If the mayor refuses, I will have no papers at all!"

Yes, I say to myself, I'll go. And I will do the other thing too... The thing we have decided on. To Papa, I say: "I can do it."

IT IS DECEMBER 15, 1943. The Alps shine in the full splendor of a perfect white winter day.

Before noon in his office at city hall in downtown Saint-Gervais, Monsieur le maire Conseil shakes hands with Emile Delachat and Clovis Perroud (two constituents of his) and Maman and me. The mayor is a medium-stout man with weary brown eyes. His lids betray his fatigue.

"What can I do for you?" he says.

And he motions Maman and me to the two straight chairs opposite his desk. Emile Delachat (the butcher), and Clovis Perroud (our landlord) stand behind us — berets in hand.

I am here to help an elderly mother. At forty-eight, Maman looks older because of the war. She also speaks French with as strong a German accent as Henry Kissinger.

It is 11:30 AM. Dressed in my ski outfit, I ooze respect toward authority.

"*Monsieur le maire*," I say in a sweet voice, "yesterday my mother fell in the snow walking up to Le Champel to get our bread rations, snow must have entered her coat pocket..."

(I produce Maman's ID card).

Blots of illegible ink.

Monsieur Conseil picks up the blotched paper.

"*Oui... en effet!*"

"*Oui, Monsieur le maire.*"

186

Non-committal, the mayor looks at his two friends, Clovis and Emile. They both nod.

Briefly, he glances again at the snow-laundered document. The hands on the wall clock show twenty minutes before twelve. The mairie closes at noon. Time is running out. It must not go the other way.

The mayor shrugs. His tired face is drawn. He hesitates.

Slowly, he unlocks the top right-hand drawer of his desk, takes out a blank ID card, and lays it on top of the bureau. "Let's start!" he says.

Surname? — "LENGEL."

Fleetingly I think, What's in a surname? Life or death is in a surname!

Maiden name? — "SCHMIDT."

"Née Schmidt" is the maiden name we chose for Maman around the kitchen table at Chez Nous. For my mother it will do nicely. Schmidt is a good German sounding name, easy to remember and common as sour Kraut.

First name? — "MARTHE"

Profession? — "Without"

Birthplace? — I spell GEMMINGEN for the mayor.

Quickly I add: "It's in the Bas-Rhin, Alsace, *Monsieur le maire.*" (Say "Baden, Germany," and you write a ticket for deportation; say "Alsace," and you give a chance to your mother).

The mayor writes down all the data as I tell him.

Nationality? — "French. Of course."

To the question, PREVIOUS DOMICILE? I answer: "75 BOULEVARD MALESHERBES, PARIS," to better lose our tracks. The Boulevard being a beehive of Paris city dwellers.

A difficulty arises with the line "Proof of identity." Maman has no livret de famille, no birth certificate. Nothing. At this instant, Mother is undocumented. Maman looks pale. Monsieur le maire Conseil leans back into his armchair. Above him the stern image of Marshal Pétain looks down over his shoulder. For a moment the mayor stares into his boss' eyes. He rubs his chin with the right hand. If he wavered at all between his oath of allegiance and his

187

heart, he speedily resolves the dilemma. Below, and very close to the line "*Pièces justificatives produites*, proof of identity" he writes in a fine hand: "In residence at Bionnay."

The other vital statistics: Color of eyes — Hair — Height — Forehead — Eyebrows — Mouth — are his choices. He is generous; he describes Maman as having a rectiligne nose.

Time for the signature.

Maman looks whiter by the minute. Messieurs Clovis Perroud and Emile Delachat are the witnesses. They have known Marthe Lengel, née Schmidt, for months. Maman signs her name. I stare at the puddle of water that forms around my boots on the wood floor in the mayor's office. The ice is melting fast.

Now fingerprinting.

Maman's index-tips get inked. She rolls her lines and whorls on the ink pad; physically she lays claim to her false identity. Mother is near fainting; she bites her lips to hold on.

It's five minutes before noon. The mayor hits the document with a series of dull plunk, plunks — rituals the French are so fond of. Eight times he formalizes the document with his stamp set. This punctilious public servant now holds up the card to his eyes. A frown appears on his brow. What now?

"Ah, Bionnay, it's inside the prohibited Alpine frontier zone! I better make a note of it," he says calmly.

I fold my hands on my lap and watch Monsieur le maire Conseil write in a neat penmanship in French and in red ink:

"*Zone réservée alpestre.*"

The mayor knows that the Germans are methodical. The document must be perfect. "Ah, I better stamp it in German as well...!" he says.

And he turns the carrousel round and round for yet another rubber stamp. He selects an ink pad color purple, and, plunks *Alpensperrzone* above BIONNAY in purple ink.

By now Maman's new ID card looks like a piece of period op art. Red, blue, purple, and black seals set against a white background. I am fascinated to watch a local mayor help defeat the enemy. All within the norms of the present-day political culture.

The two hands on the grandfather clock point to twelve.

Lunchtime. The mayor rises; everybody rises.

"Merci, Monsieur le maire."

"A votre service, M'dames, Messieurs."

An assembly of five has just created Identity 00736 using a blank, rubber stamps, colored ink pads, and a heart. We shake hands.

Outside on the sidewalk Maman and I thank Emile Delachat and Clovis Perroud. The butcher touches his navy beret, and protests: "Avec plaisir, Mesdames." — "In these difficult times, we have to help one another," replies our landlord when thanked, "it is the least we can do," and he sets his navy beret back on his head.

An officially issued, false ID card now belongs to Maman, the only one in the family. I still see the mayor on the back of my eyelids when I go to sleep because all I want to do is thank him.

Under white trails of clouds crisscrossing the blue sky, Maman and I trek home to Bionnay on the freshly plowed D 902. We pass two Wehrmacht officers walking downstream. One holds a powerful Alsatian on a leash — by then German COs venture out of their Le Fayet-Saint-Gervais-south garrison only with attack dogs. Both officers wear daggers over their fine wool coats, the blades bounce in step off their behinds. Tick-tock, tick-tock! Stiff military caps top their arrogant bearing. Maman pales. In the distance the glacier of Bionnassay shines through the clouds. I have won a battle of wits. Inside me I jump up and down, I scream for joy.

>   One can
>
> >   outwit
> >
> > >   the Germans!

I wish to communicate my elation to Mother. An over-the-shoulder-look to see if the two Wehrmacht officers are out of hearing, and I turn to Maman playfully.

"Bonjour Madame Schmidt!" I say.

Maman's face looks like Edvard Münch's painting, *The Scream*. Ghostlike, she murmurs: "Marguerite, I'm afraid."

At Chez Nous, still dressed in her coat, scarf and hat, Maman sits down on her unmade bed and starts sobbing. "If my good *Mütterle* knew that I had to give up my name Oppenheimer, she would roll over in her grave," she cries. Tears run down my mother's cheeks and form little drops at her chin.

I can't think about scruples. Scruples don't count right now; the will to live counts. Deep inside my teenager's pride, I resent Maman's self-pity. I feel it's weak to displace your own outrage onto the body of your dead mother's. Young, irreverent, I am convinced one must take the power of defiance against evil into one's own hands without any sentimental effusion, preferably with a beat of mischief in the heart. Aren't Churchill and Roosevelt using deception to win?

At the same time, albeit less heroically, deep founts inside me ache to say, Oh Maman, don't cry!

The pressures of the opposing feelings in me explode. Standing under the door frame to my parents' Savoyard bedroom, I burst, "Grandma is dead! She can't roll over in her grave!"

Papa throws a glacial stare at me, and then withdraws his gaze as if he didn't recognize me. Seated in shirt sleeves, next to his wife on the edge of their unmade bed, he clasps his strong arms around her thin shoulders. "Come, come, all is well; soon you will be a née Oppenheimer again."

Maman lets out her sobs; Papa cradles her. I fuss on the threshold, dismissed; understanding that from the tight embrace of Papa and Maman united against a fiendish world, exclusion is enforced against a fresh teenager.

I walk away.

To Bonne Maman. On the way back I kick the compacted snow on the valley road. I mutter, "They could at least have thanked me."

In the distance, I see the cable cars moving up and down through the forests on Le Bettex and Arbois gently swaying like small red toy wagons suspended from ropes. My skis need waxing and the rusty metal edges need sanding down. My thoughts focus on the wooden table, and the flat iron behind the door in the basement at Bonne Maman. Is there enough dark brown cake of wax left from the last season?

This episode still fills me with a strange richness. When — for this book — I pick up with my fingers Mother's official false identity card number 00736 established in Saint-Gervais-Mont Blanc on 15 December 1943 by the mayor and witnessed by Messieurs Emile Delachat and Clovis Perroud, and I close my eyes — it isn't just the playfulness, the generosity, the courage, and the family drama that I relive, it is rather the "normalness" with which some human beings meet their moral convictions.

Eventually, Monsieur le Maire Conseil had to flee, barely escaping through the back door of city hall as two Wehrmacht officers entered through the front entrance with an order to "invite *der Buergermeister*" to enter their staff car. A quick thinking employee alerted the mayor.

Chapter 12

The Classics of War:
"How Many Soldiers Inside?"

(1943-1944)

I live by my wits, yet classical education is going on all about me. Other refugee students in Saint-Gervais are working towards their baccalauréate. My sister has her Bac. She uses hers as a class ring. Round. Finished. "I am a graduate."

Le Bac or *Bachot,* in the French school system, is the degree at the end of the secondary cycle required to enter college. Its level of academic difficulty lies somewhere between an American high school and a B.A. degree.

The examinations are tough, competitive, and only thirty-percent of the candidates are awarded the baccalauréate diploma each year. With the Allies' win in North Africa and Sicily, and the climate of ordered respect established by Madame Vachette, I again feel a future.

At Bonne Maman in my room, I ask myself: what will you do when the war ends? My intellect hungers for knowledge; I can't help it: I like to study. It's the joy of learning that sustains me in my precarious present-day situation.

Flat on my back in my bed, I see myself going to university after all. Six hundred kilometers away from Paris, I dream a luxurious minute of "Science-Po," the colloquial abbreviation for l'École des Sciences politiques, the Social Sciences University, one of the famed graduate schools in Paris.

The following Thursday on my day off, I burst into the kitchen at Chez Nous and without closing the door behind me explode: "Work bores me stiff! I want my Bachot!"

"What's holding you back?" responds Maman, perplexed.

To Mother's credit, I must say that she instinctively encouraged me. Whether she realized the enormity of the task, I did not know, but she heard her daughter's distress, and responded: if you want it, you can do it!

I will have to master French literature, philosophy, history, anatomy, and a second language without the help of a correspondence course since I have no money; besides, I can't get any mail. A lycée in Saint-Gervais? There is none!

In the parlor of their private school, "Les Chamois," the Demoiselles Dejey express their regrets: "We only teach as far as the third form, the tenth grade."

They recommend someone named Henri Baud. "He's one of our very best teachers. At present he's at home convalescing from TB."

Off they send me with a burst of flowery French language, "We hope you will find in Monsieur le professeur Henri Baud, a mentor able to guide you through the shoals of the baccalauréate examinations!"

"Allons, enfants..." Onward to exams!

A two-story grey stone house behind a low iron fence on the Mont Pacard slope above Saint-Gervais in an older neighborhood shows a white ceramic plaque in the upper right corner. The name on the tile reads: La Roseraie, the Rose Garden. Wintering rose bushes shrivel sadly in the small front garden.

A slender young woman with wavy-blond hair lets me in while drying her fingers wet from chopping celery roots. "I'm Dédée!"

We shake hands.

I tell her why I have come. "The Demoiselles Dejey from Les Chamois recommended Monsieur le professeur Henri Baud to me. I would like lessons in philosophy and French literature for Le Bac."

Dédée Baud lends a sympathetic ear. "It will do Riri a lot of good to interrupt his studies. He's working too hard."

193

She leads me through the dining room past her two children René and Françoise eating lunch at a long polished dark wood table in their blue and white checkered grammar school uniforms. The Fiz mountain range enters through the windows, tooth after jagged tooth of limestone.

I have taken the first step.

The professor sits in the far corner of his study behind a desk piled high with papers. He has a taut, ascetic face under straight black hair combed backwards over a high forehead, but it is his intense dark brown eyes that impress me most. They are eyes that have known pain. His skin is yellowish as of someone bedridden. He wears a grey hand-knitted wool scarf around his neck; he is in his early thirties. "I can't give you lessons," he says on that first visit, "but we can discuss books from time to time."

Books! A surge rises in me.

Henri Baud has just returned home from a two-year stay at the sanatorium on Assy, "I function with one lung only, the other has collapsed," he simply says. "I underwent a thoraco." He's under strict doctor's orders: bed rest, no exertion.

Longingly, I gaze at the books. Books weigh down the shelves. Stacks of books lean against the baseboards. Books the size of hands in leather covers; a large book in hard cover. Books in Greek, Latin, and French. Books give his study both a well-ordered and a much-used look.

At home, first at 18 Richard Wagner Strasse, Mannheim; then at 76 avenue de la Bourdonnais, Paris, Papa's library contained one huge glass-enclosed Chippendale armoire filled with red leather-bound volumes of Shakespeare, Chaucer, Goethe, Schiller, Lessing — the classic authors. As a child I would crane my neck or kneel to read their names and titles written in golden letters across the spine.

Ever since early life, I have been surrounded by books.

I got books for presents. In Mannheim I owned *Pinocchio, Heidi,* the *Grimm Fairy Tales,* and many more. In Paris, I read avidly Jules Verne, George Sand, Madame de Sevigné, Alexander Dumas, Merimée, Sir Walter Scott, Jacques London, and Gide. I bought books with my allowance. From my lycée library I borrowed armfuls. I devoured adventure stories, fables, biographies, anything. In Roanne, every day to and from Chez Jacques along the avenue de Mulsant, I memorized a few stanzas of poetry out of my two thin volumes of the Romantics or the Symbolists as an exercise for the mind.

In Henri Baud's study, I stand with arms hanging by my side. Again, I feel I'm a student facing a respected teacher. I lower my eyes. He has a Master's degree in Latin, Greek, and French literature. However illness constrains him. All I want is to learn.

For a moment he looks down at his desk. He touches an earmarked paperback. Am I dismissed? Surely in Saint-Gervais there is no one else with a degree in classical literature.

When his deep brown eyes lift and glance up at me out of a drawn face, I hope personality and passion will play in my favor.

"I am rereading Homer. Are you familiar with the Greek classics?" he says finally.

"We... I... studied ancient Greece in the fourth form at the lycée in Paris," I mumble. Maybe I named Socrates or Plato or Aristophanes' *The Birds,* and out of intellectual honesty added: "In the translations of course!"

He asks: "Are you aware that Homer already acknowledged that superior force allows man to treat others as objects or corpses or slaves, and that violence eventually boomerangs and destroys the agent of destruction?"

This is a dream come true. A teacher in his study actually sharing with me the wisdom of the ancient Greeks.

Surely I have nothing to complain of. I'm a Jew and I'm free under the Nazi occupation of France; but I haven't been inside a regular classroom since May 1940, and this is the winter of 1943.

On my feet I fleetingly see three and a half years of pell-mell reading, makeshift shelters, false ID cards. I'm aware that I'm pinning my hope on expansion of the mind. So far I have imparted knowledge, preserved human dignity, and made this world a better place to live in for the children at Les Bruyères and Bonne Maman; I feel vibrant in the company of my passion. Silently I implore:

195

Please teach me! Tell me about Greek thinkers. Romans. French. Anything.

"Violence boomerangs and eventually annihilates the agent of destruction," echoes in me. I try to look calm, but in my chest, my heart pounds. Henri Baud is talking about our present-day circumstance. Haven't the Allies annihilated Rommel's Panzers in North Africa? They have liberated Sicily!

In my soul this experience feels holy; it can't be fragmented and analyzed. The chasm between the meaning it had for me, then, and what the reader might see in it today, is too great. *Henri Baud is using the blue Mediterranean sea of yore to make me understand my current condition.*

"Did it strike you that Homer describes war as an infernal cycle that has the implacable and purely mechanical inevitability of fate?" he asks.

My ears hear, my mind sees, my war explained by a five-thousand-year-old bard, and I understand the illumination.

Like most Europeans, I believe in the myth that war is an inevitable part of life. Hadn't each generation of European men waged war since the dawn of the tribes?

On the cobbled La Forclaz, back up to Bonne Maman, the joy of learning accelerates my step.

Henri Baud surely possesses the lucidity of the French, also their shrewdness: not once did he allude to Hitler's Panzers — death penalty for incitement against the occupying forces. Instead, he wraps our horrific present in an ancient Greek cloak.

Next time at La Roseraie, no mention is made of whitewashed rooms in sanatoriums. The teacher dives directly into the topic that is on his mind that day: "I have been researching the battle of Tours (732).

Like every French schoolgirl I know about *The Song of Roland* which tells the saga of Charlemagne's Spanish wars. I have learned about Roland, Oliver, and the ambush in the Pyrénées mountains at Roncesvalles — called in French "Roncevaux" — written circa 1100, and sung by the troubadours at the courts during the early Middle Ages. *La Chanson de Roland* is a part of that battle in the

Loire Valley in 732 when Charles Martel routed the Moors back across the Pyrénées into Spain. At first, I can't see the relevancy. I don't know what to say. I'm excited but paralyzed. The teacher looks at me intently.

"Charles Martel saved our Greek-Roman civilization from the Moors and galvanized the western world into self-defense," he says slowly.

A star-struck moment. I connect the battle of Tours — when Frankish spears drove back the Moors — to the battle of El Alamein in the desert of Cyrénaica North Africa last November 1942 when the Allies stopped the eastward push of Rommel's Panzers toward the Suez Canal. I see the British, the Free French under General Koenig, the South Africans, and the Jewish brigade of Palestine saving our civilization from the onslaught of Hitler's Huns.

I'm eighteen years old, I live in a vortex of disasters; I'm trying to make sense out of my crumbling world. At *La Roseraie*, I'm learning historical truths older and wiser than my own perceptions; vérités funneled through the prism of a scholar. It is as if I saw for the first time a painting by Rembrandt with the light source directed on his dark subject.

We are at a time when Cardinal Liénart declares: "To leave for the STO (le Service du travail obligatoire, the compulsory Work Service in Germany) is not a conscientious duty." When Field Marshal Friedrich von Paulus surrenders one million men to the Russians. When Tunis and Bizerte fall to the Allies. When the weekly meat ration in France is four ounces. When deportations east accelerate for Jews. When over six hundred and fifty thousand French workers are sent as slave laborers to Germany or "volunteered," and another hundred thousand are snared into building the Todt Atlantic fortifications. When young men are escaping to the maquis (the bush) rather than helping the German war machine. While other young French men join the Vichy militia and commit horrible atrocities. When informers sell out their compatriots for a set price, while patriotic railroad workers derail Wehrmacht troop transports. When defiant men cut telephone

197

wires and gun down traitors, while infiltrators decimate the Resistance. When high schools and university students rebuild the devastated Resistance networks. When names of executed hostages are broadcast over radio Vichy or printed in newspapers almost daily to frighten the population, and I routinely look over my shoulder to see who is following me. When evil lurks and I prick the soft fold between thumb and index finger to harden myself so as not to talk under torture.

Nothing has changed, yet everything has changed.

I am still in hiding, still living under a false name, but last week, when Churchill thundered defiance at Hitler on the BBC, inspiring the defense of England — invoking the glory of the British Empire, praising the navy, the RAF, and the Eighth Army — I said to myself: he blows the horn of history. Like at Tours, our entire civilization is at stake.

When de Gaulle extols the courage of our valiant young men fighting in North Africa as being hale, fit, and trim in their khaki uniforms — I see a revitalized France climbing out of a shameful defeat.

At night, in my room at Bonne Maman, I read Voltaire's *Pamphlets, Les Letters* by Madame de Stael, and Diderot's speeches against tyrannical masters. Their defiance inspires my own.

One noon I return Saint-Exupéry's *Pilote de Guerre* on my lunch hour to Henri Baud. He is busy writing an essay. I have hidden the forbidden volume under my ski jacket. I shift my weight from foot to foot, a starved youngster who yearns for knowledge more than for rutabagas with ground tripe.

Henri Baud is annoyed at my insistence. He stares at his notes; they lie on his desk. He fingers pages. I can see in the distance the point of Varens emerge from under a thick fog. Suddenly, an animation enlivens the teacher's mien. In a passionate voice, he asks: "Are we 'men' because Man exists, or is it the other way around?'"

Imagine you are a youth with a strong desire to learn, but you must be careful not to be found out because you and your family could be deported. You wonder: is my teacher referring to dogma and the notion of baptism or to a premise of Man responsible for his own actions? Now that the world is shaken by deep suffering, thinkers seek to redefine the relationship of Man to man, and Man to God. Some, like Camus in *The Stranger,* think there is no higher meaning at all to man's existence. Henri Baud is Catholic. I feel nervous at expounding a philosophy based on the premise of individual sensory experiences excluding the Christian tenet of salvation through spiritual redemption. What if Henri Baud engages in a debate about original sin — I could be in deep trouble. I know very little about his passions.

I hesitate.

Abruptly, Henri Baud leans forward on the edge of his chair, tense like a tiger ready to pounce.

"Have you seen any activity on Lachat when you went up to Mont Blanc?"

"No. No activity!"

Henri Baud settles back into his seat. His pupils veil over, he draws two blinds, and mask-like, makes haste for St. Ex.

"Did you read that long excerpt about the 'significance of our civilization?'" he asks.

"Er... yes, it's very lyrical..." I answer, thinking,

"Better safe than sorry."

Moments pass. I must say that those whose freedom has never been threatened will never know the care, the cunning, we used to protect ours.

Henri Baud, book in hand, turns the pages. Half to himself, half to me, he mumbles: "How does St.Ex. word this... his social testament?" He finds the place he is looking for and says, "There it is!"

In his deep resonant voice, he reads the paragraph aloud: "My civilization is founded upon the reverence for Man present in all men, in each individual... And this is the true meaning of my civilization. It has little by little been forgotten. It is Man who must be restored to his place among men. It is Man who is the essence of our culture..."

Dangerous words in 1943.

Gallimard (the French publisher) under pressure from Vichy had had to withdraw the second printing of *Pilote de Guerre* (*Flight to Arras*), because the idea of human self-respect drew the ire of the censors. Henri Baud may have obtained a copy from the first printing. We knew that Vichy and the German occupation forces allocated scarce print paper to Lucien Rebatet, Louis-Ferdinand Celine, and Brasillach of *Je Suis Partout*, a far right Parisian newspaper — all muckraking anti-Semites who sold their pens to the Nazis — but print paper is denied to André Malraux, Elsa Triolet, Louis Aragon, Jean Paulhan, Paul Eluard, and Vercors, the authors who buttress our spiritual strength.

Yet, seen through a certain looking glass, France enjoys special privileges. French literature is sorted out by German censors before being permitted entry into Belgium, Holland and elsewhere in the "New Europe." In 1940, publishers in Paris signed an agreement with the authorities of Occupation to police themselves. At the time, we were told, "The compromise enables French thought to continue its mission." I know that Madame Pierre, the librarian in Saint-Gervais, keeps Romain Rolland, Stefan Zweig, and Georges Duhamel on the shelves. You could read and think in private, but you couldn't let go and exclaim: Humanism, that's my philosophy. I'm for a culture based on freedom and human dignity!

"I understand St. Ex." is how I answer Henri Baud.

A teenager in a distant mountain society, living on the fringes of that society — I yearn for acceptance. I try to ingratiate myself with my teacher whose interest for things military hasn't escaped me.

The following week in Henri Baud's study, I blurt: "Two German army trucks drove by Chez Nous yesterday!"

"How many soldiers inside?"

"The flaps were drawn. I couldn't see!"

He stares at me; processes the response. Quickly he draws a veil over his intense dark brown eyes; and back to... LaFontaine.

"Did you notice how the writer avoided his fate — ?"

200

After the fourth visit, I stop going to Baud's house for private lessons in French literature. The course curriculum for Le Bac requires philosophy. I also start to feel ill at ease thinking five steps ahead before each response is restrictive and it is potentially dangerous.

Although I continue to see Henri Baud in a group with other students, I find a teacher of philosophy in Mégève. He is a young Ph.D. from Paris. In winter, on my day off, I take my skis to his chalet on a cable car up to Mont d'Arbois then schuss down to his very doorstep; in summer, I weekly walk the ten mile round trip on the road through the forest. I intuit he's Jewish and that he lives with false papers; likewise he steers clear of making eye contact with me. We mutually practice "No see. No hear. No tell of the other's clandestinity." Just Leibniz, Spinoza, Kant, and Hegel.

A serious group — mostly made up of students from Paris sent to Saint-Gervais to heal TB: Yves, Ginette, François, Armand, Annette, Françoise, Pierre, Jean-Claude, Martha, and I — we gather around Henri Baud. We call ourselves "Henri Baud's *petit groupe*." As is the custom of the day, we do away with surnames.

A yellowed photograph shows the girls' hair coiffed high above their foreheads, the boys' trimmed short and combed back. We roll our socks over climbing shoes. Ginnette at seventeen is the youngest; twenty-four-year-old Yves, the oldest. Henri Baud is just a dozen years our senior. Thirty-two, he was born in 1912 at nearby Les Cluses. His features are fine and sharp. In the picture I have of him, the little group is standing and Henri Baud is seated on the edge of a table, a bit removed, aloof. He has a Roman nose with a high prominent bridge; his dark eyes stare into the distance as if focused on matters beyond his little group — a star-bound *Little Prince* wearing a hand-knitted grey scarf around his neck.

Sometimes Henri Baud and the little group go on outings into the mountains. Once, we chip in for dinner at Martha's restaurant, the "Crystal de Roche" at les Pratz. I'm reserved. My dinner partner, François, asks me: "Marguerite, why are you so quiet?" I had been waiting for him to start talking to me. In boy-girl matters,

201

I'm a bumbling teen who draws a chalk circle around her. No intimacy, please! If anyone had guessed my true identity, I and my family's lives would have been in jeopardy.

On another special evening, Ginette's parents invite the Little Group for a drink at the Splendid Hotel downtown opposite the esplanade. At the bar, Madame Splendid confides in me that her daughter Ginette is not serious. "All Ginette wants to do is flirt," she says. "She sees me at night here at the bar mingling with guests, but she doesn't realize how hard I work each day to run this one-hundred-room hotel."

I am barely a year older than Ginette. A good listener, I'm flattered that Ginette's mother takes me into her confidences.

Moments later Henri Baud pulls me aside: "Ginette is using me," he says. "Her mother just thanked me for letting her daughter sleep at my home because our meeting ran past curfew last Wednesday. Our meeting was over at 8:30 PM!" He implies that Ginette had slept with her boyfriend. Ginette's mother is revealing herself to me; Henri Baud confides in me. This trust bestowed on me by two grown-ups whom I admire creates a real dichotomy within me: one part of the adolescent quivers at being accepted by adults; the other says: but I and my people are unworthy pariahs. In *Le Juif Süss,* a German movie reviewed in a Parisian paper which a visiting parent from Paris had left behind at Bonne Maman, the reviewer cited the German actor as saying: "Jews drink the blood of Christian children." Ginette's mother and Henri Baud could have picked any member of our little group to tell their feelings to. Yet they chose me. The anti-Semites are dead wrong! This vampire was so innocent, she felt ill at ease just sitting on a bar stool. It was a first for me.

Whenever Armand, Pierre, François, Annette, Martha and I meet on the cobbles, we shake hands. We exchange a few words. We smile. We part feeling better for the encounter. No one suspects that one of us is a camouflaged Jew whose mother lights Shabbat candles in the pantry. I accept their scarred lungs. I ask Armand: "How did you find out you had TB?" "Blood in the spittle, a cold that wouldn't heal!"

202

I can't talk about what it is like being Jewish.

About our families — we all feel equally concerned, and we share the same pains of defeat. The shame. The fears. The guilt: why do we let others do the fighting for us?

On the night I ski down the Voza Pass I lose my way in the forest. Hair disheveled, pants torn, face scratched, I knock on the door of the Mont Pacard rest home about 9:30 PM, well past curfew. It's a pitch black moonless night. In ankle-deep snow by flashlight with chivalrous selflessness and much laughter, Armand and Pierre escort Marguerite back to Bonne Maman.

A burning question however remains unanswered in my mind: would they have accepted me as one of theirs, had they known that I am Jewish? Would they have helped me? Whatever! I thank my Christian friends in Saint-Gervais for their friendship.

No one asks any questions. The people are accustomed to winter skiers, summer tourists, TB patients, and war refugees. The Alps sheltered us all.

Henri Baud is well-regarded in the community. People say: "Henri is serious, well-educated." He has a degree in Greek-Latin and in French literature. On Sunday after church lets out, under the portal, the locals approach him courteously. "Henri, how are you?" "Ça va!" he answers, never stopping.

Yet, there's a mystery about Henri Baud.

On the day we climb through the dense Prarion forest to the high mountain village of Motivon, "Riri" as the boys call Henri Baud, disappears.

Twenty minutes later he comes out of an old farmhouse at the far end of the trail, way off the path. He has the subtle grin of a man who has accomplished a secret goal.

On the summer morning when our little group hikes up to the plateau of Passy above the Chamonix valley, we may have walked for two or three hours over the Arve river bridge, the railroad tracks, in meadows, all spread out — the Parisians with rolled-up pants cuffs, the locals in rough alpine garb, amidst the red poppies and the blue corn flowers and the purple gentians reciting poetry,

203

singing melodies of bygone times, old folk songs of love and chivalry, battles won and lost, and hardships overcome — our joie de vivre carrying us on as we crawl through hedges and around clumps to see the great views one has from the Fiz range over Saint-Gervais and Mont Blanc — when Henri Baud once more leaves le petit groupe. This time in Assy at the sanatorium.

For half an hour we mill about on the asphalt.

No one says a word.

He returns, a veil drawn over his sparkling eyes, his Adam's apple moving. He has the manner of a man who is pleased with himself, but hides it.

One afternoon two weeks later in the kitchen at *La Roseraie,* while I am talking to Dédée, he enters, the grey hand-knitted wool scarf tied around his neck; he leans against the icebox.

"Do you type?" he asks me point blank.

I nod.

He leaves, lips sealed, without giving anything away.

In the Baud's dining room, we rehearse *Mountain Crest,* a play by Jacques Donnault.

Performances are to be given over two weekends in Le Fayet-Saint-Gervais-south at the local community center.

The script is about eight young people stranded by an avalanche at a mountain refuge. Isolated, passions erupt, relationships break up. Fresh bonds form. After four days outer and inner storms subside, the eight return to the valley below changed, and with new partners.

Madame Vachette at Bonne Maman burns my text on the afternoon she has to supervise the rest period. "By mistake," she says, but I'm sure it's intentional: she's fed up with my frequent absences. I don't dare make a fuss; I'm Marguerite (Lévy)-Lengel. I spend a whole night typing a fresh script off another actor's. *Merde*!

In the play I land the leading role, a beguiling ingénue, a *jeune première*, but two days before the opening I'm asked to switch with Annette because, having never been kissed by a boy, I giggle in the love scene with Pierre. The loss hurts. I still have a good part, although not the leading one. I tell Papa and Maman: "Come and see my performance!" My parents are clearing dishes off the dining table at Chez Nous. Papa coughs, Maman purses her lips. They let me understand that acting in a public play, at a time when Jews are being deported, is morally reprehensible. While I try to lead as normal a life as possible in order to retain my sanity. I would have liked to see my parents in the audience. Zut!

When the play opens, I bring the house down anyhow with a deep deep look into my new partner's eyes on stage. Still, I'm smarting from my wounds. I have been demoted. Marguerite, I tell myself, distance yourself a bit from Henri Baud. He ruthlessly took the première role away from you; he cares little about other people's feelings, and a lot about the goal. THE GOAL!

On the morning of 25 October 1943, in this small town nestled deep inside an alpine fold — this narrow glacial valley of little strategic value which harbors no Gestapo, no active militia, no visible hatred, and where an eighteen-year-old Jewish girl without an identity can act in a public play and discuss the classics with a seriously-ill professor of Greek-Latin-French literature — a plainclothes trio rings a doorbell.

Marie, at lunchtime, stops by the small table Ghis and I occupy near the window in the dining room at Bonne Maman and, her head bent low over a basket of brown bread, she whispers: "Did you hear about your guide? His farm has been ransacked. They fled."

Out of curiosity I walk up to rue la Toile near the Viallet farm at Les Pratz during the rest period. By chance Henri Baud on his motorcycle stops there at the same moment.

"Have you heard about the black notebook?" he asks me.

"The Black Notebook?" I shake my head.

We stand outside under a pine tree, a ways off from the Viallet farmhouse, lest the Gestapo is still inside.

A year later at the secret headquarters of the local Resistance on LeBettex I find out that Henri Baud is the head of our district's

205

Armée Secrète (de Gaulle's faction). Baud worried that the black notebook had fallen into the hands of the Gestapo. The spiraled notebook contained the names and vital data of each maquisard sheltered by the Viallets. "Somebody had to be able to inform the next of kin in case of an accident!" Julien Viallet protests later on, "ALL IN CODE!" A buddy retrieved the metal box later. "Always outside, never in the house," Julien insisted.

I recall how Louis had written "Marguerite Lengel, Bonne Maman, for Mont Blanc" into a black spiral notebook on the day in August 1943 when I had visited him at his farm to humbly ask if he would take me on for the summit.

You should know that the black notebook had been hidden in a box outside under the very pine tree where Henri Baud and I were standing.

In hindsight, as I think about our strangely interlocked mountain culture, I realize that the young fugitives from the compulsory Work Service in Germany hid in the maquis (the bush) in a group, while the Jews individually handled their own fate.

"And how imprudent we were at times!" Baud, horrified, once laughed.

In his dedication to me of his thin volume *Batailles pour le Mont Blanc* — Henri Baud wrote: "En souvenir de moments heureux mais tourmentés de notre Jeunesse, In memory of happy but tormented moments of our youth."

COPIE.   SERVICE ADMINISTRATIF

Extrait

du registre des personnes réintégrées de plein droit
dans la qualité de Français
en exécution du Traité de Paix du 28 juin 1919.

Commune de   Soultz

Nº 4379

M r   Albert Lévy

né à   Soultz Haut-Rhin

le   25 avril 1885

Le Maire

Signé : G. Fritsch

Pour copie conforme :

Soultz   le   16 décembre   19 38

(Sceau)   Le Maire :

IMP. E. LOHLATTER—RIBEAUVILLE

1 This page is taken from the registry of persons
reintegrated by law to the full rights of French
citizenship by virtue of the Peace Treaty of 28 June
1919 that ended World War I and returned Alsace-
Lorraine to France.

RÉPUBLIQUE FRANÇAISE

DÉPARTEMENT DU HAUT-RHIN

ARROND. DE GUEBWILLER

SOULTZ (Haut-Rhin), le 30.11.1939

Affaire Administrative

Certificat

VILLE DE SOULTZ
MAIRIE

N°

        Le Maire de la Ville de Soultz Haut-Rhin,
certifie que :

1° Mr.Louis Lévy,est né à Soultz Ht-Rhin,le 10.6.1881.

2° Mr.Albert Lévy,est né à Soultz Ht-Rhin,le 25.4.1885.

3° Mr.Edouard Lévy,est né à Soultz Ht-Rhin,le 26.12.1891

    Le père Joseph Lévy,est né à Soultz Ht-Rhin,le 24
mai 1832.

    Le grand-père Félix Lévy,est né à Jungholtz,annexe
de Rimbach Haut-Rhin,le 10 Pluviose A VI,de la
République Française,comme fils de Simon Lévy,
domicilié à Hartmannswiller Ht-Rhin.

    Lévy Félix a contracté mariage à Hatmannswiller le
27 janvier 1825.

                         Le Maire

 # 2 Papa's ancestry is from Alsace. My great grandfather Felix Lévy was born on 10 Pluviose year VI of the French Revolution in Jungholtz, Haute-Rhin (Alsace). Before 1789, civil records were kept in synagogues and churches.

 # 3 I am 2, and my sister Ghislaine is 6, in Mannheim, Germany

 # 4 Maman, me, Ghislaine and Papa at home   Richard   Wagnerstrasse   18, Mannheim, circa 1932

 # 5 Family vacation in Garmisch, 1929

209

 # 6 In Paris on the Champs de Mars 1935, the École Militaire in the background. I am second from left with sister and friends.

 # 7 Roanne, southern Free Zone, France 1941-1942. I am (seated, center) with my young Scouts on a picnic cookout.

 # 8 At a Girl Scout summer leadership camp in Mermidol (Vaucluse) France, Free Zone, August, 1942. I am far right kneeling by the shore of the Durance.

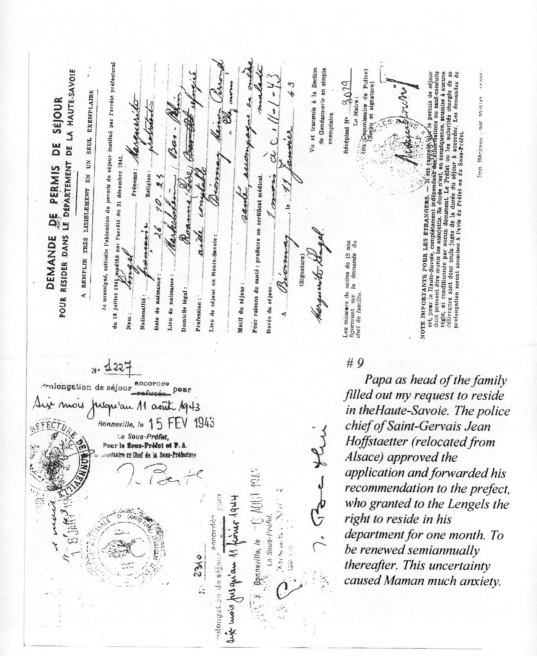

9

    Papa as head of the family filled out my request to reside in the Haute-Savoie. The police chief of Saint-Gervais Jean Hoffstaetter (relocated from Alsace) approved the application and forwarded his recommendation to the prefect, who granted to the Lengels the right to reside in his department for one month. To be renewed semiannually thereafter. This uncertainty caused Maman much anxiety.

211

 # 10 At Bonne Maman with the children. I am standing far right. August 1943

 # 11 My Christianized ID.

 # 12 Henri Baud and our little group. I am standing in white coat, third from left.

 # 13 Certification that Marguerite Lengel (Lévy) served in the Resistance, military district of Saint-Gervais, FFI – AS.

213

 # 14-15
right: Maman's
official false ID.
Issued by the Mayor
of Saint-Gervais in
December 1943.
Annulled after the
war and replaced
with her authentic
data as shown above.

#16 Papa's war ID, made out by me, camouflaged Lévy into Lengel.

17"Chalet Chez Nous" Bionnay near Saint-Gervais Haute-Savoie, French Alps.

#18 Maman and Papa on the D 902 road Saint-Gervais, winter 1944.

#19 Papa 1942.

 # 20a and 20b Mont Blanc and our surroundings.

Gr. LENGEL
"Chez Nous"
BIONNAY
par St Germain-en-M¹
(H⁴ Savoie)

Le 14 Décembre 1944.

Monsieur Lengel
au Général Delattre de Tassigny
Service Social
75. A⁷ᵉ des Champs Élysées
PARIS VIIIᵉ

Monsieur,

J'ai l'honneur de vous adresser
ci-inclus les trois certificats:
1°) Bonnes vie et mœurs
2°) Extrait du casier judiciaire
3°) Autorisation paternelle
de Marguerite Lengel, dont vous avez
bien voulu accepter l'engagement.

Veuillez agréer, Monsieur,
l'expression de mes sentiments
très distingués.

JHLengel.

*# 21 Letter to General de Lattre de Tassigny's Enlistment Office
in Paris, written by my sister on my behalf. The cover letter
includes the three documents required for a girl to enlist in the
French Army in 1944.*

217

LS 73598

MAIRIE DE SAINT-GERVAIS-LES-BAINS.
(Haute-Savoie)
-:-:-:-:-:-:-
CERTIFICAT DE BONNES VIE ET MOEURS.
-:-:-:-:-:-:-

Le Maire de la commune de Saint-Gervais-les-
Bains, arrondissement de Bonneville, département
de la Haute-Savoie, certifie qu'il est à sa
entière connaissance que Mademoiselle LENGEL
Marguerite, née à Markelsheim (Bas-Rhin), le
vingt six octobre mil neuf cent vingt quatre,
fille de Lengel Albert et de Schmidt Marthe,
sans profession, domiciliée en cette commune
depuis le premier janvier mil neuf cent quarante
trois est de bonnes vie et moeurs.

En foi de quoi le présent certificat lui a
été délivré.

A Saint-Gervais-les-Bains, le treize décembre mil neuf cent quarante quatre.

Le Maire,

 # 22 Document # 1. The Mayor of Saint-Gervais declares to his full knowledge that Marguerite Lengel, née at Markelsheim (Bas-Rhin) Oct 26, 1924, daughter of Lengel Albert and of Schmidt Marthe, residing in his district since the first January 1943, is of good morals and reputation. Based on these facts, the present certificate (of good behaviour and morals) is issued on Dec 13, 1944.

218

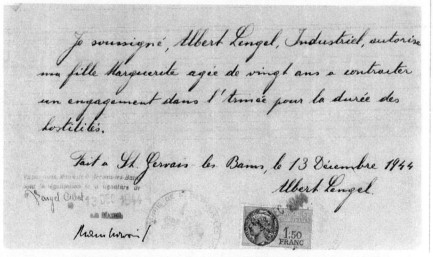

 # 23 above: Document # 2. Papa certifies on his honor that his daughter has never been the object of any judicial or other proceedings.

 # 24 below: Document # 3. Papa authorizes his daughter Marguerite, twenty, to enlist in the army for the duration of the hostilities.

Chapter 13

Dangerous Encounter

(Spring 1944)

"Why don't we visit your parents in Bionnay today?" suggests Henri, one of my charges at Bonne Maman. "Perhaps we can dig up some onions in the garden, and eat them raw as we do in the Midi."

I hear happiness and we trek up the D 902.

Already once before the children had unearthed the smelly bulbous roots in Papa's garden and consequently adopted my parents as their favorite alter-elders, the more so, since their own grandparents had remained at home in southern France.

However that day in the vestibule at Chez Nous, Clovis Perroud, our landlord, had left standing his ladder to the hayloft.

The youngsters immediately clamber up the rungs and, through the open trap door, shriek to their heart's delight:

"Hay, Henri!"

"Hay, Gaston!"

Papa, coming out of our rented half of the chalet into the foyer, quickly steadies the wobbly wooden crossbars with his foot.

Boys! Boys!

I leave my acrobats aloft and go inside to talk to Maman.

Seated at the long dining table by the window, she is busy darning socks. Even though she tries to smile, Maman looks stricken. I sit down beside her.

After a short pause charged with fear, she explodes:

"Marguerite! Yesterday in Saint-Nicolas-de-Véroce, I met…" and she pushes the brown socks across the table in a gesture of dejection. Pupils narrowed with fear, she glances at the door to make sure no one is listening.

220

"Who, Maman?"

Again she eyes her surroundings.

"A what?"

"... A Jew!" she gasps, anguish spread over her visage.

As far as I knew, we were the only Jews camouflaged in Val Montjoie, at least until yesterday.

Maman appears desolate. She doesn't see the fresh green shoots on the pine trees; despondent, she holds her hands over her face and, head in her palms, fingers outstretched, she fiercely lets fly: "I stared him down! Marguerite, nobody is going to inform on us!"

I'm by her side, but I can't enter her suffering. Because that pain of loneliness, isolation, and fear, I have to keep at bay. From salt, I must protect my own raw, open wounds.

"Maman, where did it happen?"

"At the hunchback's farm below the Cross."

And my mother rubs her right thumb with her left fingers. "My rheumatism" is how Maman calls the angst of getting caught that settles in the fleshy part at the base of her right thumb.

I understand that the incident occurred in a small two-room farmhouse at the end of an unmarked lane above Saint-Nicolas-de-Véroce at a place known as La Croix at 3,900 feet altitude.

"As soon as I saw him come in, I picked up my Alpenstock and I walked out..."

"Good for you, Maman!"

After a pause, head still in her hands, elbows on the table, she sighs. "Marguerite, do you think he lives on the Bettex side?" she says.

Maman is not reckless; she just needs the daily exercise as a form of mental and physical therapy. She reproaches herself that she shouldn't have been up there at La Croix, that she compromised the security of her family.

"Maman, he doesn't know your name. He doesn't know where you live..." I say, trying to console her. — Distraught, she goes on justifying her actions. "I was trading a cotton blouse for half a small Tomme (local cheese) and six eggs when he came in..."

221

I get the picture: a knock on the door, the heavy hinges creak. Through the shaft of light Maman sees a visitor. He has Semitic features. Instinctively, they both sense they are co-religionists. The newcomer smiles amiably and extends his hand. Normally, before the false papers, my mother would have said some polite words or other like: "Fancy meeting you here in this out-of-the-way farmhouse. Where are you from?" Instead, as the times were perverse, Maman picked up her Alpenstock and fled, afraid to meet a member of her tribe.

"But Marguerite, such bad luck, and it had to happen to me! What if he's caught? He might tell the Gestapo that he knows of other Jews in the area... the Gestapo will find us."

I see the terror in my mother's eyes; I pat her hand. "He isn't going to be caught, Maman," I say soothingly.

In a flush of despair, my mother explodes: "I hate what they are doing to us. Always living in fear. Always being persecuted or being killed. Sometimes I wish I could jump out of my skin!" Mouth drawn, Maman shakes her fist in the direction of the outside world, the world beyond the glass panes of *Chez Nous*. The Nazis.

Steeped in her grief, she insists:

"What do you think, Marguerite? We can't run the risk of being recognized!" and she bites her lips into a tight pinch. I notice how her loving, sensuous mouth has shrunk due to worries.

"Maman, our cover is safe," I say.

"What if the hunchback tells him we live in Bionnay?"

"She won't."

"What if he asks her?"

"She'll pretend not to hear."

Maman looks doubtful.

She resumes massaging her anguish. I rise and stroke her dull white hair. "What if we are caught, Marguerite?" she repeats in a low plaintive tone of voice. I reassure her that he couldn't possibly have seen her features inside a dark room through a crack of the door.

Of course he saw her Semitic traits in the beam of light, and his own sharpened instinct instantly perceived her ancestry.

So, Maman, with much delay, I wish to say to you forthwith: you hiked into the mountains to barter goods and sympathy with the locals; you returned home before dusk with bits of news, cheese, butter or bread. Teasingly, as family does, we called you "our long-distance runner," cognizant of the fact that the isolated mountain folks enjoyed your visits. You listened to their ills, and you acted as a social worker, and always you dispensed good homespun remedies. To them, your Semitic features meant nothing: they had never met a Jew. They did not pre-judge you.

Instead of patting your hand and reassuring you with cliché words, I should have taken you into my arms and laid your anguished head against my shoulder. I am sorry, Maman, I couldn't. For to accept in others feelings that I rejected in myself — was beyond my ability.

And Maman in 1981 —

There, Marguerite, I am handing you our false papers..." and her lips quiver. I look at my mother standing by the closet of her Philadelphia apartment, and I see a lonely woman still devoted to her family body and soul but whose children have long left. "Perhaps you can use these documents and tell the story," she says with a glint in her eyes. "The story of living with fear in France during the War..."

"But Maman, I thought you liked it in the Haute-Savoie. Didn't you say, "For once I have Papa all to myself?" I look at her wrinkled face, at the rounded shoulders, and I touch her elbow. "It wasn't all that bad, we were never caught... nobody betrayed us... and the beautiful French Alps sheltered us," I say.

"But the fear, Marguerite, the raw fear..." she answers terror dilating her pupils still thirty-seven years later.

Chapter 14

Furlough in Annecy

(Spring 1944)

S pring comes slowly to Val Montjoie that year. Every day, the white mantle of snow retreats patch by patch ever upward toward Le Bettex and Arbois. The landscape resembles one vast checkered handkerchief. Above Bionnay the thin Bon Nant, fed by the thaw of the Bionnassay glacier, cascades down the forested mountain side splashing like a torrential stream. Along the D 902, ice sheets slide off the steep roofs of the chalets and crash onto the ground beneath. In the spongy pastures, on the muddy footpaths, and in the cobbled streets around Saint-Gervais, rivulets run everywhere. Doctor Tissot calls the period *stationary*: on the X-rays of his patients' lungs, the shadows refuse to shrink.

War news compounds my gloom. In Italy, the battle for Rome is stalled. A combination of enemy fanaticism, intense cold, and sheer slopes cut down the single-file Allied soldiers who must bring supplies and weapons up the Apennines by mule.

The assault on Monte Cassino turns into a slaughter. When wave after wave of B-52s and Hurricanes level the Benedictine monastery atop the mountain, the very next day, German parachutists re-occupy the ruins.

Once General Juin, the commander of the CEF, the French Expeditionary Corps and its Moroccan troops, meets with some success: his forces reach the Belvedere of the monastery. *There, France is rehabilitated*! But in the end support on his flanks fails to materialize and his cliff-hanging positions have to be abandoned.

Twice, General Kesselring breaks the British–led offensive and American General Clark's meets with the same fate.

On March 23, General Clark orders the end of the frontal assault on the Gustav line. On the BBC the newscaster says: "The Italian front has stabilized." To me "stabilized" sounds like "stymied." Has the Occupation also *stabilized*? Doesn't anybody care about us?

I can't afford a depression. Who will take care of the children and of me? The more so that I can't unburden my frustrations within the family. Papa and I do not discuss private feelings. Maman expects me to be her Sunshine-child, so that with my mother I play the role of confidante. I listen and cheer her up but rarely voice my own worries. What to do? Quoi faire?

"Ghis, why not a trip to the city? You pack your knitting, and I — my thin 19th century volume of Romantic poets. Madame Vachette will grant us an extra day off (to be made up). We both have saved some money." I fancy reading Lamartine's *Le Lac* on a bench under a weeping willow by the lake.

In Annecy we'll visit the 14th century castle of the Princes of Savoy, the one built with the four tall towers on the high promontory. We'll explore the 12th century Palais de l'Isle that tells the history of the Savoy region. "You and I will stroll along the famed canals that meander through the cobbled streets of the old city." I already hear the water lapping at the pebbles along the shores.

Papa and Maman pepper their reluctant consent with good advice. "Take a small room at the best hotel in town and lock your door as soon as you get in.

"Oui!"

"Oui!"

In a nearly empty carriage marked Annecy via Sallanches-Cluses-LaRoche-sur-Foron, we sit down in a compartment occupied by a young Savoyarde. She wears a head scarf tied under her chin and the usual pair of wood-soled shoes over thick wartime cotton stockings. Ensconced in the corner curtain by a window, her little snub nose is moving up and down the pages of a book. About

225

twenty, average height, and with an honest transparent face, my instinct tells me: you can trust her.

Discreetly, Ghis and I cover our heads with a scarf: do as the locals. You could say the three of us resemble *Cézanne's Les Joueurs de Cartes* — a tableau that shows each player as being separate yet connected to the others by horizontal lines. Alone, yet together.

Before La Roche-sur-Foron, our train is sidelined. "Why?" The ticket controller shrugs, and walks on. We stay on a spur track for what seems a very long time.

Eventually, a German troop transport rolls by and our carriage moves on.

I keep on reading Lamartine open on my lap:

O lake! The year has scarce attained its term,
By thy beloved waves, that she should have beheld again...

When, suddenly, Ghis sits up very straight; listening closely, she whispers: "I hear shouts in German."

Abruptly, the door to our compartment slams open, and a black uniformed SS man, the skull and bone insignia pinned to his cap, commands:

"Heil Hitler, Papiere Kontrolle!"

Razor sharp eyes fix their gaze on the Savoyarde, on Ghis, and on me. I see the veins on each side of his short heavy neck stand out like blue rods. My breathing stops.

The young Savoyarde bends to the floor and pulls a well-worn ID out of her old leather purse. With contempt sneaking over her lips, and a subtle flush of indignation on her face, she hands the document over to the black uniform and turns her head away to the window, her eyebrows raised into a soft arc.

I copy her gestures.

My identity card shows my photo, Christian name, and fudged birthplace. I hand the card over to the SS and, like the local, I stare out the window pane at the landscape streaking past. (*He has no*

226

inkling... I order myself secretly. *You are not afraid*! *Count telephone poles! Count...*)

One, two... three... four... nine...

"Next, please...!"

From the corner of my eye I see his red bony hand stretch out toward Ghis. I know Ghis's ID card bears her photograph and the data is filled out in her own cursive hand. LYON-CALUIRE is stamped on Ghis's ID, although our Saint-Gervais seals are identical. Seated on her wooden bench, Ghis crosses her arms on her chest as if in protest.

Mouth twisted into a crooked scar in a smooth white face, the SS examines both Ghis' and my ID cards. His paranoid eyes compare the handwriting. (It's different, all right)! Twelve... thirteen... The ID covers likewise are different. *You are not afraid. Fear drives them mad with aggression!*

I feel his stare on my back.

Fifteen...

Red spiny fingers hold Ghis's and my IDs. Heinous eyes dart to and fro the sisters.

He hands over our IDs...

"Heil Hitler!"

Right arm raised, he leaves the compartment.

"Alles in Ordnung!" he calls out to a fellow SS member who is in the corridor. "All is in order!"

A miraculous blindness.

I pocket my ID.

I'm a hollowed vessel. Vacant of emotions, I fixate a pastoral photograph of Lake Annecy on the opposite wall above Ghis's head.

Little by little the cognitive brain functions again. I see two wooden benches, the fold-up table, the dark flowered curtains, the white headrest covers, and the brown-framed luggage nets re-enter my consciousness. Later Ghis tells me that I said to her in a toneless voice *"Il fait beau dehors*! The weather is nice outside!" and that a small grin of subversive satisfaction lifted the corners of my mouth.

For the Savoyarde's sake I pretend this was just another routine paper check under the Occupation for me too. I bend over Lamartine's *Le Lac,* as if I could comprehend:

Toward new shores we wend our relentless way,
Into the eternal night borne off before dawn,
May we then never on the ages' ocean cast?
Anchor for one sole day!

In the pleated folds of her corner window curtain, the local girl scrupulously lowers her eyelids. Her thin Mona Lisa lips cut a slight ironic smile. If she noticed anything at all, she doesn't let on.

At 9:30 PM, past curfew, we arrive in Annecy-Gare. At the turnstile of the railroad station a clerk hands out late passes. Ghis and I step into the darkness of the Place de la Gare, two Jewish girls without a place to stay in a strange city.

The moon reflects our shadows on the cobbles; a star-studded sky shines above. At the curbside I double up with laughter. Unstoppable. "Ghis, the nerve to question our home-made papers... They are authentic! WE fabricated them!" I hiccup.

When finally I sober up freed from my pent up tensions, the Scout in me tries to get her bearings. I identify the familiar Orion, that huge human figure with shoulders and three blinking buttons in his belt close to the great Dipper. I point at the "W". "See the Cassiopeia? The bluish North Star twinkles! I say to Ghis. "It's a good omen."

Wrong! Unexpectedly in the distance a series of loud clangs jar the night. Metal tips hit the asphalt. Instinctively, Ghis and I take each other's hand even though we hold late passes. After nearly four years under the boot, we know the clang.

Ghis and I run around one corner, and then another, until a dimly-lit red-lettered sign — faintly glimmering in a window — stops us in our tracks: "HOTEL."

At the end of the long corridor, behind a small desk, sits a woman with pasty make-up, her hair: flame red. A brass comb with colored glass stones sticks out of her perm; and a pair of piglet's eyes, close-set, hunger to know why two *Bécassines* (naïve country girls from the sticks) are out at night past curfew and select her hotel.

She gives us a thorough going-over.

"*Mesdemoiselles?*" she enquires.

"We wish a room, *s'il vous plait,* Madame."

In an effort to pre-empt her request for papers, and expecting a contrarian response, I offer "Do you wish to see our identity cards?" And I put my hand into my purse. "Never mind!" she replies. "It's twelve francs, to be paid in advance!" She doesn't even give us a crude smile.

We could return into the night of the Germans, but my life force warns, "Don't."

The patronne tucks the bills into her ample bosom and, with false respect, mews: "Follow me, Mesdemoiselles."

Up the dark wooden steps the bulging monument moves, we in tow.

The double bed is covered with a frayed pink chenille spread, an old pine dresser leans against the wall. A single light bulb dangles above a small table at the end of a cord inside a torn paper shade. The weak glow on the shabby furnishings gives the room the yellowish tinge of a horror movie.

"Here's the bidet, here's the wash basin, the W.C.'s at the end of the hall," and brightly ringed fingers pull a washed out paisley curtain open.

Ghis and I look at each other.

"Merci Madame."

She leaves.

All at once I feel free and wild. From deep inside my guts rises a laugh. All has come together: the garish make-up, the general air of malevolence, and a hole the size of a baby's fist above the door knob where the lock had been taken out.

Images of 76 avenue de la Bourdonnais, Paris 7ème; of 18 Richard Wagnerstrasse, my *comme il faut* bourgeois past, rush me. Mischief chuckles. If Madame Vachette could see, huh, her two

Demoiselles Lengel, teachers to her very proper private paying guests, huh, dwell in this wickedness...

Index fingers on our lips, Ghis and I warn each other not to speak. We mime: "Push bed against door."

On the other side of the grimy wall, a sharp bang hits the floor. A second bang follows after a short interval. The noise of boots dropping makes us very quiet. I hold my breath. A man's voice curses, "*Donnerwetter*! Damn it!"

I nudge Ghis under the torn coverlet.

"Ghis --"

"What?"

"Don't fall asleep."

At 6:00 AM, after a fitful night, we tiptoe down the stairs.

"Au-revoir, Madam. Merci Madam."

The Madam sits at her little worm-eaten desk leafing through a tattered tabloid with plump fingers adorned with glass ruby and emerald rings; her blotchy make-up, a sorry sight. She slowly turns her small slits, barely concealing an appetite for two sassy virgins. With a gesture of the hand and a crude smile, she shoos Ghis and me away without further ado.

"Allez, Mesdemoiselles!"

Got you!

At the corner bistro the steel shutters are being rolled up for the day. We select a table in the little café just opening after the 9 to 6 AM curfew. *"Deux cafés au lait, s'il vous plait!"* The waiter brings the chicory brew on a traditional café tray imprinted with a Pernod advertisement. We unwrap our brown bread and a chunk of Tomme de Savoie. I joke: "Ghis, weren't we lucky business was bad and Madam rented us a room for the night instead of by the hour?" In the streets, on that morning, droves of Wehrmacht are saluting each other "Heil Hitler." The boots, the Heils, the uniforms — the sheer numbers of them — send shivers down my spine. In comparison, Saint-Gervais is not physically occupied; the F 4 soldiers at the hydroelectric power plant sleep under our roof. In Annecy the Swastika flag flutters above the Hotel de Ville (city hall), and the four-star hotels near the lake where their officers are billeted. "Just as well we didn't go there to ask for a room!"

My sense of humor freezes quickly when I see a shop window rue Royale showing posters: "JOIGNEZ LA MILICE FRANÇAISE, JOIN THE FRENCH MILITIA." Intuitively I reach for Ghis' hand. On the other side of the street, we melt into the crowd. I had never seen a real militia display.

Determined to open my thin orange-bound volume of the XIXth Century Romantic Poets, I find a bench under a weeping willow by the lake. I barely start reading

... But I demand in vain a few more moments, yet...

when sounds of goose-stepping soldiers singing the Horst Wessel Lied pierce the air. To the infamous words: "When Jewish blood spurts under the knife..." a platoon leader yells to his men, "One-two-three! That does our heart good, that does us good! One, two three..." I draw back. It's my blood they are spilling. I can't

Implore time to suspend its flight,
And propitious hours to stay course...
Taste the swift delights of this day of ours.
Call it the fairest of days...

In the streets all about us, Anneciens are transporting roped parcels on their bicycles; they carry heavy valises in their hands, lug loads like beasts of burden. A sullen worker in threadbare blue overalls grips his lunch box in his fingers. He is thin, and his shoes are wooden-soled. Everywhere, grim people walk about under a yoke of silence.

"Let's go, Ghis!" I say, and I crease the top corner of page seventeen. On we move, part and parcel of the shuffling crowd.

With Lamartine, I monologue.

"Sorry, mon ami, I have to shut you, *c'est la guerre*! It's wartime, 1944. The Boches are here. You wrote "As the river gushes, as the bird sings, as the soul longs" in 1817 after the

231

Napoléonic wars had ended and peace finally reigned in the land; while I find myself caught up in an occupied city. Yet when I read your poetry, fresh air enters my lungs; your warmth displaces the cold within me. Alas! I can't dwell in your company for angry eyes are staring at my leisure. Single girls 18 to 35 are supposed to work or study full time or raise children or be sent to work in Germany. In the backcountry, this rule is not applied. Here, in Annecy, it is no joke."

At the castle of the Princes of Savoy, on the heavy wood door, a sign reads in German: *Eingang Verboten,* entrance prohibited. Entry to the ancient Palais de l'Isle is likewise prohibited. Later I learn that the thick walls muffled the screams in the basement cells of the resistants being tortured. Ghis and I climb down the cobbled pavés hand in hand into the silent gait of the anonymous throng. Shaken. Thinking.

Back in Val Montjoie, almost overnight islands of crocuses, spring anemones, and buttercups had broken out in patches. A warm wind is blowing along the valley floor. On the crest of Arbois the snows had melted. The Dome of Miage and the other high ice-clad summits around Mont Blanc glisten in the yellow-purplish after-glow of the setting sun. That's how I remember it.

By the door to my room my charges grin like Cheshire cats. "Mademoiselle, we haven't done our homework, ha!" And they grimace with laughter.

A glass bowl filled with short-stemmed violets sits in the middle of my room on the table. The children strain their necks. "Did you see our flowers?" they rush. "We picked them for you in the forest this morning." And Henri leaps over the sill into my bedroom: "Smell, the woods!" he says, pushing the wild fragrant purple blooms under my nose.

"Thank you, boys! Merci!"

I sleep soundly between two clean sheets, in my own bed, safely tucked in behind a locked door. I had been deprived of culture, and went to the big city in search of civilization. I found instead a threatening, oppressive silence, and a desert of soul. I return to my U-shaped valley aware of the difference between a Nazi-occupied metropolis and the mountains where nature rules.

My universe is filled with the Bon Nant cascading down the mountain sides splashing melt waters against the Devil's Bridge, and ice sheets sliding off the chalets' steep roofs onto the ground beneath. There is isolation and boredom in my existence. And I chafe at the immutable laws of the seasons — they impose their rhythm of spring, summer, fall, and winter on me. Out of sheer frustration I often kick rocks on the D 902. In November, my landscape resembles a Corot grey-greenish-brown painting with forests wet from the rains that make the children and I suffer from colds. But sunny summers also are part of my existence.

How extra-ordinary Saint-Gervais really is, I only become fully aware later on when the ashes of Hitler's monstrous deeds are uncovered.

The next morning, Ghis and I telephone Maman and Papa at chez Dave in Bionnay.

"Yes... a small room at the best hotel. Yes, we locked our room right away..."

"Oui! Oui!"

We giggle.

Chapter 15

Kitchen Politics

Spring 1944

S ix-year-old Eric complains of a stomach-ache in the dorm at Bonne Maman. "*Mademoiselle, j'ai mal à l'estomac,*" he says. It's bedtime.

In France, the remedy de rigueur for all childhood ills is a sugar lump sprinkled with a few drops of *crème de menthe liqueur.* Marie dispenses the magic cure in the downstairs kitchen. "*Je serai de retour dans un petit moment,*" I tell Eric. "Be back in a moment."

That night in the kitchen, Marie's husband, Raymond, an ex-POW *évadé*, sits perched atop a stool by the heavy country table, his arms spread out over an open newspaper. In a halting voice he's reading aloud, using his index finger to underline the syllables, *Hel... den tat... un se rer...*

Marie stands at the sink doing dishes. Her back is turned to me.

Raymond hears me first. He moves his square head toward the threshold where I stand.

"Do you understand German?" he says.

Automatically the lid shuts tight on Margot Gerda Lévy born in Mannheim, resident of that city until the age of nine who reads, speaks, and writes German fluently. I swallow hard and without haste advance toward the wooden table. Curious but cautious I peer over Raymond's shoulder.

I liken Raymond to Michelangelo's "Slave" statues, the ones sculpted for the tomb of Pope Jules II, which I had seen with my 4th form art class of Victor Duruy at the Louvre before the war.

Raymond, the *escaped* slave, says in a frustrated voice: "I can make out single words but the longer sentences baffle me."

234

Marie is scrubbing a large copper pot at the sink; her head almost disappears inside the huge soup container. All at once, in a fit of piqué she lets fly: "Ever since I sent him to market this morning, and he brought home this rag wrapped around my leeks, he's been wasting time making out the Fritz press instead of helping me. Seems the Boches are winning everywhere." Marie's upward tilt of her little pert nose emphasizes ominously her indignation.

Dark-haired Marie is a quick-witted, intelligent, hard-working woman from the Savoy. She and Raymond are the pillars of Bonne Maman. Marie cooks, cleans house, does the laundry, and serves the meals. Raymond plants a garden and takes care of maintenance; he also gives a hand to Marie in the kitchen. Together the couple looks after the physical well-being of twenty plus children and staff. "I'm lucky to have them in my employ," Madame Vachette says.

But that evening, instead of helping Marie, Raymond reads phonetically syllable by syllable: *Sch la a ch t — duu r ch brr u ck* — "They broke through. The con!" he exclaims.

"Where?" asks Marie.

"ODESSA, I guess!" And he points to the word with his index finger.

Papa had told me last week that Odessa had been retaken by the Russians. "The BBC confirmed the capture of the city." I look closer over Raymond's shoulder.

The open newspaper consists of two small double sheets. The center fold is displaying little black crosses above brief obituaries. For the first time, I actually almost touch the names of those who fell for the Führer's quest for domination: Merkel, Oberst — Heinz, Hauptman — Grupp, Lt. — Maurer — Keitel, Otto —

Marie is busy at the sink drying the silverware with a towel. I'm counting enemy losses. Raymond is deciphering so-called Boches victories, when all of a sudden Marie cuts in with feminine guile: "If you don't stop reading that trash by the time I am through, I won't sleep with you tonight!"

Raymond slaps his thigh. He laughs and goes on phonetizing: DAR FU RARE ZEEKT FER DAS FA TAR LANT, the Führer triumphs for the Fatherland.

Marie has washed all the dishes, scoured all the pots, and dried all the forks and knives. She jerks her little snub nose at Raymond, a rabbit smelling strange lettuce leaves.

"Men are stupid!" she says. "They need war to get excited, *au lieu de faire l'amour*, instead of making love."

Mesmerized, I stay on. I wish to set my hands on my first copy ever of the "Voelkischer Beobachter," the official German newspaper. I want to read the Nazi account of their victories, touch their obituaries: the names and ranks of their dead. But I have to be careful not to give away that I understand the German language.

Marie and Raymond's acceptance of my presence warms me; they go on arguing as if I were not there. Please continue pouring out your feelings. It is such a rare treat; everyone else only speaks about the weather. When I leave I write down their words. First, Marie:

"I hope they land soon. The maquisards can't stand another winter like the last one."

Raymond — The American B-17s are flying formation nose to tail, nose to tail.

Marie — Brittany is one long line of fortified block-houses, minefields, barbed wire, and steel traps. My sister told me so.

Raymond — They won't land in Brittany. There's better places. You'll see that they won't land where they are expected.

Marie — How are they going to land without a harbor?

Raymond — Oh, they have equipment the like you have never seen. They invent anything.

Marie — *Pas possible!*

Raymond — *C'est vrai!*

Marie — How do you know?

Raymond — Whispers in the stalag.

Marie — The war is going to be over in six months after the landings.

Inside metropolitan France, Marie, Raymond, and I, the vanquished people, have only the vaguest idea of the enormity of the Allieds' task. How can we? We are kept in the dark. By the spring of 1944, each one of us expects the Allies to overcome every obstacle. Once the Americans put their minds to it, they can part the waters.

And Eric? He fell asleep in his bunk without a soothing sugar cube soaked in mint liquor. When I look in on him, I suppose he is dreaming peacefully about balls and swirling kites. Did I tuck him in, pull the blanket up to his chin? It's perfectly possible. After a few minutes, I go to my room to record Marie and Raymond's banter of sex boycott, and war.

Chapter 16

"Whisper Your Name into My Ear"

(Late Spring 1944)

TO BE BARRED from presenting myself at the high school baccalauréate examinations because I live under a false name is hard on me; to drop behind a second year would be unendurable. *Mais comment faire*, how to do it?

Le Petit Dauphinois, the regional newspaper comes to my rescue in April with a front page article saying that "All resident students of the northern Alps, other than regular lycéens, are invited to register in person for le baccalauréate with Monsieur le Secrétaire-Général of the University of Grenoble (Isère), and bring their records and birth certificates with them."

I'll need luck for I have neither birth certificate nor records. But I had noticed that the Vichy authorities aren't all that smart. They appointed Révillard as *préfet* of the Haute-Savoie when everybody knew he was a sympathizer of the Resistance. Worse, André Buchet, his successor, crossed over into Switzerland altogether.

In my room at Bonne Maman, I dreamily look at Mont d'Arbois emerging from the early morning mists, and I visualize Monsieur le Secrétaire-Général of the northern Alps University as a *rond de cuir,* a middle-aged sedentary civil servant merely anointed by Vichy.

At the boulangerie the following morning I meet by chance Henri Baud. We both stand in line at the cash register.

"Tomorrow I'm taking the train for Grenoble to register for Le Bac," I whisper to him.

"Wait for me outside," he answers in a toneless voice, and he locks his gaze into mine.

Outside, in the open, Henri Baud and I face each other, safe from informers.

"Watch out for Coulon (I think this was the name of Monsieur le Secrétaire-Général), he turns students who belong to the Resistance over to the Germans." And Henri Baud departs, holding in his hand a small loaf of bread wrapped in a thin sheet of paper, the ends of his grey knitted scarf flying in the wind.

The ride from Saint-Gervais to Grenoble winds through range upon 10,000-foot towering range, each with its own ridges, shoulders, plateaus, peaks and valleys. On the right, the grey limestone mass of the Fiz fills the horizon with its twin points of Varans and d'Anterne; on the left, the 9,000-foot peak of Freney juts out of the rocky Aravis. Sheer walls give way to gentler slopes, and quaint villages of typical alpine chalets built around a church spire race past the train window like fold up pictures out of a storybook. Nearer to Grenoble, the grey limestone Chartreuses soar several thousand feet into the air, all mangled by erosion. In the valleys, the subtle mixtures of mosses, lichens, grasses, pines, ashes, oaks and larches start to shimmer in the rays of light. On my lap, lay unread, my two thin orange volumes of nineteenth century Romantics and Symbolists.

In my mind's eye I see the thousands of students who couldn't physically attend a lycée having moved from Paris to the countryside where secondary schools are not available. These etudiants prepared themselves for the examinations through a correspondence course, private tutorial lessons, or through a small preparatory school run by a retired professor who took one, sometimes two full-time boarders into his home — the so-called *boîtes à Bachot*, the baccalauréate joints. Since all the students must be integrated into the state run system on examination day, the Education minister directed that the alternatively educated candidates should register in person with their birth certificates and transcripts at the secrétariat of the university nearest to their residence.

At Place de la Gare in Grenoble I ask a policeman for the direction to the University.

"*Monsieur l'Agent, s'il vous plait...*"

Le gendarme responds with a limp hand to his worn kepi. I'm wearing my white cotton blouse, straight navy skirt under the burgundy sweater with shiny brass buttons à la mode de Roanne which I had purchased Chez Jacques at wholesale price. A leather shoulder strap purse, white gloves and, on my feet, upper leather shoes complete my attire. I look *comme il faut*, and I bet on my charm.

"It's in that direction..." says the policeman in an indifferent voice, and he stretches out his arm.

"*Merci, Monsieur l'Agent!*"

He smiles.

A positive feeling.

On the cobbled Grande Rue I stop at number 109. I read a brass plaque affixed on the house where Stendhal, the author of *Le Rouge ET le Noir*, was born. Another marker along the way reminds passers-by that on this road Napoleon was greeted by the people of Grenoble on his return from Elba to Paris, with shouts of "Vive l'Empereur." A further metal plate says: "Here the Grenoblois hurled tiles off their roofs at the armies of Louis XVI;" and there, Mirabeau, the famous orator who inflamed the Parisian crowds at the Palais Royal in 1789, saw the first light of day.

Last July 14, Bastille Day, hundreds of students hoisted the Tricolor on the campus of the University, and more recently in November Aimé Requet blew up the German artillery depot right here in Grenoble. Mass arrests followed. The Resistance in turn mounted a counter-attack on the Citadel to free their imprisoned comrades. In the streets you could see the Grenoblois walk on their ancient cobbles in brisk small steps — chins set.

I climb the wide marble staircase to the second floor of the administration building in the center of the campus. A clerk in blue overalls stops me.

"May I help you?"

"It's about a registration, Monsieur."

"*Ah oui?*" he says with quizzically arched eyebrows.

"I need to talk to Monsieur le Secrétaire-Général in person. It's special," I say.

"Ah bon! I'm going to see if Monsieur le Secrétaire-Général is available."

Just in case, I check out the wide stairway that opens onto the green quadrangle below. The glass exit door moves inward.

The square-faced clerk under a head of dark straight hair returns. "Monsieur le Secrétaire-Général will see you in a minute," he says, and he lifts a section of the counter top to allow me passage to the private offices.

Ear pressed against an unmarked door at the end of a long hallway, the clerk solemnly listens. He raps his knuckles on the door, twice. THERE'S NO ANSWER. Carefully, he opens the entrance, just a crack. He sticks his head inside to the depth of his eyes; cautiously he peers about. NO ONE IS THERE. With a ceremonial gesture of the hand, palm up, fingers extended, he motions me from the threshold into the room: "Monsieur le Secrétaire-Général will be here in a moment," he says in a mystifying tone that elevates the position of the personality about to arrive. The subordinate never sets foot into his superior's space.

I have never been inside the office of a University Chancellor. I look around. The high-ceilinged room contains furnishings that once belonged to Louis XIV, XV, XVI, and to Napoleon. On the parquet floor lays a fine antique Persian rug woven in elegant tones of rose and green. The fresh wax shines on the exposed parts of the exquisitely inlaid floor. Delicate glass-fronted rosewood bookcases line two walls; the huge Empire desk top opposite me is bare, except for a blotter and a black marble pen set. The furniture includes two Louis XIV chairs covered with green velvet; both flank the tall floor-to-ceiling Renaissance French doors that overlook the green lawn below. Too high to jump, I say to myself. That and the enigmatic Sphinx at the other end of the corridor mean to me — NO EXIT.

Minutes pass. I pinch the soft fold between my left thumb and index finger aware that here in Grenoble no one will help me, the police are his; but underneath it all, Uncle Louis' voice rises in my mind: "Marguerite is coming into her own; she's blossoming."

Pierre Coulon makes his entry dressed in a three-piece double-breasted suit, starched white shirt, and tie. Before sitting down he pulls up the creases of his trousers with great care. (There's something pedantic about Monsieur le Secrétaire-Général). I feel my heart beat very fast. This is the man who betrays the Resistance. He's here, he faces me!

"What can I do for you, Mademoiselle?" he articulates in a smooth voice.

Murky brown eyes protrude from his pale flaccid face. A wart shows on his right temple. He has a rounded head topped with dark brown thinning hair. His looks are typical middle-aged bourgeois French: flabby faced, but nobody's fool. Only his eyes didn't cry like other similar eyes did when they witnessed the victorious foe march under the Arch of Triumph in Paris on June 14, 1940. He — he turns students of the Resistance over to the Germans.

LE SÉCRÉTAIRE-GÉNÉRAL observes me keenly across the glass-topped desk. His cognitive powers demand respect.

I have no difficulty telling him the purpose of my visit.

"I would like to register for le baccalauréate, Monsieur le Secrétaire-Général."

He coughs. I have heard that dry stress cough before — it's the same sort as Papa's.

"What is the problem, Mademoiselle?" A touch of subtle sadism breaks through his voice.

"I can't furnish the required transcripts, Monsieur le Secrétaire-Général." I shrug like a helpless child.

The Vichy-appointed civil servant leans forward over his desk in a gesture of equally feigned empathy. (Marguerite, don't get fooled)!

"Why?" he asks with a silky tongue.

"I'm Alsatian!" I reply, and I make eye contact. Juvenile guile. Feminine weapon.

A subcutaneous flow of blood rushes to Coulon's pale visage, his face goes scarlet. I'm looking into his opaque brown eyes. A few sweat drops collect on his brow. My great-grandfather Felix Lévy was born in Alsace in the Year VI of the French Revolution. Coulon and I both sit on old French period chairs. The desk, the rug, and the delicate rosewood vitrines, all belonged to our kings, our emperors — his, mine. A common legacy binds us. I expect Coulon to redeem his betrayals. NO EXTERNAL POWER CAN PREVAIL.

His pupils narrow.

Abruptly he pushes back his armchair, and he steps toward the Louis XV chair on which I am seated in an eye-lowered look of virtuous reserve.

He towers over me. He orders:

"WHISPER YOUR NAME INTO MY EAR."

"Chuchotez votre nom dans mon oreille" rolls off his tongue with touching insistence. He's talking in a sweet-serious tone of grandfatherly bonhomie to me as if I were a child. (He knows my problem is that I live with false papers). One hand on the caned back of my chair, his head bends so low that his right lobe touches my lips (to better hear the whisper of my name in his ear)!

"Reich!" I murmur.

REICH is the surname of Julie and Elaine, the two sisters from Paris I met in Vignols-en-Corrèze in 1940 during the exodus. Their last name surges forward from my depth, spontaneously. My heart thumps in my chest.

Lobe to lips, lips to ear — le Secrétaire-Général caresses my right cheek with his index finger, fast, very fast, up-down, down-up, compulsive. A moist finger, soft.

The all-powerful dean of the University of Grenoble, barely mustering enough courage to issue a command, bending to touch and caress my cheek, seems absurd to me. For a moment, I hear the massive-mystic Marseillaise *"Le jour de gloire est arrivé..."*

Passive, head lowered, I stare at the leaves and the flowers woven into the pattern of an antique Persian rug under my feet, wondering: When will this game of mutual seduction end?

243

A moment passes. The secretary-general straightens his torso. He tugs at his vest and, in a resolute step, walks back to his seat of authority.

At midpoint he stops.

He looks at the starched cuffs of his shirt... and pulls, until the white border extends the one-inch length de rigueur beyond the jacket sleeve. A desire to create a good impression? On me! I watch his every move.

Behind his imperial desk again God-like, impassible, he opens the center drawer. He removes a pad and reaches for the pen stuck in the black marble base. Under the seal of the University of Grenoble, he scratches a line or two. On the narrow chair opposite him I stare at the letterhead upside down. Is he making out a ticket to the classroom or for deportation? Am I to be liquidated? Inside me, the desire to survive clings to our common past, our common heritage.

I have that visceral feeling I have had before at moments of exceptional intensity when my survival was at stake. My head is compressed. I hold my breath. I see his words flow smoothly. My eyes are glued to his large loops. He signs his name with a flourish, "Pierre Coulon," then rocks an old-fashioned blotter to and fro until the ink dries.

He hands the letter across the desk, careful not to touch fingers with me; composed again. "Please give this to registration, Mademoiselle," he says in a formal, non-committal tone of voice.

"Oh merci, Monsieur le Secrétaire-Général," I burst.

"A votre service, Mademoiselle."

He pronounces "at your service," with courteous decorum. Bayard, the 15th century virtuous Grenoble Knight in shiny armor, silk banners flying and ladies awaiting, inclines a balding head in homage to the feminine gender. "At your service."

From then on Coulon and I uphold the etiquette of bygone chivalry. He rises, I rise. He extends his fingers: we shake hands. By the door I touch the knob, a signal the lady is ready to leave. He turns it open. From his bluish lips drop perfunctory good wishes.

"Je vous souhaite un bon resultat, Mademoiselle." He wishes me good results, successful exams.

As I pass him going through the doorframe, there is a glimmer in his murky brown eyes.

The distance from the corner office to the clerk's cubicle has shrunk.

"Voilà Monsieur!" And I hold out to the gatekeeper, the signed and sealed right to present myself at the examinations.

"Ah, ça y est," he exclaims. "It's done!"

The written examinations for Le Bac are scheduled to take place at the lycée in Bonneville, the county seat of Saint-Gervais, on June 1-2 at 8:00 AM. "It's a short fifteen-minute train ride," he says. My heart skips a beat at the mere mention of "Bonneville." The twenty-five kilometer distant city means another risk-filled trip by train to me.

"Leave the line 'PROOF OF DOCUMENTS FURNISHED' blank," he says. "We'll put in something..." The sphinx-like face grins at the opportunity to create a new formal entry.

On the way back to the railroad station through the narrow streets of the old town, my nerve leaves me. My emotions vacillate between triumph and dread. You are in the system now, they can check you out. What if Coulon... what if this is his *modus operandi*... kindness before betrayal? I even question my right to academic ambition. Selfish! Marguerite, you have imperiled your family.

On Place Grenette at the sight of the Bastille Fort that overlooks the town from atop the hill, I wince. That's where citizens end up who defy the regime — in a cold cell.

Waiting for the train at the station I ponder about Coulon's motives. Attraction? Patriotism? The Alsatian chord? My enemy helped me that day: the mystery of life under the Occupation.

Vichy is often represented as one monolithic cohesive regime: nothing is further from the truth. France during the Occupation was a society ruled by a sadistic invader. Many indigenous elements crossed over to his side, many resisted. The majority found an accommodation of sorts. On my own I discover that the pressures of war bring out the best and the worst and the full gamut of human behavior in between the extremes — as individuals choose their own survival modes.

At Bonne Maman, that night, Ghis asks me:

"How did it go?"

"Fine! No problem!"

A male student may have fared less well.

Chapter 17

Reckless on the Train

(Summer 1944)

S HE stood, notebook in hand, backpack strapped to her shoulders, casually, on the platform of the old train station at Le Fayet-Saint-Gervais-south; sharp edges angle out through the canvas of her backpack. The hands on the overhead clock show 17:20. Eighteen? Yes, you could say that.

Of medium height. The usual wartime shoes: leather uppers, wooden soles over navy socks, she wears a straight skirt; a white blouse shows under a light blue cardigan smartly tied around her neck by the sleeves. She has a square head; thick dark bangs fall low over her forehead — the girl is a dimpled brunette with a strong face. Genuine. Good.

"Bonneville?" I ask.

"Oui! Oui!" she points to the books in her rucksack. "I can't wait to get rid of these and of Le Bac." An intelligent glint in her brown eyes goes with the reply.

"Me too," I say, and we both smile.

It is a fortuitous encounter. I will travel with her. The scheduled departure is 17:35.

As soon as the train pulls in we find an empty compartment and side by side, together, we settle in for the twenty-minute ride.

Books open on our laps we start cramming, studious to the sweet end.

Out of *Anatomy One* I give myself a quiz: "The name of the ball on which the hip bone turns in its socket...?" "The trochanter." Correct! "The two bones that connect the knee and the ankle are...?" "The tibia and the fibula." Right on!

At Sallanches, the platform teems with Wehrmacht. After a minute or so, three German officers sit down on the bench opposite ours. Shiny boots, blue eyes, they are very young Wehrmacht officers returning north after an Alpine R&R stay. On the spot they start girl watching. We ignore them. I feel half safe, accustomed as I have become, to living parallel to the forces of occupation.

Soon the conductor blows his whistle, the carriages roll along the wide Arly plain for the short ride to Bonneville. Le Brévent, Mont Blanc, la Verte, Les Drus, and the other white peaks, all grow smaller and smaller in the distance. THEY observe the bookworms and speak in intimate voices. We, necks bent, concentrate on our textbooks. When, unexpectedly, one of the three puts a humorous question to his *Kamaraden* —

"*Wuerdest Du eine Intellektuelle heiraten?* Would you marry a brain?"

The Kamarad wrinkles his nose in good-natured dismay.

"*Eine Frau die mehr weiss wie ich*? Me — marry a bluestocking who knows more than I do?"

"*Und wer wird die Köchin sein*? And who'll do the cooking?"

"*Und die Hinteren säubern?* And clean the babies' behinds?"

The Bavarian warriors express their candid opinions about the role of women. They expect the weaker sex to rear the young, cook the food, and mind the hearth — a dull enough cliché confession in 1944, but for the comical tone of their voices and the rumpled noses.

Oops! I burst out with laughter. Loud and clear.

At once, a chill as heavy as a brick crashes the compartment. On their bench the three gemuetliche Kamaraden from Bavaria bolt upright as one body. "That one understands German!" exclaims the thinner one and he points his finger at me.

Suspicion chases Gemütlichkeit. Steely blue-eyes, now hard, glare at me. The thin foxy one jumps to his feet and sets out to uncover why I understand colloquial German. An enemy of the Fatherland! A Jew!

A tingle of cold fear slides down my spine. Marguerite, you have blown your cover; they'll take you off the train. They'll

248

interrogate you. You'll be deported. Papa, Maman, and Ghis too. So close to the end! Head lowered on *Anatomy One,* I freeze.

The three Wehrmacht officers start Jewish profiling. My nose (straight). Eyes (green). Hair (curly reddish-brown). Methodically, they dissect my body (tall, slender), and observe my behavior (assimilated French). Features and composure yielding few clues, the sly One decides to investigate me from a different angle.

He again sits down and, leaning his torso forward toward my companion the *inconnue,* the unknown student, he says: *"Fotre amee comprendre Alleman dres pien."* His French is so atrocious, it takes me a while to comprehend that he means: "Your friend speaks German very well."

His tone of voice implies a question and a command. Who is she? Where does she come from? Why does she understand the vernacular *Deutsch* that well!

The anonymous French student, a mere twenty-minute acquaintance, quick as lightening pushes her textbook under the lieutenant's Aryan nose and, in one breath, says: "We take German in class together!" Instinctively protecting me. Against THEM!

I sit on my bench, numb. From the corner of my eyes I watch the Master *Herren* recline on their seats. Book in hand, they flip through the pages of *German for Secondary Schools*; they read a sentence here a sentence there, lips tight, brows raised, convinced that the source of my idiomatic German cannot be found therein. Their slits examine the evidence at hand. Me.

Barely breathing, guilty (I should have controlled my self), my head is bent over Anatomy One. I feel trapped. Oh God, please open the floor below me. Let me drop unto the tracks like a pebble. Please! I sit across from them. We are ten minutes into the ride to Bonneville.

At that dire moment, a voluptuous blonde with cherry-colored lips and permed hair dressed in a smart beige travel suit makes a Marlène Dietrich entry into our compartment with the evincing throaty laugh. With panache, in *hoch Deutch* (Berliner-German), she inquires: *"Ist alles in Ordnung bei Ihnen*? Is everything OK in here?"

249

I know that if any one of the three lieutenants leaves the compartment under any pretext — change of venue, stretching, WC — he will do so for one reason only: to report me to her. Who will be the informer?

Eyes lowered, I see three pairs of legs slide to the floor in a slouch. And three nonchalant Bavarians answer in unison: "Everything's OK!"

The Fräulein's nostrils quiver. She tosses her bosom forward; back against the closed door, arms crossed over her chest, she keenly observes the men. She senses something is askew in here.

She singles out Foxy-Face. She addresses him in particular. "And how are things with you?"

"*Gut!*" he shrugs, palms turned upward. The vacant look in his eyes meaning, what do you expect to be amiss in here?

The Fräulein is no fool. She lets go of another peal of seductive laughter and, determined, gazes into the eyes of each young officer in turn. "*So, meine Herren?*" She goads them on. "So, gentlemen? — "

After a third attempt at sensuous baiting, she bares two healthy rows of gleaming white teeth.

The lieutenants remain quiet, unmoved.

"*So alles in Ordnung, hier*? So everything is all right in here!" She imitates them with sarcasm.

"*Jawohl!*"

And the three Kamaraden airily meet her glare.

Piqued, the Fräulein draws in her breath. The open jacket of her well-tailored suit reveals a white silk blouse decolletée at the neck.

Change of tactics. Her exasperation turns against the two French students. Blazing eyes dart from my companion to me. I feel transparent. The Gestapo takes Jews off trains!

The Inconnue and I bent on our textbooks sit still —

THEY and WE are thwarting her!

As soon as the door to our compartment shuts close behind her, the three young officers from Bavaria become vocal. The first one exclaims: "*Die ist doch ein Spitzel!* That one is a spy!"

"Der kann man doch garnichts glauben! You can't believe a word of what she says," adds the second one.

And the three let fly their hands in the direction of the corridor in a gesture of disgust. Out with the political officer! She's no good!

I'm saved, but no words can describe the terror of being cornered in that closed carriage, alone. To this day I need open spaces. I fear questions.

Shaken on my wooden bench, I hit the conclusion that the surprise entry of their own detested political agent robbed the Bavarian Herren of the time necessary to investigate me. They who dream of loyal womenfolk tending home and hearth disliked the alluring fertility goddess so much — they ganged up against her instead of against me. Unbelievable! They don't stop discussing her: *"Die Lorelei!" "Die doch*! That one!" It doesn't' matter to me what they say — I am quiet as a mouse — as long as they speak of her.

In a few minutes the train slows down. I and my friend make our way through the Wehrmacht-crowded corridor onto the platform.

On the concrete quay of the Bonneville railroad station I read the familiar signs, *Sortie, WC, and Buffet de la Gare.* The clock hangs a wee bit crooked above the worn bench; at the end of the platform the railway inspector in his threadbare navy uniform punches tickets under the tall pine tree by the gate. *The occupation forces didn't catch me. I'M FREE!*

Involuntarily, I turn around and there, leaning out the window of our compartment, stand my three Bavarian anti-Semites, a look of utter disbelief on their faces. I almost wave "Good-bye" before melting away into the crowd.

I still see the Herrenvolk's baffled faces as they stood by the open window; Foxy-face especially showed the mien of a cat that had lost its already-crippled mouse.

Beyond the barrier, I grin with the gift of life.

That evening, a group of French students and I congregate in the low-beamed bar/dining room at the old Hotel de la Gare. In the Gallic fashion, the students light up and make a song fest of the exams. Seated about the red-checkered cloth that covers the round wooden table, they sing *"Les Chevaliers De La Table Ronde,"* *"Fanchon," "C'est À Boire,"* and other traditional French drinking songs. I join. Singing makes me forget my fright in the train.

In a nearby booth, a French lady, the delicate Fragonard type, wears a chic little Chanel suit with a sparkling diamond brooch on her lapel. Her head swings like a fine pendulum between his shoulder and her own notion of propriety. Right, left, left, right, she swoons, sighs, moans, all the while rubbing her cheek against his — helplessly in the grip of love.

Her newly-wed husband dressed in an expensive suit, trim, dapper, discreetly frowns in my direction. Hmm! Privacy please! I have the bad habit of staring (I learn from observation). For the first time I understand that in wartime, intense fear and intense love coexist. Etienne, one of the students, reads my mind. He says: "L'amour, la guerre, c'est la vie! Love, war — it's life!"

We go on singing, "Goûtons *voir, oui, oui, oui, goûtons voir, non, non, non...* Let's taste, yes, yes, yes, let's taste, no, no, no..."

AND LE BAC? Before 8:00 the following morning I climb the old stone steps rue de la Gare up the esplanade to the lycée. In a drab classroom I squeeze into a graffiti-inscribed desk; I check my fountain pen to see if it's filled with ink. The candidates are waiting for the proctor to hand out the printed questions. The clock on the wall ticks away. The wooden floor boards creak under the proctor's heavy stride.

"Commencez!" he calls out.

Pens scratch on sheets of paper. Am I dreaming? For years the image of my baccalauréate had flashed before my eyes, filled with desire, as red hot as a burning sun. *LE BACHOT!* But the real thing is lonely. Suddenly I no longer have any friends. Our competing stylos scratch the paper.

I haven't been in a classroom for years. I'm nervous, not really confident about my academic preparedness, but concentration is my forte and I draw from a photographic memory. History, Anatomy, German language, English, Philosophy — I scratch away.

In the late afternoon after exams let out, the candidates band together as French students do. We stroll under the ancient arcades, past the place de l'Eglise and the Hotel de Ville. Bonneville, the former capital of the Faucigny region, resembles any other occupied town — the Swastika flies atop the German garrison. In an upbeat mood, the students come together to celebrate the end of a learning cycle. We cross over the Arve River Bridge; the banks are lined with plane trees. For me, it is a magical moment.

Yet, for too long I stand at the war memorial for those who fell in the 1870 and 1914-1918 wars. With empathy and guilt I muse how the springs of life gush forth, randomly, and how some are capped early. When I come out of my reverie, the others had left. From the nearby stone parapet over the Arve River Bridge I gaze into the water. I'm surprised at the distortion.

After the Liberation, the interim government offers a gift from the nation to the class of 1944 "in recognition for our spirit of defiance". We are spared the awful oral exams. I am jubilant. Thank you for the tribute. And the present.

The UNKNOWN STUDENT? She and I part company almost immediately upon arrival in Bonneville. On the avenue de la Gare past the railroad station we find out that we are staying at different hotels. Also our schedules differ, and our subject matters are not the same. We do not meet again.

The image is etched into me of her good square head, the dark bangs, and an honest dimple on each cheek as she shoves the hardcover textbook *German for Secondary Schools* under the noses of the three Wehrmacht officers. In that moment, she vouched for me.

I often dream of a white hard marble sculpture with spread out wings, set on a university campus in celebration of the students' swift élans of generosity.

A few days later in Val Montjoie at Chez Nous I hear on the BBC from London at the usual 9:30 PM hour, one particular message: *"Blessent mon coeur d'une langueur monotone,"* out of *Chanson d'automne*, a poem by Verlaine. "Pierce my heart with monotonous languor" is repeated several times.

It is the covert directive to the Resistance that the Landings are taking place at dawn.

Chapter 18

The Resistance Calls

(Summer 1944)

The Normandy landings are on. Through the scrambling I barely hear the BBC announcer say: "Cotentin Peninsula..." then the signal fades.

Zut! The Germans are jamming the London short wave frequency. It is morning on June 6th, 1944.

Impatient for news, I turn the dial.

La Radiodiffusion Française, the state-run Vichy radio station reports: "The American, the British, and the Canadian *invaders* are being pushed back into the sea. Tens of thousands of bodies cover the beaches."

Oh God, please make the Allies succeed!

The German High Command headquarters in France warns: "Anyone caught with arms in hand will be shot on the spot. So will those who commit acts of sabotage."

I piece together bits of BBC information: "... the French Forces of the Interior [are taking up] arms against the enemy... General Eisenhower considers them an army [placed under] his command. They [have received orders to conduct their] operations according [to] accepted laws [of] warfare... They [are provided with] a special insignia..."

It's the first time the FORCES FRANÇAISES de l'INTERIEUR, the F.F.I., the Resistance fighters, are officially mentioned as an allied fighting force. They recognize us! We count! Pride of acceptance overcomes me. In my heart I cheer as I listen to General Eisenhower's proclamation: "People of Occidental Europe, the troops of the Allied Expeditionary Forces have landed on the coasts of France. The hour of liberation is approaching..." Every word of General Eisenhower's eloquent order to his troops moves the soul. "The eyes of the world are upon you..."

They have set foot on the continent! They are here!

By evening, the Allies have established beachheads.

And a day and a night settle over what will be known in history as — Omaha, Utah, Gold, Sword, and Juno.

Next morning in town I see pictures on newspaper stands of American tanks burning in black and yellow smoke on the Normandy beaches. The front page photos show men of the 81st Airborne shot dead, dangling from trees in Ste-Mère-Eglise. I return home in shock. They fight and die, I'm sidelined!

Itchy in my room I set a pin on Pointe du Hoc and Coleville. Bayeux liberated by the British gets a third tack. They are advancing!

Radio Vichy repeats the warning: "If you help and abet the *enemy*, there will be stark consequences." The Germans are shooting scores of resisters dead.

In turmoil, ear glued to the Philips radio, I listen to the latest developments.

The BBC mentions that entire villages with their mayors at the head are marching to secret headquarters of the local F.F.I., to join the insurrection. Thus uncovered, they can't return home.

Every Western Allied leader speaks to us. Winston Churchill extols the French love for Liberté... de Gaulle (later) exhorts *les Français* with the words of: "The clear, the sacred duty is to fight the enemy with all the means at your disposal..." General Eisenhower extends his protection...

Papa shakes his head.

Where can I find the Resistance?

Every morning I walk five miles to and from tutoring my two pupils at the Splendid and the Savoyard hotels in downtown Saint-Gervais. I need my economic independence and a productive occupation, but I feel this is selfish. A flood of patriotism overwhelms me. I want to join in the liberation of my country, but I wonder how?

On D-DAY PLUS FOUR, General Koenig, the commander of all Free French Forces, including the metropolitan F.F.I., reverses de Gaulle's appeal to arms. From London, Koenig issues a communiqué: "Each one of you should carry on with his present task unless he has been given a specific order to do otherwise... Above all keep the names of the resistance groups and their leaders secret."

I glance at the dark forests surrounding Bionnay. There, somewhere, the *maquisards*, the young men fugitive from the compulsory Work Service in Germany, dwell. I am hoping for an opportunity that more and more seems ephemeral like a leaf blown by the wind.

That afternoon, Dédée Baud knocks on the kitchen door at Chez Nous. Nervous, she looks over her shoulder at the dense Prarion Mountain as if she expected to see something I don't. In a little voice, she says: "May I have a glass of water, please?"

By the window of the living room the rays of the setting sun play on Dédée's wavy blond hair. With deft hands she removes burs from her cotton skirt, and sets the prickly thistle seeds down in balled up small clumps on the edge of the table. *Tiens, how did she amass these*? It's Dédée's first visit to Chez Nous. *She must have climbed through thickets*! "The maquisards and Riquet are bringing down 250 barrels of gasoline from Mont Lachat," she says, and she raises her head and breaks into a soft laughter. "I didn't want to ride the cogwheel tram with all those Sten-toting young men!"

MAQUISARDS... MONT LACHAT... 250 BARRELS OF GASOLINE... in the kitchen I refill Dédée's glass. An image of Henri Baud at his desk in his study at the Roseraie arises in my mind as he asked me point blank: Did you notice any activity on "Lachat" when you went to Mont Blanc?

While I'm here in Bionnay shackled to the safety of my family.

Papa offers shelter to Dédée. "Would you like to sleep over-night at Chez Nous?"

Dédée declines. "I have to look in on the children first. A neighbor is watching René and Françoise."

"Henri?"

"The maquisards are taking care of him tonight," she answers. "Tomorrow he and I will rendezvous up in Saint-Nicholas-de-Véroce at a friend's house."

Dédée speaks to us as if we were family, trusting us intimately. Nobody else does this. I have always admired the Bauds. They are young, engaged in the times. They belong to one of the old local families. Oh God, please, have them include me!

Dédée says that the Haute-Savoie Resistance groups have received a coded message on the BBC to ready gasoline reserves for imminent use. "The 250 barrels up on Mont Lachat were stashed away in a cemented basement of the *Aéronautic Research Center for Deicing*." The gas belonged to the 27ème battalion of *Chasseurs Alpins.* "They stacked tons of equipment and arms in basements all over the Haute-Savoie in June 1940 for the revenge to come," she laughs.

Dédée places her empty glass on the table. "I better take the forest trail home," she shyly says

Furtive as a doe, past the apple tree, Dédée Baud disappears into the darkness of the Prarion woods. Longingly, I stare.

In my room I look at the wall map of the Normandy coast. I place a pin on Port-en-Bressin, Arromaches, and Courseulles-sur-Mer... The landing beaches are holding. I remove the white pin from Caen. The Wehrmacht is fiercely defending the strategically located town.

I am far removed from the action. I tell myself in vain that I contributed to the family's survival and more. I forged my parents' and my own IDs; provided my sister and the Dreyfuss' with blanks. I got my mother a "née Schmidt" identity... Without hesitation I have done that. I am not afraid to be free — but my wider tribe, my country?

When a call comes for me at Chez Dave I run across the D 902. Inside the tobacco shop I press the receiver of the old wooden wall telephone against my ear, "Allõ, Allõ!" and I hear a suave voice say: "Someone we both know recommended you. Can you come

258

for two or three days into the mountains, take some sténo and do some typing?" At the other end of the line the tremulous voice asks: "Can you be ready in an hour? A blue Citroen will pick you up." "Oui! Oui!" After a short pause, the Voice adds: "Please tell your parents we will take good care of you."

"Merci!"

Exhilarated, I barely thank Monsieur Dave and fly over the D 902 to tell the news to Maman and Papa.

The Resistance needs me!

At Chez Nous, Maman follows me to my room. "What if it's the militia, Marguerite?" she says. "Just a month ago the humpback's nephew in Saint-Nicholas got a phone call to visit a sick friend at the hospital in Sallanches. On his way there he was ambushed and killed. What if it's a trap, Marguerite?

"I'm going, Maman!"

In the living room Papa coughs, but he doesn't interfere. I know my father's heart pulses with patriotic fervor.

To Maman I say: "I know the caller. He's a Monsieur de la Resistance."

Au-revoir!

My parents stay inside the house. I wait outside behind the hedge for the unmarked blue Citroen. Later my mother tells me she thought she would never again see her daughter.

Good-bye!

My driver wears metal-rimmed glasses. In a modest way, he leans over and opens the back door. In the front seat next to him a bulging thing lies under a sweater.

"Let's go!" he says.

"Where to?"

"The Villa!"

Zoom! I notice a sly smile as he revs up the engine. He wears sandals. No combat boots. No special insignia.

We speed down the empty D 902 past Les Bernards and Les Pratz. By the cemetery, an image appears in my brain of my dead body sprawled out with a bullet to the head. Reflexively my hand reaches for the door handle. In my throat a scream rises. Stop!

259

Stop! Let me off! With much effort I smother the scream. Marguerite, you can't panic. Not now. Not on the way to the Resistance!

At the intersection, the Citroen swerves left past the Hotel Moderne in the direction of Mégève-Albertville. On the narrow Devil's Bridge over the roaring Bonnant my young man, gung-ho, says: "We'd better not meet a Boche patrol!"

That's when the tension breaks. *He is on my side.*

On a steep twisting track higher and higher into the mountain, suddenly the Citroen pulls into a driveway hidden by clusters of mature pine trees, shrubs, and rosebushes. A well-built one story brick chalet sits at the end of the narrow roadway.

"*Voilà*! Miquet, by the way, is my name," and my sandaled driver turns off the ignition. Nonchalantly, from under the front seat sweater, he grabs a semi-automatic.

"I'm Marguerite," I say. General Dwight Eisenhower's address flashing in my mind: "THE LIBERATION OF THE CONTINENT HAS STARTED…"

The peaceful landscape is white, golden, and green, however the air is charged with an indefinable energy as if particles that were repressed for eons are all of a sudden released into the atmosphere. The energy of liberation!

In the foyer stands a tall, broad-chested, late thirty or early forties commanding presence. Today I can't recall if he wore uniform or civilian clothes.

"CAPTAIN MONTJOIE."

Tiens, same name as our valley. Clever!

We shake hands.

Captain Montjoie introduces his wife, Madeleine, and Monsieur D'Aix.

D'Aix's handshake bares a monogrammed cuff and manicured fingernails.

Monogrammed cuffs and manicured hands, here, in the forest? I feel uneasy at the sight of such a display of wealth. I wash and dry-

260

iron my one and only white blouse at night so that I can wear it the next morning.

In the guest room I deposit my backpack. Pools of light dance on the thick carpet. The furnishings look expensive: it's a well appointed home. Along a papered wall sits an elegant white birch dresser. A skirted chintz patterned vanity matches the design of the upholstered chair; a gleaming brass bed stands on the plush rug against the inside wall behind the door, sheltered from the elements. Through the window panes enter the jagged Fiz and the Aravis massifs.

Captain Montjoie paces the floor. He dictates orders and promotions to me. Nervous, I call on my memory to fill the gaps in my shorthand. It's all new to me. I use F.F.I. letter-heads with the Cross of Lorraine inside the V for Victory. On the old Underwood portable typewriter I type stencils for the leaflets to be distributed to the population. I crank out the copies by hand on the mimeograph machine; the drum has to be filled with ink. The office furniture consists of a streaked desk, two chairs, and a rectangular table. I bring the papers to the captain. Excitement makes the hours fly.

I learn some codes. I work for Captain Montjoie. I meet Guy, Julot, Michou... and other young maquisards on guard duty. Captain Montjoie and Madeleine invite me to eat and sleep over. I'm shy at the captain's table.

During the meal Madeleine delicately shakes her wrist watch, and then presses the small gold time piece against her ear. No tick. The captain gently extends his open palm and, slowly winds up the tiny spring with his long slender fingers. As he returns the ticking watch to his wife, they both break out into a subtle ironic smile. (Just the spring, darling)! The finesse of it all strikes me. And those are the people Vichy and the Germans call "bandits!"

After a long pause at the dining table, Captain Montjoie's head all of a sudden turns red, as if pinched. Abruptly, he says: "That little bastard, so and so, I'd love to get my hands on him" and he touches the revolver in his holster. Monsieur D'Aix dabs the

261

corner of his lips with a damask napkin. "My dear captain, why dirty your hands?" he says, "Why not ask Z? He will do the task for you. As you know 'Z' did a first class hit on Mademoiselle Alain, made it look like a stray bullet."

So, it's the A.S. who killed Mademoiselle Alain! I nearly choke. I'm afraid they notice my blush; head lowered, I eye the elegant Bird of Paradise painted in the center of my Havilland china plate. So my former boss with the pitch black bun who gave me my first job at the Bruyères was a traitor! All those heads bobbing up behind the privet hedge... So the Bruyères had been under surveillance!

And just as suddenly the captain, Madeleine, and Monsieur D'Aix speak of *Antigone*, Anouilh's new play. "The line, 'The Flower of the kingdom is in prison...' got a standing ovation,'" says Monsieur D'Aix who had seen the performance in Paris. He must have arrived recently in Saint-Gervais, I tell myself. I know he is not hiding from the compulsory Work Service in Germany — he's way too old, and he sports manicured fingernails. Monsieur D'Aix intrigues me.

The following morning at breakfast in the dining room monogrammed-cuffs-and-manicured-hands arrives late, clad in a blue silk dressing gown, and smelling of 4711 German eau de Cologne. Madeleine, the captain, and I are eating our toast. D'Aix apologizes, "Sorry, my gamekeeper at my chateau in the Dordogne kept me on the phone; he has a problem with poachers."—"I have a payroll of thirteen to take care of my castle and my three country homes," he adds for my benefit red-faced, creepy, and drooling at the corners of his mouth. Secretly I wonder, whose property has D'Aix acquired? My people's?

The part in me who believes in the purity of the Cause and in lofty ideals is struggling.

A thought slowly emerges of two school friends from the Lycée Buffon in Paris. One becomes a captain in the Resistance; the other, a war profiteer who wants to keep his ill-gotten wealth. D'Aix can avoid charges of war profiteering if he offers proof of mitigating circumstances. Captain Montjoie, his classmate, dictates a letter to me, citing the villa on Le Bettex as evidence: "He generously placed his house at the disposal of the Resistance..." Prince Charming left Paris when Hitler and the Vichy regime were collapsing; he's an ELEVENTH HOUR turncoat. A blue envelope with a June 8, 1944, Paris 8ème postmark (the Étoile arrondissement) found in the drawer of my desk confirms my suspicions. Unobserved, I read the one page scented blue note:

Mon chéri,
    Here life is still strange... Some property is getting cumbersome... am trying to dispose of certain assets...
Love and kisses,
Brigitte.

Two snapshots of a young boy and a little girl riding shiny new bicycles in the Bois de Boulogne fall out of the envelope. Cute children; clean smiling faces.

While the maquisards are suffering from bronchitis in the forests, and the Jews are being deported, D'Aix steals for his own profit. *Le salaud!* The disgusting con! I avoid him as much as I can.

One by one, the maquisards enter my life.

They all have aliases. You sense they are on the run. They wear dark trousers, a shirt, and sandals or farm boots. They are uncouth, raw. Honest, humble, and tough. Twenty, twenty-one, twenty-two, twenty-three year-olds who have grown up quickly away from home under duress.

Sten gun slung over their shoulders, they are the fugitives from the compulsory Work Service in Germany. They live in the *maquis*, the bush, henceforth their name: *les maquisards.* A price tag of 100,000 French francs and a death warrant hangs on their heads. The BBC tells them: "Defy the Saukel-Laval decree; escape to the maquis, the bush." They run away before the *gendarme* grabs them for slave labor in Germany, with nothing but blue overalls on their backs. Martin's mother called her son at work to

263

say: "Don't return home!" Martin never said good-bye. In his eyes I see the haunting pain, and I understand. Did I say au-revoir to Denise, Henri, my Brownies, the Dreyfusses, and at Chez Jacques? No! My soul also aches. In the forest on LeBettex they guard us.

LUC, thin, awkward, with wavy black hair cropped short, speaks to me with a sort of reluctant hope. Each time a pause lingers, he or I muster crucial words. "No mail, no women, no cinema," he says, and he caresses his freshly assembled Sten gun, as if it were a girl's body. Luc hasn't spoken to a female in thirteen months and eleven days. "Have to cut off all contact with the outside world."

Drones are buzzing by. Through the light in the pines I can see the narrow trail I skied last winter. Alone. Yet, I'm a thousand times better off than he. I get paid. I sleep between clean white sheets in a heated house. I'm able to visit, even live with, my parents. I work in the mainstream. Madame Perroud and Madame Vachette, great old ladies, listen to me.

At our backs loom Mont d'Arbois, Mont Joux, and Mont Joly. Their folds and dips hide us.

Luc says: "All last winter, breakfast at the hut consisted of soup cooked the night before. After breakfast there's cabin duty, then tree cutting. Have to earn a few *sous*." He shrugs. "The local who feeds and houses us sells the charcoal to *gazogène* dealers." Abruptly Luc stops talking. He's afraid to reveal forbidden secrets. "I better go inside and finish my typing," I mumble.

"Have got to do your work," he says with an intense look in his eyes, and he turns back into his forest.

Luc is an apprentice mechanic. To escape the gendarmes he pedaled from the Drôme department over one-hundred mountainous miles along back roads.

MICHOU is squatting and drawing arabesques with his left finger in the soft pine needles. He blinks, "Ah!" A month ago I'd have slunk back into the woods if I saw you coming." With a tobacco-stained thumb and index he grinds out the stub of his cigarette. Wistfully, he throws handfuls of soft ground cover into the air. Lost.

When the words come, he says: "The BBC tells you one thing from London, 'Go to the bush young man!' Reality is nobody's expecting you. You have to find your own local. You can get busted just doing that.'"

"Tell me one thing, where are the regular army officers? I bet you they are at home invoking the oath of allegiance. Don't believe it. It's the dough! Vichy is their paymaster!" He explodes: "The maquis is hell!" After a pause as if to save his pride, he adds: "Now in World War One, *there* was an army!" Michou yearns to be a well-trained soldier. "Captain Montjoie drills us only a few afternoons, whenever he's available, but that's not enough." His facial muscles tighten. Hardness sets around his mouth. He lights a fresh cigarette, inhales, and flicks the ashes away as if he was playing marbles. "After the Boches are driven out, *ça va barder! Things will get nasty," he says in slang.

Charles de Gaulle knows. Later we learn that the Allies armed over 140,000 Frenchmen; over sixty thousand found their own weapons.

PIERROT might have come from a foreign country where the men are red-haired with round clown faces and are immensely strong. He re-enacts for me their life last winter in a hut somewhere up by the Gruvaz Gorge between Bionnay and the Contamines where the glacier of Bionnassay looms over the landscape: he jumps up and down under the pines as if he were cold. "We woke up every day to a foot or more of fresh snow. You couldn't see the summits." He clatters his teeth, and shows how he got up, lit a candle, walked around, ran, talked, made a lot of noise: "I got warm, daylight rose... the morale held..." he says, clowning.

"Did you have bronchitis like the others?" I ask.

He shrugs, "We all got sick at one time or another."

We both know that there is a reward of 100,000 French francs on his head and, were he caught, he would be tortured before being shot. There are 45,000 militiamen out there who swore to fight, torture, and exterminate the Resistance. Pierrot rumples his nose, and adjusts the strap on his Sten.

JULOT has thick brown hair, he is stocky and short. A true fugitive creature, he was caught twice. The last time on Assy. The Italians killed several maquisards and pushed the rest all the way over the Bonhomme Pass to prison in the Aosta valley, Italy. When Marshall Badoglio signed a separate armistice with the Allies in September 1943, after the Americans landed in Anzio, the guards in Aosta opened the prison gates. "*C'était la filade*! Each one for himself! I stole a bicycle and off I pedaled." With his two fists he mimics wheels turning fast.

"What did you do with the bike?"

"Kicked it into the bush along the Bonhomme Pass," he answers with wry humor. The others laugh with him, laughing at their own condition.

Their genuine boyishness has pup-appeal.

TONTON picks his teeth. He's in an insurgent mode. Everything he does, everything he believes in, is justified in his eyes by what is being done to him. "Ah, me, it's the little stints at sabotage that I like, *les petits coups qu'on fait que j'aime!* Sometimes it's a quickie and I and my buddies escape just in time. Beats felling trees and making charcoal for a few *sous*. Well, isn't that what it's all about? Once you choose resistance as a way of life, rather than slave labor in Bocheland, you accept the risks. Don't you?"

His hand to his neck in imitation of a guillotine blade, Tonton says: "The Boches kaput!"

At the Villa that war summer of 1944 I feel the heart beat of the Resistance. On Le Bettex, I learn a lot about human nature and a few things about guerilla warfare.

I follow Captain Monjoie's ruler as it travels over a wall map and points out to Pierrot, Luc, Miquet, Michou, Gil, Emile, Julot, Tonton, and the other maquisards under his command where they

should fight if the Boches attack. "Ambush from these heights!
Escape over that ridge!"

Rumors fly of an imminent invasion of our valley from the
Italian side via the Bonhomme Pass. "The Germans are about to
attack along Hannibal's route in reverse." Captain Montjoie and
his maquisards will defend Val Montjoie. To his early twenties-
something farm boys and apprentices, Captain Montjoie is father
and God. He is their CO.

What is a nice Jewish girl from a good family doing among
fighting men? If Maman still worries, she hasn't mentioned it
lately. Mother knows that I'm a free spirit, her "little Gypsy."

One day at lunch at the Villa, Miquet came in and whispered a
few words into the captain's ear.

"Yes, show him in!"

The guest, a robust mountain type about 5 foot 10, muscular
and sturdy, pulled a chair next to the captain's. After some small
talk he leaned over toward Montjoie, he blinked in my direction.
The captain glanced at me:

"She's all right," he nodded, "Henri Baud has known her for a
long time," and his voice dropped.

I pretended not to hear. I closed my eyes. I saw the image of
Henri Baud dressed in a grey sweater and slacks, around his neck a
hand-knitted grey scarf, as he leaned against the refrigerator in his
kitchen and asked: "Do you type?" So it's Henri Baud who
recommended me to Captain Montjoie, and the low baritone voice
that spoke into the receiver at Chez Dave: Can you come into the
mountains for two or three days? — belongs to Captain Montjoie.
My mind's eye sees Henri Baud sitting on the edge of his chair in
his study, tense like a tiger ready to spring, abruptly asking me,
how many soldiers inside the German army trucks that had passed
by at chalet Chez Nous on the D 902 en route to the Contamines?

He worried about the maquisards hiding out in the barracks of
Les Chantiers de la Jeunesse, the youth camps near the Trèlatête
Glacier at the end of the valley. Is the Wehrmacht readying an
assault on the barracks? "Did you see any artillery?"

267

Then Montjoie told a funny story to the visitor about his difficulties with Baud. He said: "When I came to see him from the army sanatorium on Assy where I was recuperating from TB, he grilled me mercilessly. I had to return three times. At first he acted as if he didn't know what I was talking about..." Laughing, Montjoie said: "I really had to work hard."

I figured out that Louis Viallet, my guide to Mont Blanc, protected the secret gasoline cache on Mont Lachat as well when Dix asked him in the TMB, What is a cement structure doing up here?

So Louis Viallet knew... Henri Baud knew... patients at the army sanatorium on Assy knew... The guest too belongs to the secret network — a web tough as wild grape vines had taken roots underground and spread.

The knowledge of how the world works gives me inner strength. I grin.

That night I have a dream. In my brass bed at the Villa I see white mushrooms swaying in the sky. They slowly drift to earth. I jump up to get a hold of one. It escapes. Others catch the swinging caps without difficulty. Finally, I yell: "I got one! I got one!" Mountains fill the picture. The people in my dream resemble Henri Baud, Dédée, Police Chief Hoffstaetter, Monsieur le Maire Conseil, Captain Montjoie, and Louis Viallet. I recognize Miquet, Luc, Pierrot, Julot, Tonton, and other maquisards. They all join in a song: "Le Chant de la Libération" written in London by the musician-poetess Anna Marly. A chorus of voices echoes in the massif, but I can't sing. Madeleine asks me: Don't you know the words of *"Ami, entends-tu?"* It's a fighting song of the Resistance. Of course I know "Friend do you Hear?" But I can't carry the tune. Open your mouth wide, inhale deeply like this... and Madeleine shows me how to breathe. It works. I sing, "… in the night liberty hears…" We clap hands. Bonfires light up the mountain ranges. Everywhere resisters sing and dance. The rejoicing spreads from summit to summit.

Slowly I wake up to the meaning of my dream: the Resistance is celebrating victory in the open. At first I can't sing the song of the resisters nor reach a white mushroom drifting to earth. I'm an outsider. I can't catch a parachute descending from the skies. Madeleine helps. After several attempts I succeed. I become a part of the group. The people are spread all over the summits into one huge circle well beyond the spot I stand on. A universal ring.

In my bed the happy mood lingers. I'm adrift in the cosmos, unfettered, and at peace. Beyond the window panes the early morning mists dissipate over the desert of Passy on the Fiz. I go on connecting the dots: Henri Baud is "Perroux;" but when my former math teacher, Paul Bertin, visits the Villa and Captain Montjoie addresses him as "Lt. Berthaud" — we stare at each other. I learn that "Xavier" is British Major Helsop, a member of Cantinier's trio. Cantinier is Captain Jean Rosenthal, son of the famous jewelry House in Paris. Gradually, I discover that Captain Montjoie is born "Henri Barbero," and that he sings baritone at the Paris Opera. A lieutenant — professional men enter the army as officers — Henri Barbero in the Resistance promotes himself one rank to captain (a common practice that makes up for "no pay"). Madeleine is an actress at the Opera Comique. The "guest" is no other than the police chief of Mégève. I never learn his nom de guerre. Our landlords, Madame and Monsieur Clovis Perroud, never mentioned their two sons: Gabriel and Marcel — both were in the maquis.

The maquisards bloom for one brief moment in history: from 1943 through mid-1945. Their place is the forests. They slink about the conifers, awkward and eager; they grimace at their days and nights filled with squalor. Farm boys, auto mechanics, and trade apprentices — they deliver the mountains and the valleys to the Allies.

The maquisards are part of the wider resistance Movement. "The Resistance" comprises different groups under one umbrella. The *Radiodiffusion Française* maligns them: "The resistance is fighting for the Jews, the British, and the Capitalists." Lies! The Resistance fights to free the territory from a hated invader. I fight for *Les Droits de l'Homme et du Citoyen,* the principles of the

Revolution of 1789 and its inalienable rights of Liberté, Egalité; a 150-year-old legacy on which modern France is founded.

MONTJOIE SAYS it all starts with the idea one has of oneself and of one's country. Essentially, each one fights for his own reasons and often for his own hide. In the A.S., Armée Secrète, de Gaulle is our leader. We are his constituency. Not the FTP, the Francs Tireurs et Partisans; nor the Communists, the most important armed branch in the Resistance and the best organized because the Communists have a thirty-year-long history of underground cells; neither are we the Corps francs de la Liberation created in March 1944 —

We are an A.S. sector because farmers and rural folks tend to be more conservative, and affiliation is decided by majority. The others and I feel de Gaulle embodied our refusal to board the raft of the vanquished.

Granted! You may say French history means different things to different people. Some Frenchmen claim Charlemagne and the Holy Roman-Germanic Empire as their legitimate antecedents. The far-righters even formed a separate military unit named "Charlemagne" which joined the *Waffen-SS* Division. Frenchmen are dying on the Russian front for the Greater Third Reich.

Here, I cross a continent and many time zones. Americans would call their young men and women of World War II: THE GREATEST GENERATION. The French refer to their people as: *Les Français sous l'Occupation,* the French under the Occupation — the resisters, the collaborators, and the accommodating masses. Into the psyche of many Jews and resisters is seared la *GRANDE ANGOISSE*, the GREAT ANGUISH of getting caught.

Later, we survivors would be told by certain historians "You weren't even deported!" No one is interested in hearing that Vichy and Berlin had equipped the Milice, the Sûreté Nationale, the G.M.R. (Gardes Mobiles de Réserve), the S.P.A.C. (anti-Communist political section), the *Canadiennes* (police inspectors), and the regular gendarmes with the latest technology connecting every unit into one cross-linked network of state-controlled police agencies joined up with Germany. A trip to Mégève, a distance of

270

six miles, or to Chamonix on the other side of the Prarion Mountain, was a life-threatening journey. The new prefect, General Marion, vowed to free the department of the Haute-Savoie from maquisards, resisters, Jews, Communists, and Freemasons. He uses his squads of police informers and C.M.Rs. to sniff out the enemies of the Vichy regime. In the expectant summer of 1944, checkpoints spring up everywhere. On certain days, I feel bullets bounce off invisible walls in the air.

Amidst the general disintegration, Val Montjoie reverts once again to a dead-end glacial valley set amidst natural defenses with limited access.

June - July - August 1944.

RETURN TO THE MIDDLE AGES. The villagers huddle around their steeple.

Whenever a call comes for me at Chez Dave, rather than speed off in the unmarked blue Citroen on the paved 902 Departmental Road, I trek the forest trail along the Bonnant and over the old wooden bridge at LaGrange. The brisk climb in the shadows under the canopy to the Villa takes an hour and a half. I type a stencil or two, crank out flyers on the mimeo, and type dispatches that a Maquisard or a courier will deliver. Then I climb back down to Chez Nous.

I feel young, strong, and intensely patriotic.

Yet years later, and after numerous returns to Saint-Gervais, I'm still known there as Mademoiselle Lengel. It has to do with fear of rejection, insecurity. I waited too long. I know there are yet darker reasons...

When I tell Henri Baud, alias Perroux, that my real name was *not* Lengel, "What was it?" "Lévy!" His jaw drops wide open.

I have thoughts about the Resistance and France. One of these is the complexity of anti-Semitism.

Another is that the brave men and women who have experienced the witchery of the underground crave the accelerated days of past common purpose.

Civil disobedience has the taste of my youth.

271

Do we know about ovens and mass exterminations? The truth of the Holocaust was revealed to us in 1945 after the liberation of the concentration camps and the photographs in the newspapers.

The mirror reflects a young woman, tall, slender, with green twinkling eyes, and reddish-brown curly hair. A little secretive smile lifts the corners of her lips.

"Everybody is optimistic," I note in my diary.

In Bionnay, Papa and Maman hike together into the mountains with their alpenstocks, Papa in suspenders and a tie; Maman in her high button boots.

Ghis hopes when we go back to Paris, she'll get married and have six children.

I would end up missing the camaraderie of our little group, Saint-Gervais, and the Resistance. I particularly enjoyed working for the Cause.

Absolument!

Chapter 19

Liberation

(August 1944)

Part I

FLIGHT TO LE CHAMPEL

"*La demoiselle du téléphone* from Le Fayet-Saint-Gervais south rang up Marcel to spread the word in Bionnay that people should scatter into the mountains because reprisals are expected."

It's early afternoon August 14, Madame Dave stands on the welcome mat at the kitchen door in the rear at Chez Nous, her round placid face brightened with emergency. Hands tucked inside the pockets of her yellow flowered cotton frock, she informs us that the maquisards had gunned down two German soldiers at Les Pratz. Their bodies lie on the grassy berm alongside the D 902. "We must flee."

I turn around and look at the Prarion Mountain. The dark densely forested mountain offers several flight paths to Motivon, Bionnassay, and le Voza Pass — which one shall we take?

In the next breath, Madame Dave calmly extends an invitation to the Lengels to join the Daves. "Marcel knows of a vacant barn up at Le Champel. Will you join us?"

Papa thanks Madame Dave for her generous offer.

Le Champel is a tiny mountain hamlet set in a clearing at 4,387 feet. I have never been there, but Maman buys her bread up there, and she barters hers and Papa's wine coupons there at the bakery in Le Champel.

"They might bring tanks up the valley later today," Madame Dave says.

My watch shows 1.30 PM. Speed is the order.

At Chez Nous, Maman sets out food, drink, tin cups and plates; a blanket and toilet paper. She has no time for her usual volley of invectives against Hitler or against whoever threatens her family: windows must get shuttered, cupboards locked. I wrap Monsieur Kaiser's wooden box, entrusted to Papa in 1940, in a coverlet and hoist it to the top shelf of the linen closet. There it looks like bedding. *Je regrette trésor, mais cette fois tu restes à la maison.* Sorry treasure, but this time you must stay at home. I wave it good-bye.

Into my rucksack I pack my diary, two books of poetry, a toothbrush, a fountain pen, my well-worn Boy Scout manual, and a sweater — a few personal things besides my share of family basics.

Single file, knapsacks on shoulders, up into the mountains we set off.

Gisèle, Maryse, and Natalie (the Daves' two young daughters, and a niece from le Midi) frolic ahead hither and thither on the goat path like butterflies. Papa carries his leather briefcase. *Tiens,* I think to myself, he carries the family's valuables which by now must mostly consist of Géo Gignoux's straw sale to Monsieur Vitipon, and the documents that show the three unpaid installments due from ALÉDY G.m.b.H., Mannheim. I wonder: have my parents any cash left? We never talk money. That topic is not shared with the children.

After a forty-five minute steep climb through the dense forest of pine, birch, and hazel, we emerge on a small knoll. An old weathered barn sits there. Dave tries to pry open the rusty latch.

Marcel Dave, in his early thirties, of medium height, and with stiff blond hair cut short, is a blend of earthy mountain-sturdiness and Gallic light-hearted irony. Sent away to trade schools, he returned to Bionnay as a certified justice of the peace, a notary public, and a land surveyor. A local son who has made good, he also inherited (by marriage) Ailène's tobacco concession which had been bestowed on her mother by the French State in recognition for the death of her soldier-husband in World War I.

Proud of his gift, Dave smiles: "How is this for a cozy shelter?" he says, when the barn door slides open unto a loft filled with hay.

Barns play an important role in World War II. There is the infamous barn at Oradour-sur-Glane in the Limousin where the men were machine-gunned to death on 22 June 1944, while the women and children were burnt alive in the church by the Wehrmacht to avenge the shooting death of two officers of Hitler's *Das Reich* division. In the Haute-Savoie, men sleep at night in their grandparents' barns to escape the knock on the door at home. Later I hear that all over Europe Jews tried to hide out in barns hoping that the hay cover would shelter them from their hunters. The weathered barn up at Le Champel facing the Glacier of Bionnassay quickly resonates with our nine lives.

From the loft, Gisèle, Maryse, and Natalie call down in their nursery rhyme singsong voices: "Why does a spider spin a web?" "No, that's not it! Nor that! Give up?" The answer to the riddle is: "Because it can't knit!" Nine, eight, and six years old, the Dave youngsters shriek with delight at stumping the adults. For a short while we play riddle games with the children.

Papa and Dave merrily joust in their own swift parries. "Why can't the miller and the baker ever be thieves?" "Because the wheat is brought to them!" Dave laughs knowingly. Papa pulls out another one from his hat. "It's far from the cannon that one finds the veterans." I sense that Papa, a World War One soldier, is embarrassed at taking cover instead of fighting. Dave quickly retorts: "Admire the heroes but do not imitate them." Dave likes happiness. Married, a father of two young daughters — Marcel Dave is not subject to the compulsory Work Service in Germany; he is neither a collaborator nor a resistant. Last winter he saved my life when I had stupidly laughed at a Wehrmacht joke. I think Marcel Dave knows much more than he lets on to. He is genuinely at ease with himself and sort of flirts around difficult existential situations. Later, when he pours a good Gamay rouge into our tin cups, he says with a self-mocking voice: "*Entre mari et femme, c'est millet et farine. Entre amis, c'est eau-de-vie et viande*. A host treats his guests."

Eventually a deck of cards appear, and our parents move to the blanket for a game of bridge. The Dave children amuse themselves in the loft; I'm bored. I think about Captain Montjoie, Madeleine, and the maquisards. I wonder: What are *they* doing? Where are the Bauds? I could talk to Ghis. No! I can't bear hitting the wall of her needles and wool.

I climb half way up the stacked hay, curl up, and unscrew the top of my fountain pen. Into my diary I jot down: "It's days since I have reported on military news. The British have liberated Florence. The French and the Americans broke through at Monte Cassino. Rome fell. The Allies are on a winning streak. The Russians have taken Lublin; Brest-Litovsk too. Inside Germany, Hitler escaped a bomb plot. Must be protected by the devil himself."

I note: "Two days ago Henri Baud took me aside and asked me: 'What are we going to do with the Germans after the war is over?' In the next breath he answered his own question: 'Let's throw them all into the North Sea! We can't sacrifice every generation of Frenchmen on the altar of Thor.'" I kept my tongue tight. I know people seek a lasting solution, but Henri is wrong. I see all those Nazis swimming in the Baltic Sea back to shore. The Germans should be made to repair the destruction they have wrought. They should be taught responsibility. I'm surprised at the absence of hatred in myself.

Father and Dave do all the entertaining. I again feel like a French schoolgirl who shouldn't speak unless spoken too. From the hay below, my father's voice rises: "Why, since April, are tobacco coupons no longer redeemed?" "The trucks don't reach the Haute-Savoie…" answers an ironic Monsieur Dave.

I can't see the glint in his eyes as his head is bent over his cards, but I could hear it in his voice. At the Villa the joke goes: "Some truckers deliver their cargo to the F.F.I. outright, others need a little help..." I know the maquisards are smoking plenty of cigarettes. For all practical purposes, since late spring 1944,

Vichy's economic and political power has ceased to be relevant here in the Alps.

Marcel and Ailène Dave do not know we are Jews living with false papers. Maman nearly gives our cover away when she sets our picnic dinner out on the blanket and Monsieur Dave's pork saucisson slides next to our goat cheese. Mother instantly picks up our *boule de pain* and holds the round loaf of bread upright in her fingers' grip, like a frozen mummy. Pork is *t'refah* (not kosher), and would defile two days of rations. I wink at her. She slowly relaxes and deposits our loaf on the edge of the quilt. For dinner Maman eats next to nothing with forced slowness.

After the meal we disappear one by one into the woods. Outside, the alpine evening is enchantingly beautiful.

I quench my thirst at a hose dripping cold meltwaters from the Bionnassay glacier through lengths of above ground rubber lines that flow into a hollowed-out tree trough. Overhead, a diaphanous yellow light sheathes the ice-clad dome of Miage.

On the rim of the hollowed-out pine trunk I test my memory. I make out le Tondu, le Vorassay, and les Penoz Mountains to the left in the direction of the Contamines. Into my mind I etch the particular shapes of their jagged peaks jutting into the galaxies.

Across the valley, tiny Saint-Nicolas-de-Véroce lies nestled in the bosom of Mont Joly like a fairy village out of *Les Contes de Perrault*. The high country is quiet. At my back the massive Prarion stretches its dark buffalo hump. Below, in the moonlight, the Bonnant shimmers as one long silvery ribbon.

A finch's late twitter breaks the nocturnal silence. Drops of water drip slowly into the trough. Plop, plop. All about, the whitish diffractions of the glaciers dispel the blackness of the night.

Bathed in the eerie light of the mountains, I muse: What will they do tomorrow? Throw hand grenades into houses? Left — right, indiscriminately? The Germans do not know where we are. If they burn down Chez Nous, I still have my two cherished books of poetry, my diary, a fountain pen, a spare sweater, and my Scout manual. Unencumbered by material things, I feel recklessly light and free.

277

Careful not to wet her skirt, Maman settles by my side on the edge of the hollowed-out pine trunk. After a moment, she sighs and says: "Marguerite, tomorrow I was going to help Barzat with the hay. He mentioned to Papa how much he appreciated you and Ghis giving him a hand last week. I groan: "Not again Maman!" I dislike raking hay. I touch my blisters. They still are soft.

I succumb to the spell of the starry night. The Alps are like a mystery theater throbbing with a thousand diffuse lights.

Before dawn I wake up in the hay to the sound of a rooster crowing. In a distant barn hoofs rustle. I pick the dried grasses off my clothes and unkink my back.

Outside on the knoll, in the shadow of the white summits, we wash our faces and hands.

Madame Dave — deep eyes blue and serene — brushes Gisèle's straight black hair, Mary's blond curls, and the wheat-colored strands on Natalie's head. When she kisses a forehead, a purr of contentment passes through the child.

Monsieur Dave kneels by his rucksack near his place in the hay, and pockets a blue-white pack of cigarettes; he hesitates. "On second thought, it's better not to barter Gauloises for milk or cheese, people might talk," he mutters to himself. The packet goes back in his sack.

Maman and Ghis return from a nearby farm with a piece of Tomme de Savoie and a pitcher of milk. The fresh foam froths on top. Papa, an unrepentant poor shopper, stayed behind at the barn. Ghis, says: "No news."

Monsieur Dave leaves. He reports back: "La demoiselle du téléphone heard from her colleague that tanks are moving out of Les Cluses." We control whatever response we individually have to that stimuli and settle down in the hay around the blanket for breakfast.

It's here at 4,387 feet altitude that Ailène and Marcel Dave give us a memorable performance of mountain folks' resilience. While expecting enemy reprisals in their valley, they entertain their guests with the story of local cheese-making. "The Tomme de

Savoie is produced from curdled cow milk warmed to mid-boiling temperature...," they explain. "The warmed milk is poured into forms, allowed to stand 24 hours. Unmolded, the soft wheels are set on a board and left to age for two to three months. Constantly rounded, turned, and washed, the cheeses ripen in the huts." I learn that all the cheeses of the higher Alps: Tomme, Reblochon, and goat, are made from raw milk. "That's what the cowherds do with the milk from June to September." "Transport?" "At the end of the season by donkey back down to the co-ops." Finally I understand why *fait par le fermier*, farm-made, means a tastier cheese than *fait en laiterie*, produced at the dairy — it's the unpasteurized milk! Later, when I live in a different land, on a different continent, I like to bring back French Tomme de Savoie made from raw milk.

In our barn, a demonstration follows. Ailène and Marcel cut a sliver off the Tomme and spear the morsel on the end of their knives. La bouchée rolls on their tongues. They smack their lips. "*Bien du gôut, ça,*" observes Madame Dave. Monsieur agrees: "*C'est à point!*" In unison they declare: "*C'est pas trop dur, pas trop avancé, juste à point.*" The verdict is rendered: la Tomme is not too hard, nor too soft, but nutty, full of flavor.

The Daves are so certain of their centuries old values that they treat each bite of cheese with the respect due to the work of a chef artisan. A CHEESE is mature, immature, according to the blending of flavors. It is called à point, just right, when the flavor has reached its ultimate peak. Perfection.

I am fascinated. What can I say? The cheese is for the Daves a form of esteem for their civilization; an affirmation of life. A stubborn refusal to yield to intimidation and to terror. On an isolated knoll at 4,387 feet, the ritual of the bon fromage shores up our morale. The Daves take us into their joie de vivre, *their* pleasure of living. In this moment I'm glad to be here in their jocund company rather than alone with my family.

The social situation takes over. My red-haired Alsatian Papa joins the celebration. "*Mmm, il est crémeux,*" Father says with a serious mien. Even Maman forces herself to control her angst and mms *à la française*.

279

Suddenly, about two o'clock in the afternoon jolts of black smoke billow into the sky. Maman bleakly asks: "Are they moving tanks up to Bionnay?" "Bionnay? I see no tanks!" answers Monsieur Dave who is adjusting his binoculars. "They are picking up their two dead at Les Pratz and marching off." (A manly smirk). Mother weakly repeats: "So they are not burning down Bionnay?"

Secretly relieved that we were spared, we amble about. Les Pratz got hit, not us! I catch myself: Do the others feel as selfish as I do? (I later find out that Yes, they did. It's a universal survival reflex).

The adrenaline rush is over. Dave closes the rusty latch on the barn door. Gisèle, Maryse, and Natalie make one last whirlwind run down the rocky trail.

Under the apple tree at Chez Nous, the two families stand and conclude their escapade into the high country with a handshake and a look of sheepish complicity. Bionnay has been spared. The Daves's house and our wood and stone Savoyard chalet — with its bright orange-painted shutters closed — sit unscarred along the D 902. Superstitious, we do not mention our luck!

Part II

LES PRATZ

At the Pratz, grim-faced villagers relay buckets of water drawn at the Bonnant. An old man, thin and stooped, wipes carbon particles off his brow with his blackened hand. In an unsteady voice he tells that the Wehrmacht wanted to burn down the entire village at first. "Their officers asked to speak to Gaby (the acting mayor). Gaby persuaded them to settle instead for the three houses near the D 902, the ones that had sheltered the maquisards who had killed the two German soldiers." He gestures toward the smoldering homes. "Look!"

At first, I don't quite comprehend that quasi-reason had triumphed. I go in search of Martha whose mother owns the Crystal de Roche Inn. Martha belongs to our Little Group. On the

280

doorstep of her mother's Inn, Martha says: "They are doing terrible things right now in Saint-Gervais."

How does she know?

"The demoiselle du téléphone — she's Maman's cousin."

I comprehend that the switchboard operators are the rural French spy network as they, by profession, plug into conversations.

A moment later, Rita — about nineteen, my age with an astounding pink Renoir face and dressed in a pretty flounce skirt — joins Martha and me.

"Oh la, it was hot down there for a while!" and she fans herself with a man's white handkerchief. "André forgot it at my place: I'm going to bring it back to him at the gendarmerie even though he forbade me to visit him at work. Tant pis! I hope the chief is out!"

Rita laughs, excited, a pretty girl on her way to a piquant rendezvous. Nearby a young boy rounds his lips and mimics a kiss. "*Elle est amoureuse*, she's in love!" he says.

I think: Two dead Wehrmacht soldiers, three houses up in flame, the villagers in shock passing pails filled with water drawn at the Bonnant River, and another disaster going on in town — all this is happening about me, but it being France — I also see petulance, red sensuous lips, and a white hanky forgotten by a policeman who had to leave his girl in a hurry.

By temperament I have a thinking bent and an action bent. Free to go where I want — I walk with Rita to St-Gervais. She needs her lover's touch to feel that in spite of the fires, in spite of the War, all is well in her world. In the parking lot of the gendarmerie on the edge of town, Rita and I part company.

"Au-revoir, bonne chance! Good luck!"

By the glass door to the police station, Rita yells: "That's how I am!" And with her fingers she waves André's white trophy at me.

Part III

SAINT-GERVAIS

The war of incidents unfurls. No clashes of armor, neither Messerschmitts nor B-52s.

Just incidents.

At the Hotel de Ville in Saint-Gervais, after the sharp bend where the departmental 902 Road descends steeply into the center of town, Armand, a student, a member of my Little Group who courts me mildly but consistently — is leaning against the wrought iron grillwork of a window at city hall. Ghastly pale, Armand's ascot hangs out from his white shirt, the broad ends open.

"Armand, what's going on?"

"Let's talk about you, Marguerite," he politely replies, forcing himself to inquire about *my* well-being. His voice cracks under the strain.

"Me? Not much! We saw the fires, the Boches marching off carrying their two dead. We thought that's it!" I reluctantly describe the meek night up at Le Champel inside the barn with the jovial Daves.

"What about you, here, Armand?"

Slowly, Armand descends into his near-death.

"*They*, they l-lined us up against the wall on the Montée de la Forclaz... arms above our heads, face turned toward the wall... we waited for the volley... I was saying my prayers when I heard boots running behind me — Next, a German officer shouted a command, and a thud of wooden rifle guns hit the ground. They l-let us go! They d-didn't shoot us." Stupefied, he brushes blond tufts of hair out of his eyes. "They didn't shoot us, they, they let us g-go," he stammers in a daze.

I fling my arms around Armand's neck. L'esprit de corps chokes in my throat. "Why did they do that to you, Armand? You are des malades?" For an instant I feel as if his and my body are one and the same. We have escaped death. Cold. Hot.

A moment later, Pierre, another member of our Little Group, likewise a TB patient at the rest home on Mont Packard, staggers over from the fountain. "Marguerite, I experienced death! I saw my life replay before my eyes weirdly fast," he says softly, trembling like a leaf.

"They made me carry a case filled with hand grenades all the way down the mountain side. I nearly collapsed under the weight."

In a voice filled with indignation, Pierre defends the pieces of his shattered pride. "I didn't want to fall. I feared what would happen to me and my companions if I slipped and fell on the steep la Forclaz carrying all those hand grenades. *'Mach schnell, schnell!'* they kept shouting. Fast, fast!'" I sense how much Pierre fears their brutalities. Oh, how well I understood that. Instinctively, I pat his arm. No words come.

"THEY thought the young men at the rest home were *the* maquisards hiding out," interjects Penz standing nearby.

The little boy from Les Pratz, in short pants and face still smeared with soot, had stayed loosely attached to us. He comes running: "Les Boches picked up forty hostages including eight women!"

"*Les salauds!* The bastards!"

This latest blow arouses the population.

The villagers pour into town. Older folks who usually toil at home or in the fields crowd the streets. The forty citizens taken hostage include Pérind-Macquet, the president of La Banque de Savoie; and Doméngey, the priest of Le Fayet. Gaby, the acting mayor of Saint-Gervais, and Father Domengey volunteered as a good faith gesture.

"There's one hostage for every Wehrmacht inside the German garrison at the Hotel des Thermes," someone in the street says.

Forty hostages. Forty German soldiers.

"They all are customs clerks in civilian life with 4-F military status." (I have seen their flat feet and short bodies under the balcony at Chez Nous).

"They are sandbagging the windows and doors at Les Thermes."

The Thermes are surrounded by the Brey Woods...

"They fear reprisals by the Resistance for the three homes they set on fire at Les Pratz." (I had no idea the German army feared our maquisards).

DID I PASS THE BACHOT?

I remonstrate myself: Marguerite, you are really obsessed with the results of your baccalauréate exams.

In the street, the poverty of the people strikes me. By the end of the war's fifth year, the women's frocks hang too long, too loose over bodies that have struggled too hard under the yoke of the German occupation. I could see patches, and then patches over patches on the elbows, the backs, the skirts. Lips tight, visages anxious, a taciturn lot by habit, today their stillness is special, they are in search of comfort. Armand, Pierre, the young boy from Les Pratz and I tread about and around the Place de l'Eglise, the old stone fountain, up and down the cobbles on rue de la Comtesse and back to the Splendid Hotel. Armand and Pierre still look white. I don't reveal that Henri Baud is the head of the local Resistance.

Des nouvelles? Any news?

That evening at Chez Nous, ear glued to the crackling Swiss radio program, I hear René Payot say: "Over thirteen thousand F.F.I. from the Haute-Savoie are about to attack the German stronghold in Annecy." Impossible! I think to myself, the number at best for the entire department is four thousand. Captain Montjoie said so. *C'est ça*! The prudent Swiss see that the balance of power has shifted: General Patton had broken out of Avranches on July 30th and today, August 15th, 1944, the American and the French forces landed in the south of France. That's it! René Payot on his popular 19 o'clock news program — listened to by both the Germans and the French — is swelling our might! *Malins*, the Swiss! Shrewd! I smile at this master piece of Helvetic disinformation.

Later that night, in the sitting room, Papa is reading Stefan Zweig's *Fouché* at the table. Abruptly, he closes his book, he clears his throat and, with a serious mien, he says: "Marguerite, I will make it up to you, now that I'm getting back the factory."

"But Papa, I have grown up. I'm independent!" I spontaneously answer. I'm nineteen. My tongue wishes to say:

Dear proud Papa, almost sixty years old, your hairline receding, the reddish golden curls turning white — you express guilt. For what? For having been unable to provide for your able-bodied daughter during catastrophic times! My steel has tempered. I have come of age. Although we were too engrossed to notice.

I look at my father's furrowed forehead, his worn freckled face, I feel: Papa, it's a long time since a fairy godmother had to take me home to 76 avenue de la Bourdonnais from the department store Le Printemps because I got lost in Paris, 1934. I would have liked to put my palms on Papa's face, but our relationship was too formal.

The following morning, August 16, a fine drizzle falls on the town. Under open umbrellas, the crowd mills about the cobbled streets. Any nouvelles? The mood is different from yesterday. Grandparents and parents move about slowly, with dignity. A sense of stoicism is in the air, subtle as the morning mist. Against the backdrop of the jagged Aravis, the steeple of the church points straight toward the sky.

Images of les Invalides, l'École Militaire, my dear Lycée Victor Duruy, 76 avenue de la Bourdonnais, the Eiffel Tower — my *quartier*, appear in my mind. In Paris, still occupied, the police have gone on strike.

I walk about aimlessly. I read the headlines at the newspaper stands: "HITLER'S NEW WUNDERWAFFEN, weapons worse than the V-1 and V-2 rockets are being readied by the Third Reich." I shiver. Surely no one, not even a madman, will dare destroy Paris, the crown jewel of Western civilization. Or will he? From exultation at our possible liberation, my mood swings to ashes and eternal servitude.

In the street, people's eyes are directed at the route du Mont Blanc winding its way up to Saint-Gervais from Le Fayet. Any news? Like in a waiting room at the hospital, the bodies twist and turn while the eyes stare at the door through which the surgeon will appear to deliver his answer. All day we stomp on the cobbles. Armand, Pierre, the little boy from Les Pratz and I cluster on the fringes of groups who surround the rare cyclist pushing his machine up the curving route du Mont Blanc. Des nouvelles? Any...?

It is 5:30 PM. The crowd shouts: "They are coming! They are coming!

I shall always see the image of Henri Baud as he stands on the lead truck, the captured swastika flag between his outstretched arms, surrounded by the maquisards — navy berets set at a smart angle, Stens slung over their backs — and the liberated hostages. Three trucks follow, each filled with jubilant maquisards (many from Mégève), and the freed captives.

The defeated Wehrmacht hang their heads or cut dejected grins.

The enemy had surrendered!

We are liberated!

On the Place de l'Église, Orsin stands next to me and calls out to every freed hostage. Gaby! Pérind-Macquet! Doméngey! Pétra...! And he crosses himself.

The GREAT ANGUISH of getting caught lifts from my psyche like a cast off my heart.

The joyous maquisards hold onto the roofs of their cabs with one hand and with the other wave to the cheering crowd. A few lean over the fenders. Girls, gaiety glowing on their faces, climb up on the lead truck, one step at a time and, as if they were tearing Hitler himself apart, rip off pieces from the swastika flag held in Henri Baud's hands.

Moving with the tide, I step around the lead truck. Collective voices sing, what else? The Marseillaise! My fingers touch the fender of the truck so that I won't lose touch with Victory. Although more intellectual than sentimental, I embrace Liberation.

Unlike the cold marble perfection of Samothrace in the Louvre, our breath, our limbs howl VICTORY.

The Wehrmacht prisoners are driven over to Mégève.

It is August 16th, 1944. The German garrison surrendered unconditionally. In Chamonix, the Resistance killed quite a few fiendish Gestapo agents. In Mégève likewise. At Les Houches, eight Wehrmacht trying to flee in a car were ambushed.

Later it would be revealed that the Resistance had been ordered to liberate the territory east of the Rhône River valley by August

17th so that the US Seventh Army commanded by Lt.General Alexander M. Patch and the French First Army under General Jean-Marie de Lattre de Tassigny — whose forces had landed in Provence on the southern coast of France between Toulon and Cannes the day before, August 15 — could race north on the Route Napoleon to the Rhine River and Germany's border, unhindered.

Some Resistance fighters encircled their enemy garrison on horseback while others attacked on foot. Most triumphed through calculated subterfuges and negotiations. A grassroots solution for each problem. The various incidents led to Liberation. Regular armies clashed south of Lyon, in the Drôme department. How did Henri Baud take the German garrison forty men strong? "As soon as they took the forty hostages," he says, "I sent a request to Mégève for thirty uniformed maquisards because Captain Montjoie and his four sections of men had had to respond to an urgent call for help from Chambéry whose maquis was threatened in the rear."

"At the same time, I ordered dozens of locals into the Brey Woods (the woods above the Thermes Hotel), so that the Wehrmacht seeing silhouettes everywhere moving behind trees and armed maquisards surrounding their besieged garrison, would think: fighting is futile." Baud laughs at his own trick and says: "Actually a few only of the thirty available uniformed maquisards had been trained in the use of the Sten gun."

At 1:00 PM, Baud sent an ultimatum to Captain Hauffen: "Lay down your arms by 3:00 PM, or we'll attack."

The German reply was carried by Heifert, an Alsatian interpreter: "We are willing to surrender but to officers only, preferably Americans."

Mégève sent over the only American OSS (Office of Strategic Services) operative and three American officer UNIFORMS (the ones parachuted on Glières).

The negotiations lasted two hours. By 3 o'clock, Hauffen agreed to unconditional surrender to the *four* uniformed Americans. Henri Baud had won the high stake poker game. He and I share a good chuckle.

The three native Frenchmen dressed in US officer uniforms had been told to merely nod and occasionally utter: "Okay! Okay!"

"I ran up the stairs to the attic expecting a blood bath. Instead, the hostages and I fell into each other's arms," Baud says.

Strategically located in eastern France between the Mediterranean and the border with Germany, some 380 miles from the Normandy landing beaches (where huge armies were clashing with each other) — the high French alpine ranges offer their natural fortresses to the inhabitants whose young men had been armed through Allied parachute drops. In addition to liberating the Alps, la Resistance liberated le Massif Central, south eastern France, the Ain department, Brittany, and other large chunks of French territory. General Eisenhower said that the Resistance saved him fourteen divisions.

Organically, I belong to Liberation. I naturally follow the lead truck and install myself at a desk in the lobby of the Hotel Moderne where the Committee of Liberation settles down with Henri Baud at its head. Supported by the maquisards, our Armée Secrète, de Gaulle's faction, simply slides into the vacuum created by the surrender of the Germans and Pétain's flight. The A.S. had been preparing for that task for a long time.

With maquisards about, Stens slung over their shoulders, the dynamics of my life change suddenly. I forget my first ride with a bespectacled Miquet in an unmarked blue Citroen. He had worn sandals and brown slacks on the way up a winding unpaved road on Le Bettex. "The Villa," he had called the hidden headquarters of the A.S. Now, we operate in full view of the public at the Hotel Moderne, downtown. Three offices are set up in the rear with Henri Baud's at the far end. The socio-political-economic heart of the town beats here at the Moderne. The Art Nouveau block and glass building erected in the early thirties has a spacious black and white-tiled lobby. All day long people stream through the revolving glass doors. They need certifications, information, reimbursements. Sometimes they are summoned on collaboration charges. At my desk in the lobby I listen to their circumstance.

Food distribution is my other task.

At the dairy Co-op by Devil's Bridge, from eight to eleven in the morning, I sit on a high stool behind the counter, and cut off little square ration coupons which I then drop in a jar. I measure out the milk. Bertie stands next to me and weighs the butter and the Tomme de Savoie cheese. The people bring their own wrapping paper. Feeding the population is our priority.

Many an afternoon I climb in the company of an armed maquisard into the higher mountain villages and requisition butter, Tommes de Savoie, and goat cheeses. On an F.F.I.—A.S. letterhead, I scribble an "I owe you" note. The cultivator distrustful, slowly turns the piece of paper around and around in his hand, undecided what to do with a promissory note signed by an unknown Marguerite Lengel on behalf of a yet nonexistent administration. (Charles de Gaulle's Provisional Government is still a mere glimmer of hope). "Henri Baud says it's all right," I add with conviction.

Afraid to act unpatriotic at a crucial moment in his town's history, the farmer reluctantly accepts the just written tender — on faith. I walk away with a wheel or two in my rucksack.

The next day I would see him in the lobby at the Moderne, the soil-stained note in his hand. "Where's Henri?" he would ask brashly as if to redress an old insult.

Butter and cheeses have to come from somewhere for tomorrow morning's distribution! I say to myself.

I still sometimes wonder if my "*I Owe You*" notes were duly redeemed by the next administration. At the time I wasn't too concerned. "Action thinks of itself only in terms of action." Everything was possible in France then.

One morning on an errand at the mairie, I notice a bright spot on the wall behind Gaby's desk. The acting mayor shrugs. "Ah Pétain!" The portrait of Maréchal Philippe Pétain, the symbol of collaboration, lay flat, face down, under the table. "Le roi est mort. Vive le roi!"

Actually, there is very little exuberant rancor in our valley. People go about their daily business. Hay has to be cut; cows need to be milked. Five-gallon cans must be picked up. The new school year has to be prepared. For several weeks, enemy cannons positioned on the far side of the Bonhomme Pass in the Aosta Valley of Italy continue to boom. The maquisards scurry up and down Val Montjoie to and from the Bonhomme Pass and the Moderne in battle fatigues.

The real threat to our orderly administration is factional strife. One noon in front of the Moderne, the FTP (Francs Tireurs et Partisans), the Communists, red bandannas around their necks, Stens over their shoulders — jump down from five trucks and start filling up their vehicles at our pumps.

They are stealing our fuel! Our maquisards and Henri Baud brought the barrels down from Mont Lachat in that risky after-hour run of the TMB, two months ago. The gasoline belongs to us! I cringe.

The FTP posts armed guards on each side of the glass revolving door. Inside the Moderne the atmosphere is tense. Baud telephones the A.S. regional headquarters in Mégève. Their orders are: "Avoid fratricidal bloodshed at all costs."

From the lobby of our besieged seat of power, our A.S. maquisards stonily watch. I swallow hard and will myself to go on working.

Within twenty minutes the FTP rolls off. The daily bustle resumes.

You should know that an earlier agreement had been reached between the various resistance factions according to which the head of the most numerous group in any given district is to be in charge of local governance after Liberation, but power struggles broke out almost at once. In our region Robert Mitterand, the brother of François Mitterand, the socialist president of France (1981-1995), was the main challenger to our A.S. rule.

One afternoon, I see Luc pushing Moreau through the revolving door at gunpoint. "A collab.!" Luc calls out to me. My former boss at the Bruyères runs toward my desk, arms outstretched. "Mlle Lengel!"

I stick my nose into a file. Moreau, I am not your friend!

290

Luc cries out: "Moreau personally watched the house of a resistant, Guy Norta. He, Moreau, was the direct cause of an attempt at his arrest. I have proof: Moreau bragged to Lecour that all Communists of Norta's type should be arrested, and he went to look for him."

Moreau's grey felt fedora rolls on the black and white tiles inside the Committee of Liberation.

The fate of my former boss intrigues me. It's serious. Baud sends him to the Fort of Mondamez. A few days later I see in Moreau's file a certificate signed by Dr Tissot. "One should take into consideration Moreau's health and the fact that he, conscientiously ["conscientiously!"] I bristle, manages a home for children, mostly underprivileged." A further note penned by Henri Baud testifies: "Moreau was a passive collaborator, a former TB patient."

Two weeks later Moreau's prison term is changed to house arrest at Les Bruyères. Although by then the evidence in Moreau's file shows that Moreau is a certified founding member of the local SOL, the Service d'Ordre Legionnaire, the Vichy militia, and that as such, he — Moreau — was in charge of nothing less than the Nazi and Vichy propaganda for the entire district. And they want to spare him! Madame A., the patissière who had been deported, did he inform on her? What about the decree of 28 August 1944 authorizing arrest of collaborators and militia men?

I gently confront Henri Baud. "What is happening to Moreau?" "I want to shelter him from the out-of-town riffraff," Baud answers, sure of himself. I bite my tongue. Protect Moreau from outside vengeful elements? What a travesty of justice!

The discovery of political accommodation disconcerts me. Parts of me admire Henri Baud. I like his courage, his intelligence; his erudition has won me over. But I reject the notion that because Baud, Doctor Tissot, and Moreau are all three born in Val Montjoie, their first concern should be to preserve the local social fabric.

291

I soon discover this mindset underpins the national governance, the Catholic Church, and other large institutions. *They* protect each other. Zut! The French talk about Justice (with a capital "J") but are afraid of justice. "The French are exhausted," says Papa. "They don't want another revolution." Accommodation fills me with loathing.

I act out my passion.

With my status pinned to my left sleeve: a white arm band marked with black letters, F.F.I. (which I had sewn from a piece of discarded sheeting), I go and see the baker. In colloquial French, I ask him: *"Ce signe sur votre volet 'Fermé, pas de farine, pourquoi?"* *"Eh, bien, c'est simple! N'y a pas de farine!"* he answers with hooded eyelids, feet stuck in worn felt slippers. His palm-up gesture suggests that I am an idiot. "It's simple! There's no flour." "May I look?" Flashlight in hand, an armed maquisard by my side, I enter the back room of his bakery. Eight — one hundred pound bags of flour! "All that is for the black market?" I stay long enough for the baker to remove "Closed. No flour," and affix a new note on his metal shutters: "Open at 7 AM as usual tomorrow."

Armand and Pierre humor me. On a visit at the Moderne, Pierre asks: "How come, Marguerite, you wear no stripes? Don't you know how to sew?" — "Marguerite, is it fun to be with all those young men? Anyone in p-p-particular...?" I enjoy Armand's attentions, but I am reserved. I know that I'm not the one Armand thinks I am. I'm not Marguerite Lengel. And names have memory. Besides, Armand, you have TB and I'm just thawing out... Ghis pays a visit to me at the Moderne, and I think Papa too. For a while, I bathe in an aura of social respect...

... until the Val d'Este hotel-dining room is closed to me. "Why?" I suppose it is in retaliation for yesterday's Chutzpah when, at lunch, I sat directly behind Bertie and his beloved. He didn't see me for a long time. Undetected, I listened to his cooing: "Chérie, let me rinse this peach for you (in a crystal bowl). Why wet your lovely fingers?" They flirt unconcerned under the boom of the big guns from Aosta on the Italian side of the Bonhomme Pass. "*Le patron mange ici*! The boss eats here!" *Merde!* Now I can't observe any longer the private life of the well-to-do.

Bertie, my boss, is suave, and worldly. In Paris, he owns a fashionable ready-to-wear apparel store for ladies on the avenue des Champs-Élysées. The budget of his fashion empire is probably larger than that of our town's. Even though Bertie had spent not one day in the actual Resistance, Henri Baud needs his expertise.

The trains do not run, henceforth, there is no mail. Daily, I pluck petals off wild daisies: did I pass? With honors? Barely? Not at all? My Baccalauréate exams.

Economic independence is essential for me. While I belong body and soul to the interim government I keep on giving private lessons to my two pupils at the Splendid Hotel.

OCTOBER 1944. The Committees of Liberation give way to appointed officials. A provisional government headed by Charles de Gaulle takes over. Political appointments follow. By then France is nearly liberated except Alsace and the Lorraine and the Atlantic coastal pockets. Henri Baud is nominated *Chef de Cabinet* to the Préfet of Haute-Savoie. Dédée tells me: "I pushed Riri to cash in his chips. He has two children and a wife." Henri Baud conquers TB. The mind helps the body. In the happy surge for fulfillment, I'm convinced his energy released self-healing powers.

Of the French Resistance one could say: "They were the people who knew nothing, did everything, and rose to the occasion without ever knowing it..." Actually, most of us were too young to know that we were *making* history. *We were engaged in the Zeitgeist.* We expected nothing from our government, the least of all protection. Our government was the bad guy. Initiative, luck, and secrecy were our most trusted friends. The fact that my life was like this, didn't seem strange to me. It was the only way I knew. I took for granted that in order to live I have to break rules, defy, and resist and fend for myself.

Ironically, it is de Gaulle who, as newly appointed head of the new Provisional Government, immediately issues an executive order: "Surrender all arms!" Possession of a Sten becomes a felony.

Thus ends the era of the armed Resistance in France. Most Frenchmen comply with de Gaulle's decree.

Then one day, Michou shows up at the Moderne in a freshly-issued uniform of the regular French army. His dream of becoming a soldat de métier, a professional soldier, come true.

Pétain and Vichy are gone. The far right is finished. We'll soon live under the Fourth Republic, we think. Too fast! Because the threat of the far left is swelling. Daily, Henri Baud must change the route his préfet is travelling on to and from the préfecture. On the national level, de Gaulle escapes five assassination attempts.

A POLITICAL LESSON I learned — after four years under a foreign dictator, a nationally recognized strong man is needed to hold a liberated — yet deeply divided — country together again. The occupier having used the passions that split the citizens before the war — left-wingers versus right-wingers — to arouse deep hatreds. "Divide and rule."

A personal lesson — there is no sadness in rebellion. There is self-confidence, solitude, and determination.

Like the frogs in Papa's story that fell into a pail of milk and swam until a ball of milk churned to butter, then hopped out — Papa, Maman, Ghis, and I survived as a family. With our traumas. Our scars and our achievements.

ON A WINTRY NOVEMBER day, Joe Barzat carts my luggage to the train station on his one horse-drawn sleigh. I walk the four kilometers alongside the brown mare and the shiny five-gallon milk cans. Down the D 902 valley road, I go alone with my desires. Papa, Maman, and Ghis stay behind until the trains to Paris once again run on schedule.

The engine starts with a jerk on its journey. On a wooden third-class bench I open my purse. I read once more my army enlistment forms signed reluctantly by Papa; I touch my Baccalauréate diploma. Yes, I passed! Mont Blanc, the Dome of Miage, my ice-capped valley, grow smaller and smaller.

Ahead stretches the wide Plain of Sallanches. The war is still raging in the north of France, in Alsace-Lorraine, in Belgium, and in Holland. Eager, I wonder: Is the old Scout local rue Mouffetard in Paris still there? Shall I see René, Simon, Agnès — my girlhood — again? What happened to our apartment, to my Lycée Victor Duruy? Where will I be most effective: enlisting in the army or continuing my studies at the Sorbonne? The vital forces urge me onward.

 # 25 Papa 1945.

#26 Maman and Papa 1946.

 # 27 On the Champs Elysees, I stand (left) with friends 1947.

Chapter 20

Paris Encore

PARIS is built in space and in time with such an exceptional concern for beauty that even Von Choltiz, Hitler's military Commander for Greater Paris, disobeyed the Führer's orders and saved the city from destruction.

If you walk the magical stretch from the Palais Royal to the left bank of the Seine, through the Tuileries gardens, and stop and view the full length perspective of the Champs Elysées to the Arc de Triomphe at l'Etoile through the Arc du Carrousel — you can't but feel enchanted.

Post-liberation in that cold winter of 1944-1945, the liberated city lay under yellow and grey rain clouds.

The day after my arrival, hail the size of golf balls falls on the Boul' Mich. After four years and some of Occupation, the city seemed desolate. Morose.

My return to Paris both excites and depresses me. At the Army recruiting office near the Rond Point des Champs Elysées, dressed in my new navy wool jacket trimmed with rabbit fur sewn by a little country dressmaker in Assy, I push open the plate-glass door. I feel self-conscious.

Inside the sleek office, an elegant female captain of the regular army in a dashing khaki uniform sits behind a desk the size of France. "I'm interested in enlisting," I candidly say to her.

A ten-inch-high stack of Manila folders sits brooding on the farthest corner of her desk.

The female captain points to the pile, and aloof says: "We have hundreds of applications to process. It'll take time." And she turns away to powder her nose.

For weeks I had harbored a rose-colored dream of serving my country at the front. In Saint-Gervais, the Resistance had made me feel individually essential to Liberation. This is different. Very different. I hold my ground. "Please give me the names of one or two enlistees presently on furlough in Paris."

The first recruit agrees to see me the next day at her parents' apartment on avenue Hoche, Paris 8ème near the Etoile.

In the ornate high-ceilinged salon, the young Parisian lies stretched out on a day bed, charmante, à la Madame Récamier, surrounded by a circle of doting aunties — her much autographed cast resting on a pink, silken down coverlet.

"What happened?" and I direct my chin at the white thigh-high gypsum cast, ready to pay homage to the hero.

"A skiing accident on the Schlucht, in Alsace," she replies sweetly.

A skiing accident! My heart sinks.

"What do girls *really* do in the army?"

"I... we... type and ski," she says graciously.

That's not for me. I need to do productive tasks that count.

In turmoil, I walk for days along the quays of the Seine. What shall I do? *Quoi faire*? Goals charged with energy yield reluctantly. They keep on charging: "It's selfish to study when others fight. You must do your bit. A girl is as good as a boy." The reality-bound streak in me that accurately had perceived the limited role of girls in the 1944 French army, contented: "You are not a typist, you are not a nurse. You have no other skills. You like to study, and you are good at it. The pursuit of knowledge sustained you during the War. You worked hard to pass Le Bachot. Register at the Sorbonne...!" The inner conflict rages — until one day I could give myself permission to further my education, guilt-free.

On the Left Bank near the Sorbonne on the rue Champollion, I find a small room in a student hotel. My eight by ten-foot long cubicle is furnished with a studio couch, a wooden table, a straight chair, and a washbasin. Heat is rationed. I study in my 30 inch wide bed tucked in my sleeping bag, alternating the hand that takes notes with the one that thaws in the feathers.

PARIS, NOVEMBER 1944. The period of my life as Marguerite Lengel ends officially here in Paris at the police station of the 7th *arrondissement*. The chief writes "annulée" across my false ID, then issues a new document to Lévy (Margot Gerda), 76 avenue de la Bourdonnais. He looks up my old name and address in the hardcover burgundy ledger sitting on a table nearby in which he had recorded the data in his own hand, years ago, before the War. Et voilà! ONLY IN FRANCE! When I thank him with a warm smile, he lights a cigarette and, pragmatic, shrugs: *"C'était la guerre!* It was wartime!"

The next day at the post office I walk up to a clerk behind the counter, and ask her to please dial the Daves' number in Bionnay for me. I wish to speak with Maman or Papa. Waiting on my chair I hear: "Mademoiselle Lévy, cabine numéro 2," twice repeated. I look around at the crowded room to see where that dumb girl who doesn't proceed to booth number 2, is. The operator points her chin at me. My reflex hadn't responded to LÉVY.

PAIN IN PARIS lurks beneath the timeless architectural magnificence. Throngs of displaced persons, forced labor slaves, concentration camp inmates — the masses of returnees from hell — stomp the rue de Rivoli, the boulevard Haussmann, alongside the quays of the Seine. Everywhere I look, I see the human wrecks of Europe. *You must help, Marguerite!*

I adopt a godchild. My fourteen year-old-Lorrainer orphan girl from Nancy, is tiny and shriveled. She lost her mother, father, and eight brothers and sisters in Auschwitz. At the time of the round-ups of the Jews in German annexed Alsace-Lorraine, she lay in a Nancy hospital undergoing a thoracotomy. I take my godchild out for walks; buy her small presents, and write her encouraging notes. The social worker tells me that I'm helping with Charlotte's recovery.

BLOOD is needed. Twice I donate at the Red Cross. It takes me weeks to recover my strength.

A student and I meet trainloads of prisoners-of-war at the Hospitality Center of the Gare de l'Est — the railroad station that connects Paris to eastern France, Germany, Poland and beyond. At

299

6:00 AM at the BUFFET DE LA GARE, Jacqueline and I serve red wine and sandwiches. I choke when I greet the bearded, emaciated men on their return from five years of captivity in a Stalag. "Welcome home!" I say with a smile. They look so lost, so guilty. "I better not drink," says one POW in his oversized khaki long coat. "I don't know what I'll find at home."

At the Buffet de la Gare, I hear the anguish of the POWs. *Est-ce que ma femme a trouvé un autre homme*? Has my wife found another man? *Les gosses vont-ils me reconnaitre*? Will the children recognize me? Has the world forgotten me?

My own homing instinct attempts to return to its sacred grounds. At 76 avenue de la Bourdonnais, the elevator lifts me to the third floor. On the familiar red carpet that covers the stairs, I press my ear against the closed door. Strange voices reach me.

Downstairs, the concierge, dish towel in hand, informs me coldly: "Your apartment is occupied and there's a law that protects new tenants."

At the Chasseloup-Laubat synagogue, the caretaker answers: "Rabbi Cohen, your former youth group leader? He's a chaplain in the army of General Delattre de Tassigny fighting on the Rhine."

I check out my dear Lycée Victor Duruy. I walk the yellowed hallways hoping to encounter familiar faces. In the office I recognize the secretary. "Bonjour." For a short moment she stands across the counter from me. She glances at my transcripts and smiles at *"Excellente élève," "Élève très intelligente."* I leave with fevered longings. Good-bye!

At the old Maccabées Scout locale Rue Gay-Lussac I recognize four or five female members. Their energies emit sounds and smells directed at attracting the opposite sex. In a state of competitive fertility, the young women display in all directions. Look at me! No, at me! The buzz is all about vying for a mate to get married to. There is one only male present. He's in the uniform of a French army captain. I stand apart. I do not fit. In the intervening years I had climbed mountains; channeled energies towards studying, worked with children, and rendered services in the Resistance Haute-Savoie.

Stunned, I leave my Maccabées with the awareness that my scouting years are over. I did accept the captain's offer to escort me to my next class. He was moved by my "radiant a-loneness," as he called my self-sufficient a-partness. He had escaped from a cattle wagon to Auschwitz by unscrewing two center boards with his pocket knife.

The uniformed captain and I, together, walk up and down Le Boul' Mich. Over the next weeks we go for a few more walks. I ask Papa to visit him at the offices of the Wizo, a Jewish charity the captain heads. But I didn't like my captain so much.

At the Sorbonne, I again find Agnès and Simon, my prewar childhood friends. Agnès studies physics. Simon: math. I, philosophy. We engage in theoretical disciplines, the real world being too awful. Agnès and her parents survived the War in Monaco where her actor-father, Daniel Lecourtois, occasionally found work performing character roles with the Monaco Theater. Simon escaped with his parents and brother in a fishing boat to England. Another friend, René, fought with the Free French in North Africa. René wanted to get married at once. "Or I enlist to fight in Indo-China (Vietnam)."

I meet Nicole, a Huguenot, and Jeannine and her brother Jean-Pierre, Jews, at law school. We become friends. Jeannine, Jean-Pierre, and their parents had lived with false papers on the other side of Mont Joly in the Haute-Savoie; Nicole had stayed with her family in Paris. Together we visit museums, go to Art shows; attend openings at galleries the so-called *vernissages*. We purchase discount student tickets to *le poulailler* (literally: the chicken coop," the upstairs gallery in theaters). At intermission we scramble downstairs to the vacant seats in the Orchestra.

Immediately following Liberation, Paris explodes with artistic creativity repressed during the Occupation. Ionesco, Genet, Chekov's works are staged, plus a plethora of new plays from authors who had been banned. At Les Deux Magots on Place Saint-Germain-des Prés, we glimpse Jean-Paul Sartre and Simone de Beauvoir.

Mostly we study.

301

Paris occupies a rather small area: 41 sq. miles (105.4 km2.). J.T., my former patrol leader of the non-denominational Scouts "The Robins" to which Ghis and I had belonged prewar, recognizes me on the avenue des Champs Elysées. I had been J.T.'s assistant. J.T. invites me to lunch at her parents' apartment near the Etoile.

Over a sparse meal of rutabaga and Brie cheese, her mousy-faced, thin-bearded, graying father rants on non-stop about the present-day bad times. He says: "Five thousand people are interned at Drancy awaiting trial." (Drancy had been the transit camp for 70,000 Jews sent to their death at Auschwitz). Collaborators are now housed there. J.T.'s father gripes: "They have arrested Sacha Guitry (the playwright); Louis-Ferdinand Céline (a novelist); Charles Maurras (the former editor-in-chief of l'Action Francaise) — and he names several other prominent hatred-spewing pro-Nazi writers: "All innocent great litterateurs."

Throughout the meal, Mousy-face complains non-stop that American soap is available only against coupon E, *enfants,* children; that gas is still restricted to the hours of noon to 2:00 o'clock and 6 to 9:00 PM. "Where is the promised help from our so-called liberators?" My chair itches.

J.T.'s mother wears a Givenchy silk scarf over her head tied at the nape with a chic bow. For lunch, at home! I stare at her coiffe. J.T. blushes. I understand that her statuesque mother was a female "collaborator" who, as punishment after the Liberation, had had her hair shaved and with French flair, hides the stigma. In Paris, many elegant silken coiffes like hers are seen in the streets shopping.

I leave directly after the meal. To HELL WITH COLLABORATORS!

Hunger hallucinations overcome me one gray rainy evening on the rue Soufflot on the way to visit my friend Agnès. Suddenly a giddy white light envelops me; I sort of float. I stop in my tracks. What gives? When did you take your last meal, Marguerite? I had forgotten to eat for two days. Oh!

Mostly I cook my food on a folding stove in my hotel room. Some meals I take at the student cafeteria on the rue Mouffetard. The cost is one dollar per voucher. You must buy a carnet of ten.

Finally women get the vote. General de Gaulle is rewarding the French women for their role in the Resistance. The elections will be held in April 1946. Merci. It's about time!

But on the Boul'Mich, I see a man hit a poor girl who protects her head with her arms; it's dark. She pulls a few francs from her black coat pocket and reluctantly hands them to him. He hits her once again. She walks away. To earn more money for her pimp. Bastard!

One day the bell tolls for me. A weird looking student in philosophy with a huge deformed head offers to loan me a book difficult to find: a critique of *Kant's Critique De La Raison Pratique*. I can't recall the exact title. "Come with me to my room, I'll give it to you," he says. Naïve, I go with him. Without preamble he tries to push me onto a large dirty-looking bed. Furious, I resist. He picks up a cold boiled potato on the windowsill and hands it to me. He tries to pull me down again. "Stop!" I yell at him. I just stand there a few feet away from the dismal unmade bed, arms crossed on my chest. A smirk cuts across his boorish face. I swallow hard. We leave together. For an hour or so, up and down the Boul'Mich, we go on discussing — Emmanuel Kant. Of course I don't acknowledge him again when I pass him in the halls or on the Boul'Mich, but on that day my goal had been to clarify the Kantian theory. These are the weeks and the months when the bewitching city's narrow escapes push me back into loneliness.

At the Sorbonne, the huge amphitheater is filled with hundreds of students all taking notes. If you arrive late you find standing room only. When Professors Le Senne or Bayer or Wahl enter through their office side door, the class rises as one body. At the end of the lecture the same homage to erudition is once more bestowed on our teachers. Learning at the Sorbonne is an anonymous event. Students do not ask questions. Teaching consists of a series of formal lectures.

303

Professor Le Senne, a disciple of Henri Bergson ("*L'Evolution Créatrice*") examines me for the orals in Ethics. In his side office, he says: "*Je vous reconnais, vous avez suivi mes cours regulièrement.* I recognize you; you have attended my lectures regularly." (I always make eye contact). He seems happy. I pass Ethics.

Suddenly, in December 1944, French newspapers and radio broadcasts are censored. On the Boul'Mich at a corner kiosk, I daily read the headlines in Le Journal de Genève, a Swiss paper: THE GERMANS TAKE ST. VITH — BASTOGNE ENCIRCLED — BRIGADIER GENERAL ANTHONY McAuliffe SUMMONED TO SURRENDER — McAULIFFE ANSWERS: 'NUTS!' — A dense fog covers the Ardennes.

In the Quartier Latin, the street lights are off. Heavy war curtains cover the windows. In the yellow winter dampness the silence is eerie. When I walk up the rue Soufflot toward the law school on Mont Sainte-Geneviève near the Panthéon — the wet pavement is deserted. I live through the BATTLE OF THE BULGE, Hitler's surprise attempt to retake the port of Antwerp and push the Allies back through Belgium to Paris — the biggest battle and the costliest in American casualties of World War II, lasting from December 16, 1944 to January 5, 1945, and in which one million men participated — as a mute and anguished witness in Paris.

Papa, Maman, and Ghis arrive at la Gare de Lyon from Saint-Gervais in early JANUARY 1945. I present Maman with a small bunch of multicolored dewy nosegays which I bought at *le Marché aux Fleurs*, the Flower Market along the Seine behind the Tribunal de Commerce. "Welcome!" We hug. I am happy to be reunited with my family. In the night we go on directly by train to Savigny.

At Géo Gignoux, the iron gate is closed. We four stand there on the outside. Papa pauses. Lips pursed, deliberate, my father slowly takes out a small key from his vest breast pocket and inserts it in the keyhole. Half a key-turn later, the steel hinges creak. I hold my breath. With a decisive step, Papa sets foot on the grounds of his factory he had left on a June morning four and one half years ago.

Across the moonlit yard, Papa, Maman, Ghis, and I go up the wide staircase to Papa's office. Not a chair has been moved. The green curtains hang the same. After a moment's hesitation Papa sits down at his desk. He removes the black and silver pen still stuck in his desk set and, with a furrowed brow, he jots down notes on a pad. Already my father is concentrating on tomorrow. That night we sleep on the leather furniture on the landing.

The following morning, Papa and I go to the shipping room. One by one his workers file in on the concrete floor. They touch their caps and shake Papa's hand. Some pump his fingers for a long, long time. When I look up, I see Papa's energetic light grin. The boss is back at work with his men.

"Papa I got a marriage proposal today..." "Papa this is the third one in two weeks..." I come out feverish but disinclined. I wish to finish my studies first... First things first.

I have enrolled in philosophy and in law at the Sorbonne. "Papa I want to become a lawyer." "Papa..."

But Papa dies of a hiatal hernia within a year and a half of the family's return. I am rigid with grief. The protrusion could not be repaired during the war. We had no money and the risk of talking under anesthesia was too great. Papa had worn a painful hernia truss until the danger of a rupture threatened his life.

On July 2nd, 1946, at the age of 61, my father was operated on by a highly recommended surgeon at a private clinic in Paris. At the time, I was a guest of the British Council in Chester, England, attending a conference on British Democratic Institutions organized for deserving students in Europe who had been active in resistance. On July 13th, my cousin Ilse in London telephoned me to say she had received a telegram from Maman: I should come home at once.

A blood clot had lodged in Papa's lungs. He died in the night of July 12th. "Impossible! I have just received a letter from Mother in

305

which she told me that Papa is doing fine. He's coming home in two or three days." Papa!

I am not sure how I returned home from London.

All the extended family from Alsace, London, and Paris, all the workers at Géo Gignoux, pay their respects to Papa at the graveside cemetery of Thiers on the outskirts of Paris.

By the open grave, as the casket is being lowered into the ground, I ask: "Where is Papa's head?" and there I throw my shovel of earth as my final adieu to the humane genius who had been my father.

Edouard, Father's younger brother and partner, had always existed in Papa's shadow. Bookkeeping was his profession. At Géo Gignoux he managed the accounting department. Naïve, fidèle, I go to work at Géo Gignoux under his orders. Maman had asked me to. I had graduated from the Sorbonne with a *license,* a degree in Liberal Arts. I decide that I would write the short thesis to obtain a diplôme d'études supérieures (an intermediate step for the doctorate) at night in Savigny, and on Wednesday afternoons, I would attend the one required course on metaphysics at the Sorbonne.

At Géo Gignoux, Edouard occupies Papa's chair. He thinks he is both the head of the family and the new CEO. I'm churning with sorrow. I know, I won't submit to Uncle Edouard's rule for long.

We sit Shiva, the week of mourning. Many people come daily. Each one admired Papa. The prayers recited in Hebrew (which I do not understand and cannot translate) feel ritualistic and stale to me. I yearn for hugs and human warmth. I'm cold.

Instead, Uncle Edouard declares: "I am the eldest now."

For Maman and the Albert Lévy children, the fall is sudden. Ghis has an easier time of it: she is engaged to get married to Oscar Jacob of Bruxelles. She soon will be moving away. I am angry at the pettiness of it all. I have a lump in my throat, but I can't cry.

I bow my head as a tribute to my father, Albert Lévy. Alone in my room I try to recite a verse from the Kaddish, the old Jewish prayer for the dead. From childhood memory, I extract:

"Yisgadal, v'yiskadash shemei raba" —

306

That's all I know. The translation: "May your great name be made great. May your great name be sanctified," and the sonorous cadence of the prayer are lost on me.

The Fates had allowed Papa to survive the War, only to let him perish under a well-known surgeon's knife at a private clinic in Paris. In 1946, anti-clotting drugs were yet unknown in France and the operation had been performed in the heat of summer.

Backpedaling to our safe return to Paris after the War, when we four slept on cots in two offices at Géo Gignoux for months, and Maman cooked our meals on a two-burner hot plate — Papa, in gratitude for his family's survival, offered at once Tzedakah, charity, to his less fortunate brethren.

The list of recipients includes the Wizo Children of the Deported; the Jewish Orphanage in Paris, les Déportés et Orphelins, and several more. I found the receipts in Maman's papers after her death. Papa had offered his first after-war earnings.

I need to build my own niche; I can't go home again. Now is the time? The options I consider are a doctoral thesis in Philosophy, a law degree plus four years of apprenticeship in a French lawyer's office, and various marriage proposals. I liked none of the above.

EPILOGUE

The passion to survive drives us
to start again and again and
then presses us to try once
more, all over, elsewhere

Unknown

Professor Albert Bayer, my thesis supervisor at the Sorbonne, touches his coat pocket:
"Columbia University Graduate School sent me two scholarships in sociology 'tuition only,'" he says puzzled. "Do you know anyone interested?"

I see myself in New York doing research on John Dewey, the American philosopher whose premise emphasizes learning through both theory and practice. My own studies had been mostly theoretical steeped in Plato, Spinoza, Kant, Fichte, Schopenhauer, and Bergson, although in psychology we studied the Gestalt theory which demonstrates that the dynamics between the parts affect the total, and that therefore the whole is larger than the sum of the parts. John Dewey attracts me and I am curious about the USA.

Mother sends me gift parcels of French Limoges china miniatures to New York because of strict French currency exchange rules. I sell my imports to Bloomingdale's and pay for my room and food. Maman helps me once again and, innocently paves the way to my much-desired adult independence.

Leonard Feibelman, a childhood friend from Mannheim, is studying for his engineering degree. At the end of a lonely year in New York at Columbia University Graduate School where everyone is married, holds down a job and hurries to and from classes, I visit Leonard and his parents in Cincinnati. Cupid appears with a bow and a quiver of arrows. Leonard's sister Senta has earned a PhD in psychology — and I know Leonard supports my aspirations to be an entrepreneur.

I return to Paris — and Leonard and I stay in touch. Within two years, he passes his exams in electrical engineering. I decide to publish a shorter version of my research (on John Dewey) in *Les Temps Modernes*, the well-known Paris scholastic Review connected with Jean Paul Sartre. No doctoral thesis. In Paris, I also sell articles to *Combat*, Albert Camus' newspaper. A front page piece fetches thirty-five dollars. I show how American society is based on organized teamwork and the spirit of community.

Beneath the journalistic debut, a deep personal need to rebuild my lost childhood garden pulses on. I unload the pain of the forthcoming rupture in a full length manuscript, *Les Dieux de Capri,* The Gods of Capri.

Marriage to Leonard happens, complete with the bliss and slavery of an entrepreneur passionately driven to survive in the New World.

The balance sheet shows —

Gains. Retailers in America demand European home accessories: British brass planters, candlesticks, and wall plaques; British dinnerware. Bone China cups and saucers, and Biersteins from Germany — all augment the French Limoges miniature china line. Consumers decorate their homes with Mercator Imports (my company's name). I employ five people, hire commission salesmen. I enter the economic fray. I exhibit at wholesale trade shows in New York, Chicago, Dallas, Atlanta, and Detroit. The competitor is pulled into the marathon race in the field of floral, gift and home accessories.

Losses. I lose my beloved language, culture, and French crusty baguettes with à point unpasteurized goat cheese. My friends, relatives, and Paris. My life-style. I am frequently exhausted.

Leonard chooses to leave engineering and join Mercator Importers. In 1986, Mercator Inc. is sold. Freed-up, I self-reconnect and rappel into my spiritual and emotional font; I return to writing.

I tell myself: throughout the shoals of time, we humans did transplant dreams of lost Edens into distant lands. Then built bridges.

The courage to change is hard to assess. To France, I return often. France is so beautiful.

Leonard and I have raised three children and have six grandchildren. My oldest granddaughter Tamar is inscribed in my Albert Lévy *Livret de Famille* (the legal French family record-book).

In America, I have earned what I didn't have during the War in France, first class citizenship.

Always in the eternal deal — joys, sorrows, adventures, challenges — to me as a survivor everything in my life is still with me. Existentially, I believe nothing ever gets lost. Lévy, Lengel, Feibelman — all fuse into a woman of passion, authentic, no façade. I think — what? We human creatures are built one nano at a time. The things that happen to us make us different.

At peace with myself; understanding the universal challenges to life: wisdom under strands of gray hair nods — the Great Liberation of 1944 was just a beginning… "Whisper your name into my ear," no more! It is time to step up to the witness stand and bare the dynamics of hiding out in France during World War II. Because the whole feeds on the parts and the dynamics of each part feed into the whole process of being —

Today, I'm proud to be

MARGUERITE LÉVY-FEIBELMAN,
Daughter of ALBERT & MARTHE LÉVY
née Oppenheimer

RESTITUTION

The story of spoliation and amends is delicate. France was one of the last Western European nations to agree to the restitution of Jewish assets confiscated in World War II. It took legal and diplomatic pressures from America for the French to nominate a commission and secure funding from the French banks and the French government. This didn't happen until the year 2000. The set amount was $ 630 million.

End of 2001, the program's first year, I filled out the forms, sent proof of losses, photographs, pages of explanations, and detailed lists.

The process of data verification passed through Berlin, Mannheim, Paris, and involved the ministries of Interior, Finance, Taxation, Defense, and the ministry of the *Anciens Combattants,* Veterans Affairs, a well as several Jewish agencies. Many a morning, I set the alarm clock for 3:15 AM in order to find the person in Paris at 9:15 AM who knew anything about my file.

After four years of thorough investigations, my claim was eventually assigned to a rapporteur (magistrate).

My 'Rapporteur' used a complex official formula that began by taking off 50% from the estimated value of the losses.

In negotiations which followed, I learned to defend my side when my *Rapporteur* scaled down our six-room, two-and-a-half baths, one-and-a half kitchen luxuriously furnished apartment at 76 avenue de la Bourdonnais to a modest bourgeois logis of five rooms with one room for a maid. The larger Géo Gignoux bank accounts were altogether omitted.

In addition, I had to learn again the sensitive art of prodding without irritating the French staff at LE SERVICE DE SPOLIATION who handled upwards of 20,500 claims. "Madame, you must write nice letters," one clerk remonstrated with me because I had sent off rather raw words of frustration at the delays.

The French could make me feel that I was just out to gratuitously get *their* francs while they were working very hard to reach an equitable settlement.

"But that money belonged to my family!" I protested. "It was stolen from us!"

From 1940 on, and for all the four years of Occupation, the French State had actually deducted the confiscated value of Jewish properties and bank accounts from the daily war reparations imposed on France by the Third Reich.

"The State profited!" I blurted out to one secretary who had vexed me.

When I dared complain to my magistrate about several omissions on his list of losses, he mumbled to himself: "*On leur donne de l'argent, et ils ne sont jamais contents.*" He didn't think I understood what he was saying: "One gives them money and they are never satisfied..."

"It was our money to start with," I interrupted.

Yet, on the whole, I must say, most French staffers at le Service de Spoliation were sincerely helpful. "You have phoned several times now," one female employee in Paris said to me on the telephone. "Monsieur le rapporteur should know of this!" and she set my *dossier*, file, on top of his desk.

When I visited personally the office in Paris, I fared less well. An unctuous male employee felt he should punish me for having had a father who worked extremely hard at building a paint and lacquer factory in France. *"Oh la, c'était une grosse boîte! Avec un capital versé de 9.000.000 de francs en 1934 et pas de dettes*! Oh la, that was some large enterprise with a fully-funded capitalization of 9.000.000 francs in 1934, and no debts!" he said with a sadistic nuance in his voice. He forgot to take into consideration that the capital was tied up in the business. Buildings, machinery, and raw materials. "It's going to take time to review *that* file!" and he flipped four inches worth of pages in my manila folder with a smirk. (It is impossible for me to calculate today's value in US dollars.)

312

The coefficient for all confiscated bank accounts had been fixed at X 1.8 of their original value. Although a devaluation of the currency in the late forties had chopped off two zeros from the value of the French franc. However, in other ways, a concern for justice underlies the program: any Jew who lived in France from 1940 to 1945 and had a bank account — has a right to an indemnity of 3,000 euros even though his balance may have been less than ten francs.

My Rapporteur initially offered a settlement of 23,454 euros. After a lengthy telephone conversation and additional proofs of losses, he upped the figure to 36,214 euros. This sum included all the Lévy furnishings, paintings, valuables, the private, and the smaller Geo Gignoux bank accounts (the larger Géo Gignoux bank accounts were ignored altogether). The amount included a one-time only 160,000 French francs salary which the German-appointed administrator paid himself two times.

Incidentally, the Nazi manager had sold on the black market for his own account the barrels of gasoline and precious resins which Papa had stored in the cellars at Géo Gignoux, and paid for with our own private money. My Rapporteur, on the telephone, called the Nazi-appointed French administrator *"une véritable fripouille, a real scoundrel."*

My Rapporteur also told me that for two years Géo Gignoux had two rival CEOs who were not on speaking terms: the German appointed administrator, and Monsieur Vitipon—the client of Papa from the Côte d'Azur to whom Father had deeded the factory in 1940. "They sat in different offices at Géo Gignoux until the French courts backed Monsieur Vitipon as the legitimate, legally appointed CEO."

The intervention in Paris of the Simon Wiesenthal Center for Tolerance and Justice helped my case. The mixed French Commission "For the Compensation of Victims of Spoliation due to anti-Semitic Laws in place under the Occupation" made up of one representative of the French government, one of the Jewish community, and one legal expert was willing to listen to the evidence presented by the Wiesenthal spokesman and agreed to

313

increase the amount of the spoliation to 48,500 euros ($64,000) each for Ghis and me. But the larger Géo Gignoux bank accounts were still denied, as were the thefts committed by the Nazi "scoundrel."

Hundreds of documents. Ghis told me: "I don't know how you did it."

US $64,000 in 2005 is the equivalent of US $2,818 invested at 5% for 64 years!

In 2005, I was 81 years old; Ghis, 84. The fruits of Papa's life-long labor had been mostly stolen.

GLOSSARY

A la mode de Caen. Sausage in gelatine.

Alpensperrzone. Alpine frontier zone with Switzerland and Italy. Forbidden area for Jews and foreigners in World War II.

Ancien combattant. Veteran, ex-serviceman.

Armee Sécrète, AS (abbr.) Secret Army, de Gaulle's faction in the French Resistance.

Arrondissement. District.

Au-revoir. Good-bye.

Bachot or **Le Bac.** (abbr.) Baccalauréate, French degree at the end of the secondary cycle, between an American high school and a BA diploma.

Bien du gôut ça! It's tasty.

Boche. French hostile name for a German.

Boulangerie. Bakery.

Bureau de Tabac. Tobacco shop.

Camion. Truck. Van.

Centre d'Accueil. Hospitality center.

Consistoire Central des Israélites de France. Organization of all French Synagogues.

Dumkopf. (Germ.) Dullard.

Edict 108. The infamous law 1077 published in the Official Registry on December 11, 1942, ordering 'all Jews in the former Free Zone to get their IDs stamped *Juif* by January 11, 1943,' popularly known as 'Edict 108.'

Eclaireurs Israélites de France, EIF (abbr.) French Jewish Scouts.

Etudiants. Students.

F.F.I. or **FFI** (abbr.) French Forces of the Interior.

Flânerie. Stroll. Promenade.

Gare de l'Est. Railway station in Paris carrying easterly traffic, namely to Germany, Poland and beyond.

315

Gendarme. Policeman.

Gendarmerie. Police station.

G-d. Jewish conservative custom to not spell out God.

Goy. (Hebrew). Christian.

Jamais. Never.

Journal Officiel. The Official Registry that publishes all laws and decrees issued by the French government.

L'École Nationale d'Administration, ENA (abbr.) French prestigious Graduate school for civil servants.

Les Bruyères. The Heathers.

Les Droits de l'Homme et du Citoyen. The rights of Man and of the citizen.

Mairie. Town hall.

Malade. Sick person.

Maquis. Bush. Refers also to the French fugitives from the compulsory Work Service in Germany who hid out in the 'bush' during World War II rather than go and work for Germany.

Maquisards. The above young men.

Milice. Militia.

Nouvelles. News.

NOZ. Non-occupied Zone.

Oh mon Dieu! Oh my God!

Patisserie. Pastry shop.

Quoi faire? What to do?

Pain de Campagne. Loaf of country bread.

Rapporteur. Magistrate.

Science-po, (abbr.) **L'École des Sciences politiques,** the famed political Sciences Graduate school in Paris, known as the Institute for political Sciences.

Service du Travail Obligatoire, STO (abbr.) Compulsory Work Service in Germany during World War II.

Sous. Pennies.

Tant pis! Too bad!

Tiens! Strange!

TMB. (abbr.) Tramway to Mont Blanc.

Tomme de Savoie. Local French cheese from the Savoie.

Tout ça! All that!
Union Générale des Israélites de France, UGIF (abbr.)
Association of French Jews to which membership was made
compulsory by Vichy.
Voilà! There!

DRAMATIS PERSONAE

ALBERT LÉVY, my father, a Paris industrialist, died as a result of a hiatal hernia operation on July 12, 1946. During the War we lived with false papers, had no money, so that surgery could not be performed.

MARTHE LÉVY, my mother, passed on in Philadelphia on July 5th, 1981. She was 85 years old.

UNCLE LOUIS, Papa's oldest brother, senior rabbi of Brno (Czechoslovakia), a renowned scholar, a friend of Sigmund Freud, chaplain of the Free Czech brigade in France, suffered a stroke in Périgueux at the end of 1944. He died in Paris, December 1946.

AUNT GRETL, his wife, succumbed to cancer of the stomach during their exile in the Dordogne.

UNCLE EDOUARD, Papa's younger brother and partner at Géo Gignoux, died in Nice in the eighties.

The extended **DREYFUSS** family (of my Brownie Isabelle) survived in the suburb of Riorges-Roanne. After the War, Pierre Dreyfuss served as minister of Labor; Industry and Commerce, then as head of the Renault factories.

HENRI and **DENISE LEVI**, the Jewish Boy and Girl Scout leaders in Roanne, and their baby son Jean-Michel born at Drancy in August 1943, were gassed on arrival in Auschwitz. Henri and pregnant Denise had been caught at a Gestapo checkpoint near Lyon, when they decided to use their true papers rather than the fake IDs in their coat pockets.

MADAME FEIST and her children survived in Roanne. **Monsieur Feist** stayed behind in Paris where he was caught in the great Round-up of 1942. He perished in Auschwitz.

JENNY and **ELIAS STRAUSS,** Maman's older sister and husband whom Papa rescued from Camp Gürs in 1940, survived at 9 Rue de la Chaise (Roanne) in our apartment after we had left for the Haute-Savoie. Stateless, they immigrated to Philadelphia in 1946.

ROBERT, HÉLÈNE and **LOUIS MEYER,** my French-Alsatian Cousins, survived the War in Périgueux and returned to Strasbourg. **JULIEN,** my cousin Hélène's husband, an officer in the French army, a Christian, the head of the Resistance in Strasbourg, was arrested by the Gestapo, tortured and executed. Julien Ruffel did not talk.

Monsieur KAISER, a friend of Papa's who entrusted us with his wooden box, came and claimed his treasure after the War.

Many of the **POLISH JEWS of ROANNE** were handed over to the Germans by the Vichy authorities. They are among the 76,000 Jews deported from France who did not return.

HENRI BAUD, the head of the Saint-Gervais Resistance, was appointed Chef de cabinet, then sous-préfet (administrative prefect) of the Haute-Savoie. He died at age 83 in Grasse (Cote'd'Azur). **DÉDÉE** passed away earlier, weakened by TB.

CAPTAIN MONTJOIE, the military commander of our district's Resistance, a baritone at the Paris National Opera, divorced Madeleine after the Liberation and married a younger actress. **BERTIER** returned to his fashion store on the avenue des Champs Elysées.

LIEUTENANT BERTAULT, my math teacher in Saint-Gervais, a lycée professor, a member of the local Resistance, returned to Paris. He left behind his girlfriend and young son; both died soon thereafter.

PIERRE COULON (As I recall his name), le secrétaire-Général of the University of Grenoble, was executed after the Liberation for crimes committed against the Resistance, so told me Henri Baud.

LOUIS VIALLET, my guide to Mont Blanc, led the rescue operation in the eighties that recovered the bodies of a downed Indian airliner in the French Alps.

PAUL PERROUD, a relative of Clovis our landlord in Bionnay now lives at chalet Chez Nous.

MONSIEUR LE MAIRE CONSEIL, mayor of Saint-Gervais, fled through the backdoor of city hall as the Germans arrived to arrest him for helping the Resistance. He survived the war elsewhere with false papers.

POLICE CHIEF JEAN HOFFSTAETTER and his family took flight by night without saying good-bye.

Villagers of Saint-Gervais-Mont-Blanc (Haute Savoie), most of whom have since died but whose descendants still live there: the Perrouds, the Viallets, the Daves; the Orsets, the Orsins, the Brispierres. Among the people in the Resistance: Grandjacques' son built the Igloo resort hotel on top of Mont d'Arbois; Gaby Orset's son built the Hotel-ski resort on the Prarion; an older brother became mayor of Saint-Gervais. The maquisards returned to their own villages.

CPSIA information can be obtained at www.ICGtesting.com
Printed in the USA
BVOW04s2333300314

349207BV00001B/4/P